Restoring the Story

T0356687

Restoring the Story

The Good News of Atonement

Anne van Gend

scm press

© Anne van Gend 2024

Published in 2024 by SCM Press
Editorial office
3rd Floor, Invicta House,
110 Golden Lane,
London EC1Y 0TG, UK

www.scmpress.co.uk

SCM Press is an imprint of Hymns Ancient & Modern Ltd
(a registered charity)

Hymns Ancient & Modern® is a registered trademark of
Hymns Ancient & Modern Ltd
13A Hellesdon Park Road, Norwich,
Norfolk NR6 5DR, UK

British Library Cataloguing in Publication data
A catalogue record for this book is available
from the British Library

ISBN: 978-0-334-06619-4

Typeset by Regent Typesetting

Contents

Part 5: A Whole New Kind of Rabbit: *The Story of* Theosis

Part 6: Final Thoughts

To my mother, who has lived the Story all my life

Acknowledgements

I have discovered that writing a book demands a great deal of patience, tolerance and grace on the part of close friends and family. While it is an act of vulnerability to give something you have written to another to critique, it is an act of courage and love for that other to respond honestly. I am blessed to have friends with all those necessary qualities.

Thanks first to my friend and husband, Mike, who has been unfailingly encouraging no matter how many doubts I have had, and to my sons Julian and Jonty, who have dealt admirably with growing up with two priests for parents – especially ones with insatiable appetites for learning and writing. I owe my fascination with fantasy books primarily to them, and to my sister Marie who introduced me to Harry Potter when his name was still relatively unknown. Thanks beyond words to Lisa Emerson and Gerald Morris, whose writing skills I respect deeply enough that I took to heart the smallest suggestions they made. They patiently worked their way through draft after draft of this book, and years earlier they, together with the wonderful Leisa Lance, did the same for my PhD thesis. They have truly proved their friendship! Thanks to Ellen Clark-King and Sally Miller for being early readers and encouragers, and to Paula Gooder whom I suspect is a key reason this book has reached the point of publication. Ongoing thanks to my mother, to whom this book is dedicated, not only for her response to this book, but far more for the living example of grace and faith she has been all my life.

Finally, thanks to David Shervington and the SCM team for taking a chance on an unknown author and for making the whole process so painless!

Foreword

One of the most fascinating parts of working in a university is hearing the stories that new generations of students tell about themselves and the world. Much of the current content is about identity: unsurprising within the context of the world of distorting mirrors that is the reality of social media. Students search for the story that makes sense of who they are and that gives them hope for becoming the person they long to be. Sometimes this quest takes them deeper into the traditions they have inherited in their families, either in acceptance or opposition, and sometimes it winds through the fantasy worlds of books, films and games where the choices seem simpler and the happy endings more within reach.

In this accessible, original and profound work, Anne van Gend's quest has been to explore the rich story-telling tradition within the Christian doctrine of atonement and find ways that it resonates with our contemporary stories. Identifying the 'bad news' that the original theory was created to counter she shows how some past iterations of 'good news' may no longer answer present-day questions or speak to contemporary understandings of what happy endings look like.

This is not a book that knocks down, though. In so many ways it is a book that builds up. A book that finds the ongoing good news in stories that the Church may almost have forgotten, providing narratives that speak directly to the needs of contemporary hearts; telling of a God of grace, forgiveness and unbounded life. There is a real happy ending here, rooted in the deepest reality of God's own being, that is not to be derailed by any human misunderstanding or misbehaviour.

Woven in through the chapters are bright threads drawn from works of fantasy, from the familiarly Christian storyland of C. S. Lewis to the magical realms of Harry Potter and Garth Nix. Van Gend shows how their fabulous depictions of right and wrong, of hope and despair, and of how life is redeemed hum on the same wavelength as many of the traditional accounts of God's atoning work in Christ. All this helps keep the focus on imagination, story, poetry and mystery as the key interpretative lenses rather than on the intellectually abstract and analytical.

Or to put it another way:

Once upon a time there was a wise and loving being who wanted to mend the creation that their beloved creatures had broken. When this was accomplished those creatures, who were not always wise or loving themselves, tried to share their understanding of what had happened. Being story-telling creatures, they produced narratives that made sense at the time, though they were always partial and incomplete. Sometimes their descendants got so caught up in these stories that they lost sight of the reality outside the narrative. Today we can listen again to all these stories and hear the pure notes of truth that continue to ring out amid the distracting static of their time and ours: the truth of that world-changing act of love capturing the imagination of our hearts as much as the reasoning of our minds.

This is a book full of good news. I hope you find in it some that speaks into your own particular story.

Revd Dr Ellen Clark-King
Dean of King's College London

PART I

Getting Ready

Definition of Atonement

NOUN

1 satisfaction, reparation, or expiation given for an injury or wrong

2 Christian theology

(**a**) the reconciliation of humankind with God through the life, sufferings, and sacrificial death of Christ

(**b**) the sufferings and death of Christ

https://www.collinsdictionary.com/dictionary/english/atonement#google_vignette

I

Mystery

If you take a lift in the Ministry of Magic to the lowest possible level, which very few people do, you will come out at the Department of Mysteries. It is a place of silence, of dark, featureless doors that swirl and change positions at unexpected times. We know that behind one door is a room containing minds: brains carefully preserved in a tank of green liquid, able to inflict lasting wounds if touched. Another room has shelves of misty prophecies: evidence of the rare times when true insights into present actions and future possibilities have been discerned and captured. Another is filled with clocks and a tiny bird that repeatedly hatches and is re-enclosed in its egg.

The only room to be kept locked at all times, we are told, 'Contains a force that is at once more wonderful and more terrible than death, than human intelligence, than the forces of nature', a force constantly under-estimated and dismissed by Voldemort who can neither understand nor accept it.[1] Dumbledore calls it, simply, 'Love'. And in yet another room, on a stone dais at the base of something like a stone amphitheatre, there is an ancient archway with a veil hung across it. Some can hear faint voices beyond it; some are strangely attracted to it as the veil moves gently. We are never told directly what it is, but when Sirius passes through it there is no coming back.

Those who work in the Department of Mysteries are called Unspeak-ables.[2]

Deep at the heart of Christianity are mysteries: mysteries of love and death and time and space and worlds beyond our imaginings. Deep in the heart of many faithful believers lies the conviction that the mysteries of God are beyond words, 'unspeakable'. If God is God and therefore infinite, how could the mysteries of God ever be contained in finite words, creeds and doctrines? It can only be done by shrinking them to a manageable, and therefore inadequate, size. The appropriate response, they say, should be awe and silence.

This – one of the great dilemmas of religious thought – could be a rather discouraging start to a book crammed full of words about one particular Christian doctrine. However, we shouldn't be too worried. On the one hand, yes, if we're going to delve into something as mysterious as atonement – the whole complex, interwoven story of what Christ's incarnation, life, death and resurrection achieved – we do need to remind ourselves regularly of the limitations of human words and human minds. Most of us are not mystics, and we are far more likely to fall into the trap of believing our particular expression of a Christian belief is the ultimate, complete Truth, than to fall silent before the inexpressibility of it all. But on the other hand, Jesus and his followers seemed content to use words to get their ideas across. His followers were even happy to commit these words to a written form – fortunately for us, 2,000 years later. Maybe words are clumsy and inadequate tools when it comes to expressing great mysteries, but with such an example before us we should be encouraged to do what we can with them.

So, how do we start? If we were talking about 'Love', the mystery studied in a locked room in the depths of J. K. Rowling's Department of Mysteries, we would have some idea of how to go about it. We know instinctively, for example, that scientific treatises which analyse love's hormonal or evolutionary source are valuable for certain purposes, but show no resemblance to love as we know it or experience it. We know that love cannot be forced into being by rules, regulations or reason. Analysis and reason are good and helpful things but, as centuries of experience show, mysteries such as love lead us to reach instinctively for story, poetry, music and art to express and understand them. We reach for those things that spark our imaginations: imaginations that are perfectly capable of taking reason into account while building something that reaches beyond reason. When it comes to mysteries, 'We murder to dissect',[3] but the gentler, allusory arts can grant us foggy windows through which the living truth can be glimpsed. This, then, points the way for the direction of this book. Reason and analysis will play their part, but so will story and poetry, music and imagination.[4]

Especially imagination. In one of George MacDonald's novels, a character sees it as his life's mission to argue religious believers out of their misguided faith. MacDonald writes:

That region of a man's nature which has to do with the unknown was in Bascombe shut off by a wall without chink or cranny. He was unaware of its existence. He did not know, apparently, that Imagination had been the guide to all the physical discoveries which he worshipped, therefore could not reason that perhaps she might be able to carry a glimmering light even into the forest of the unknown.[5]

That glimmering light will be our companion through these pages.

Why atonement?

This is a book about one Christian mystery – atonement – and how the Christian stories of atonement may still be 'good news' today. Why atonement? Mainly because it is the heart of our 'Good News'. 'Atonement' is about *what Jesus did*, what he achieved through his incarnation, life, death, resurrection and ascension. Unless what he did was something remarkable, life-changing, *world*-changing, we have Fairly Feeble News, or One Inspiring Message Among Many. Some people are able to build their lives on that sort of foundation, but our spoiled-for-choice younger generations are more likely to flick through those ideas and pass on, as they would the next inspirational meme. Whatever has drawn centuries of Christians to lives of love and sacrifice, it was more than that. Whatever has given centuries of Christians hope and purpose through happiness and extreme suffering, it was more than that. Whatever transformed the first bewildered, and then terrified, followers of Jesus into men and women with no fear of death, it was not Fairly Feeble News.

And yet, in many parts of the Church today, we avoid talking about it. Atonement is a good example of a mystery that has suffered from being 'shrunk' into words – or, at least, into the style of words we have chosen in recent centuries. The lessons we have learned when speaking of love are, for some reason, often overlooked when it comes to atonement. With love we know that it is best expressed through stories, poetry, music and art. Yet we have insisted that atonement be understood as a logical, even legal, process. With love, we welcome a new story or poem which allows us to glimpse another facet of the great mystery. Yet Christian history is littered with debates and arguments and wars over loyalty to one expression of atonement over another.

This has led to a certain reluctance on the part of many Christians to refer to atonement at all, except in very hazy terms. Not only do we want to avoid yet another painful debate that highlights our differences, but discomfort with the most common expressions of atonement may give rise to a disquieting, if unexpressed, question: is atonement still good news? This question can apply to descriptions of how atonement 'works' from either end of the theological spectrum. Are stories laced with ideas of judgement, punishment, sin and a father killing his son still received as 'good news' in our secular world? Or is holding up Jesus as one among many long-since-dead moral examples for us to follow inspiring enough that our young people would dedicate their lives to following him on his demanding path?

My work in recent years has been with school chaplains: people who deal on a daily basis with an audience who are ruthless in their demands for authenticity. Unless the stories we tell 'ring true' for them as genuinely good news, young people have no reason to bother with them. Given the difficulties surrounding commonly held atonement theories, then, perhaps we should quietly shove the whole thing under the carpet and focus on nicer aspects of our faith.

This book is an attempt to lift up that carpet, give it a good shake, and deal with whatever has been hidden beneath it. It does so in the hope that we may discover a few dusty lumps, long pushed out of sight by all but dusty theologians, which, when polished, show gleams of gold.

Good news?

What we find under that carpet may be surprising. The extent of the richness and variety of the New Testament stories of atonement is still largely unknown to most Christians despite the wealth of theological writing on it in recent decades. This is partly because few Christians count themselves 'theologians' and so veer away from overtly theological writing, presuming that it will either be incomprehensible or obsessed with academic quibbles. It is admittedly difficult to sift out the good news through a thick mesh of multi-syllabic words. However, if we want to know more of God we are automatically theologians, and if that is a genuine desire we should be willing to give our minds to this search as fully as we do to anything important in our lives. I am writing this, then, for those of us who are juggling a multitude of responsibilities yet still want to engage our minds, when we can, to learn more of God and the good news God has for us.

For I am convinced that atonement stories are brimming with good news. I am convinced that Jesus' life, death, resurrection and ascension *did do something* that radically altered our relationship with God, one another and creation; and that this 'something' was good news then and is good news today. If there are hesitations in our minds over how 'good' atonement really sounds, then we need the courage to dig deeper rather than push it to one side.

Having said that, atonement *is* an uncomfortable doctrine, inasmuch as before we can understand the good news we have to grapple with the existence of 'bad news'. Bad things happen. We do bad things, and nowhere in the Bible is God a doddering old grandfather patting us benignly and vaguely on the head as we wreak havoc around his feet. God takes bad stuff seriously and atonement stories bring us slap up against that uncomfortable fact.

But it is also a doctrine whose good news is so good that we barely dare believe it. Remember when the disciples met the risen Lord? 'In their joy they were disbelieving' (Luke 24.41). They had encountered the depths of darkness, and for a moment the light when it came was too dazzling for the eyes of their hearts to open to it. As you read on, I will be describing scenes of darkness: ways of understanding the world that try to make sense of how death and suffering exist. These parts may be uncomfortable for you, but darkness is real and Christianity is thoroughly realistic in its acknowledgement of its existence. Push on, because atonement is God's grace poured into the world's need, the lotion that heals the gaping wound, the love that enters the isolation and uncertainty and failures of our lives and brings us home.

What to expect

Each section of this book will be looking at a different 'dusty lump' from under the carpet, a different way of speaking about atonement. Every reader will find some ways appealing and others distinctly unappealing, and that is natural. The first step for all of us is to remember that one poem or novel or artwork cannot communicate all that love is, and that the particular atonement story that is dear to us is also not the full story. There is no one depiction of the 'how and why' of Christ's atonement that explains it completely: it is too big for that. Instead, the New Testament gives us the central story of 'what happened' in material terms, followed by the attempts of various followers to explain the inexplicable, to break the flood of white light into its spectrum of colours, to use human tools to communicate divine truth. It was clearly not a straightforward task! So much to say, and only awkward human words with which to say it. The early followers of Jesus approached the challenge in every way they could: through rational discussion, yes, but even more through story and imagery which could lift their readers' imaginations into realms that mere logic cannot reach.

This does cause difficulties for us, 2,000 years later. Logic remains logic over time and can be passed, with some adjustments, between cultures and across ages. Pythagorus' theorem is as easy to use on twenty-first-century triangles as it was on the triangles he worked on. Stories and imagery, however, are dependent on a shared lived or imagined experience.

There is a Māori proverb, '*Ka mua, ka muri*', translated loosely as 'Looking back to move forward' or 'Moving backwards into the future'. For us to begin to grasp what the New Testament writers wrote, we have to attempt to start where they started, looking deep into the Hebrew scriptures and writings and keeping our eyes fixed there as we move 'backwards' into the New Testament and beyond.[6] Alternatively, think of that journey as being like following footprints in the sand. The tracks will show a definite continuity between the Old and New Testaments, and the New Testament writers believed that if we traced those Old Testament footprints through to their day, we would discover the One who had made them: the Reality and Cause and Goal of it all.

Let me illustrate why this is important. Imagine that you are aching with fear about something, and a friend assures you, 'It's only a boggart.' How would you respond?

(a) You haven't a clue what they are talking about.
(b) You picture a harmless little otter-like creature and wonder what that's got to do with anything.
(c) You think they're telling you that if you can laugh at a fear, it may go away.

Depending on your response, I can tell something about your teenage reading. If you answered (a), you didn't enjoy fantasy books much. If it's (b), you read the Septimus Heap series by Angie Sage. If you responded (c), you have read (or watched) at least book 3 of the Harry Potter series – and so has your friend.

Unless you and your friend are both familiar with the same story, the term 'boggart' is either completely meaningless, or communicates a false message. If you *do* know the same story, then you will not only understand what your friend means, but also bring to that meaning a wealth of imaginative associations, emotions and memories you may have formed while reading that part of the story. You may remember reading it for the first time. You may remember laughing at a spider in roller skates or cringing at a rotting mummy or delighting in the fact that one particular character, who is normally weak and fearful, overcomes his fear and for a few bright minutes becomes the star of the class. With that victory in mind, you may be moved to see if you too can conquer the fear by laughing at it.[7]

On the other hand, those of you who are reading this and have not read the Harry Potter series will have no idea what I'm talking about. That is exactly the situation we often find ourselves in when we confront apparently bizarre portions of the Bible.

The New Testament writers made full use of the imaginative power of their shared stories when they wrote of what Jesus had done. Our problem is that we often have not heard or read the same stories, so may well be picturing the equivalent of an otter-like creature when the writers were referring to a terrifying shape-shifter. Even if we take a good stab at the meaning, we lack the imaginative and often emotional associations that the shared stories would have given to the first readers. Our first task, then, as we polish up our dusty atonement fragments, is to dig into the stories these writers shared and see what we can find there to spark our own imaginations. As we move from those ancient stories to the New Testament, we will take with us some fragment of the imaginative associations the New Testament writers had in their minds as they sought ways of communicating the mystery they had encountered in Jesus.

Throughout the discussion, I will be using illustrations and allusions from books and, occasionally, films. Many of these will be children's or young adult books, and many will be fantasy works. There are two main reasons for this. One is that I find it fascinating how the footprints of Christ have continued to appear even in secular writings up to today, and I hope that this discovery will be encouraging for you. Writers who have no apparent interest in Christianity still use the imagery and ideas surrounding Christ's atonement in order to make sense of atoning stories within their own created worlds – suggesting that these ideas are perhaps more appealing to contemporary minds than the Church realizes. That these parallels appear most often in fantasy works does not imply that the biblical story itself is some sort of fantasy, but rather that the cosmic and world-changing nature of Christ's work is difficult to communicate within the limits of a purely material existence.

The second reason relates again to imagination. While we will be able to develop some of the imaginative associations with which people of biblical times enriched their stories and history, our associations will naturally lack their depth and emotional complexity. We do not live, breathe and inhabit the stories as they did. However, if we find a similar idea embedded in stories that we know and have immersed ourselves in since we were young, that can provide us with a type of short-cut to understanding. Any of us, for example, who read the Narnia books as children will remember the *feel* of them as much as the plot: something that it is impossible to reproduce in words. I hope that by bringing various stories like these into the conversation, those 'feels' will enrich your otherwise cognitive understanding of stories from another time and culture.

Having said that, if you have not read any of the books alluded to, don't worry. The illustrations may still be helpful to you; but, if they are not, skim over them and move on.

This leads to one final thing to keep in mind as we enter this ancient Hebrew world: many of these biblical stories themselves contain things that some readers will find as fantastic and unbelievable as any fantasy work. That doesn't matter in the slightest. The message of the boggart story, above – that fears can often be conquered if we can laugh at them – is true regardless of the means by which we were given that message. As we study these background concepts, the 'factual truth' of them is not important. What *is* important is how the New Testament writers used them to communicate the factual and beyond-reason truth of Christ.[8] You will need, then, to suspend your disbelief as we explore some frankly mythological-sounding backgrounds to New Testament concepts.

First up, I will take you on a rapid and drastically over-simplified tour of the past 2,000 years of atonement theories, looking specifically at how the 'bad news' of each time was met by good news in Christ's atonement. Then we will look in more depth at some key atonement stories, approaching each in three stages. We will start by exploring some of the relevant stories shared by the New Testament writers, dipping into the Hebrew scriptures, Apocrypha and Pseudepigrapha.[9] This is the least familiar part to most of us, so will take the longest to unpack. We will then see *how* those stories were used by the writers, and by later Christians, to speak of atonement. Finally, I will 'wonder aloud' how each story of atonement could still be good news today. Those final 'good news' chapters of each section will be the most speculative, and I do not expect or even hope that you will agree with them all. I am content if they are discussion-starters for a conversation that could be, above all, life-giving.

So, sit back and prepare for a rollercoaster tour of 2,000 years of thought.

Notes

1 J. K. Rowling, 2003, *Harry Potter and the Order of the Phoenix*, London: Bloomsbury, p. 743.

2 Rowling, *Order of the Phoenix*, pp. 681–8.

3 William Wordsworth, 1950, 'The Tables Turned' in Mark van Doren (ed.), *William Wordsworth. Selected Poetry*, New York: Random House, p. 83.

4 My own complete ignorance of visual art is the reason for the gaping hole in that area. Music, which I do know something about, is harder to incorporate in a soundless book, so story, poetry and imagination will dominate.

5 George MacDonald, 1876, *Thomas Wingfold, Curate* in Michael Phillips (ed.), 2018, *The Cullen Collection*, New York: Rosetta, p. 18.

6 'Hebrew scriptures' and 'Old Testament' are used interchangeably in this book. In general terms, if I'm writing about Jewish people using them, I'll use 'Hebrew scriptures' and if I'm writing about Christians using it, I'll use 'Old Testament'. Sometimes, however, as here, the borders are blurred.

7 Angie Sage, 2005, *Magyk*, London: Bloomsbury, pp. 160–72.

8 No one believes the Narnia books are 'factually true', but think of how many truths about God you absorbed while reading them. The Old Testament is not fantasy by any means, but there are elements in it from a culture 2,000–3,000 years ago that are as strange to us as fantasy – and that's OK. Don't stress about it, just see what truths you can absorb from it.

9 A fascinating collection of stories that didn't make it into either the Hebrew or Christian canon, written in the few centuries before and after Christ.

2

Bad News, Good News and Atonement through the Ages

The world of the first-century Church was as messy as our own, with a rich mixture of languages, religions and cultures trying to coexist. Even within Judaism there were factions who argued passionately about theological questions, who favoured variations in their sacred writings, read these writings in different languages, and who traced the ills of the world to different sources. That should all sound familiar, since Christianity inherited most of its parent's traits. The centuries that followed the time of Jesus showed Christianity engaged in ever more passionate debates held in an ever-increasing range of languages and cultures, and even today we haven't completely agreed about what should be part of our sacred scriptures.[1]

What has shaped the changing popularity of various atonement stories most strongly, however, has been the variety of ways in which people across time and cultures have traced the source and centre of the world's ills. What was their understanding of 'bad news' for which they sought 'good news'? We cannot understand or begin to discuss atonement until we are aware of just how different some of the explanations we have used for it are, and why different stories have made so much sense at different periods of our history. If, however, your eyes begin to glaze over before reaching the end of this chapter, feel free to skim through it and move on as soon as you've got the general idea. The details will become clearer as the book progresses.

Sacrificial theory of atonement

The earliest Church was largely Jewish, so it makes sense that our first atonement story is the most obviously 'Jewish' of them. What was their bad news? Physically and socially there was plenty to choose from, with foreign oppression a prize contender. But for Second Temple Judaism there was a deeper, ongoing problem.[2] Sin and impurity polluted the people and the world, and a holy God would not dwell in a polluted land. Fortunately, God had given them the sacrificial system to cleanse themselves and their land. Unfortunately, sacrifices were always incomplete and needed to be repeated. The good news, then, was that Christ was the complete and sufficient sacrifice for the whole world, cleansing it from sin and allowing God to dwell with his people for ever.

This is one of the atonement theories that seems strangest to us, not surprisingly. It was already strange to the men we call the Latin Church Fathers (Tertullian and Augustine are two of the better-known ones). So strange was this to them that some began to re-tell the story according to their own understanding of sacrifice: not as a gift from God with which to cleanse the people and their land, but as a way of satisfying the honour of the gods (or God, in this case). This is our first classic example in atonement history of mistaking a hairy otter for a shape-shifter.[3]

Victorious theory of atonement

Over the first three centuries AD, a second, complex atonement theory grew in popularity alongside sacrificial atonement. The human predicament was seen in terms of a battle between supernatural powers. Anyone who reads the Gospels must notice the prevalence of demonic forces in the everyday life of the people. These were not understood as metaphors for sickness and evil, but as actual forces or beings, and they were not pleasant to have around. The glorious news of Christ's atonement, then, was that he had defeated Satan, 'bound the strong man', and given his followers the 'armour' with which to do the same.[4]

Not content to leave the story as a story, the early Greek and Latin Christians sought to analyse exactly how this victory had been achieved. Debates raged. Some favoured the idea of 'recapitulation' while others focused on 'ransom'. This will all be discussed in more detail in Chapter 8. What is important to understand is that the means of this victory were debated for centuries. While recapitulation theories grew in favour in the East, the idea of a ransom was followed to its logical and illogical ends in the West, giving scope to much boggart-style confusion. Some decided that God paid a just ransom to Satan; others that God tricked Satan into accepting a ransom; and yet others that the ransom was paid *to* God, not *by* God. This final development paved the way for a new theory of atonement: the satisfaction theory of atonement.

Satisfaction theory of atonement

The Satisfaction theory of atonement grew slowly as a logical result of developing the first two atonement theories down alternate paths. First, sacrifices came to be understood primarily as a way of appeasing God's anger, or of satisfying the divine dignity or honour that was wounded by humanity's sin. The 'bad news' the world had to grapple with was, essentially, a justly and dangerously angered God. The good news, then, was that Christ's perfect sacrifice restored God's honour and satisfied him. Adding weight to this was the growing belief that the ransom Christ paid was not to Satan, who had humanity in slavery (the usual reason a ransom was paid), but to God, as payment for the sins of the world.

This theory reached its clearest and most brilliant expression in the writings of a man called Anselm of Canterbury (1033–1109). His world was one whose social structure depended on the maintenance of proper respect from one tier of the hierarchy to the next. Any breakdown in that order was seriously 'bad news'. To contemplate such a breakdown on a cosmic scale – where the ultimate Lord was not given the respect that was his due – was to envisage a crisis that would lead to the whole beauty of the universe being destroyed. The good news here is that God, like any good feudal lord, arranged it so that the balance could be restored. He provided restitution for the world's inability to honour him aright, through Christ's sacrificial payment. Note, however, that this is a voluntary payment, not a punishment. The idea that Christ was punished came seriously to the fore many centuries later.

Moral influence theory of atonement

Not everyone liked Anselm's ideas. Around the same time, Peter Abelard (1079–1142) was exploring a quite different atonement theory. Abelard, a priest, is famous for his correspondence with Heloise, a nun: a correspondence that showed the depth of the love they experienced and denied themselves. It is perhaps unsurprising that the clinical, judicial understanding of 'God's love' within Anselm's teaching sounded more like bad news than good news to Abelard. Instead, he explored an idea that had been present throughout the centuries as a component of other atonement theories. He suggested that it was the example of Christ's life and love, set before the believer, which 'provokes the response of human love' and leads to salvation.[5]

Later developments of this moral influence theory of atonement made it more extreme, suggesting that Christ's death and resurrection were not necessary; that Jesus' life alone was enough. That was never Abelard's view. He simply believed that the demonstration of God's love through Christ's life was a key part of the redemptive process.[6]

Penal substitutionary theory of atonement

Move forward a few hundred years and we have a different world. Nationalism is on the rise, pope and emperor vie for power, leaders further down the pecking order start showing uncomfortable signs of making their own decisions. The Renaissance has launched new ways of thinking into the world (or, rather, ancient ways rediscovered). There is, then, political and social unrest on a large scale, there are no standing armies, no police forces, and into this powder keg comes Martin Luther (1483–1546) to light a few sparks.

It is unsurprising that the Church that grew at this time worked closely with the local magisterium: the one place capable of upholding law and order. That is why you may hear the Lutheran and Calvinist part of the Reformation referred to as the 'Magisterial Reformation'. It is also unsurprising that their good news should be shaped in magisterial, legal terms. Abelard's quiet Christ who 'influences' people was not robust enough to tackle the bad news of the Reformation world. Peace, they believed, could only come through those who perpetrated injustices being appropriately punished through proper legal channels, or anarchy would break loose. Yet no human could meet the demands of divine justice, so how could peace be restored on a cosmic scale? Only through appropriate punishment. But who could bear such a punishment? It would destroy us. Therefore God, in his love, chose to punish his own son in place of the world. Hence the penal substitutionary theory of atonement entered Christian thought, and has been holding on with determination ever since.

Natural religion

By the time of the Enlightenment, philosophers and certain theologians had begun to reject ideas of the complete helplessness of humanity and its reliance on an act of God for salvation. As breakthroughs in science and industry wowed the world, it was wounding to human dignity to think there was anything beyond our capabilities, including salvation. The 'bad news' of this time was that humans kept letting themselves down by not living up to their own ethical standards. The 'good news' was that we are able to 'repent', turn around, and seek to be better human beings.[7] God was not completely out of the equation: at least in the writings of the philosopher Kant, God is operating within us.[8] But the Christian story became a symbol of the struggle (death) and victory (resurrection) of humanity's progress towards a greater humanity.

Christ the healer and Christ the reconciler

The closer we get to the modern day, the harder it is to speak in generalities. However, two key developments in the nineteenth and twentieth centuries can be seen in the language and stories that have become a part of everyday Christian vocabulary today. One grew from the 'bad news' of Freud and his ilk. Humans are sick. Every ill, whether it be physical, emotional or psychological, can be conceived of in clinical terms. Therefore, the good news is that Christ is the great healer. Atonement came to be understood in terms of our inner healing, the healing of relationships with one another, and the healing of our relationship with God.

The second development was the growing recognition of the harm done by groups of people to one another: colonization, invasion, apartheid, assimilation, genocide. In the face of that 'bad news', the good news of Christ was that he was the great reconciler. Terms like 'reconciliation' replaced 'confession' in the Catholic Church. Christ's work was understood in terms of reconciling God to humanity, and us to one another.

As is the case with the majority of historical atonement stories, these developments are thoroughly biblical. 'Healing' and 'reconciliation' are used frequently by New Testament writers and have been used to describe Christ's work for millennia. However, they came to the forefront of atonement language in response to the particular 'bad news' of the last century. So, in their day, did stories and language of restoring cosmic order, or conquering Satan, or cleansing the world, come to the fore in response to the bad news of *their* day.

In the interests of simplicity I have not touched here on the importance of covenant stories or the Eastern understanding of *theosis* (both important atonement ideas), nor have I summarized the possibilities of exile and the state of peace, called *shalom* in the Bible, all of which I will explore later. But these examples should be enough to give us a glimpse of how Christ's work can be understood in quite varied ways, yet each way can conceivably point to the one, beyond-words act of God. Different facets, same gem.

What now?

What stories, terminology or images do we need today if we are to uncover the facets of Christ's work that will meet our present bad news and atone for it, make it right? What is our good news in the face of the climate crisis? What is our good news in the face of our increasing isolation, our growing suicide rates, our obsession with 'well-being'? Can any of the old atonement stories speak to our present need? Are there 'treasures old and new' in our scriptures to draw from?

Let's have a look and see. It's time to examine more closely what was revealed under our carpet, pick up our first odd-shaped fragment, and dust it off. I'm afraid you may find that it is bleeding. Unpleasant, I know, but then blood was always meant to be shocking.

Notes

1 Catholics and some Anglicans include the books of the Apocrypha. Protestants do not.

2 'Second Temple' refers to the period between the return from exile and rebuilding of the Temple (539 BC) and that second Temple being destroyed (AD 70).

3 If you've forgotten what this refers to, look back at the discussion on 'boggarts' in Chapter 1. Or read the Harry Potter and Septimus Heap series. Go on. They're great.

4 Matthew 12.29; Ephesians 6.10–17.

5 Steve Cartwright in Peter Abelard, 2011, *Commentary on the Epistle to the Romans*, Steve Cartwright (trans.), Washington, DC: Catholic University of America Press, p. 30.

6 Cartwright, *Romans*, p. 38.

7 Paul Fiddes, 1989, *Past Event and Present Salvation*, London: Darton, Longman and Todd, p. 10.

8 Colin Gunton, 1988, *The Actuality of Atonement*, Edinburgh: T&T Clark, p. 4.

PART 2

Cleaning Up the World

The Story of Sacrificial Atonement

3

The Backstory: Blood is Life

Our shocking behaviour

Imagine for a moment that you have never been in a church, and never heard anything about Christianity. You see a group of harmless-looking people entering a building, and you draw nearer, wondering what they are going to see or do. A friendly woman invites you to join her and you have nothing better to do so you follow her in and find yourself in a kind of mini theatre with rows of chairs facing the front, and costumed people acting out one of those dramas where the audience is invited to partici-pate. At first it is harmless enough, if a bit obscure. But soon something begins to sound a little off. They appear to be celebrating the memory of a blood sacrifice – a *human* sacrifice. They sing a song about being washed in someone's blood, as if it was a good thing. Finally – and this is the point you decide it's time to sneak out the back – they perform some ritual on a makeshift altar at the front, and invite everyone to drink a cupful of blood. If, as is likely, you are familiar with Dracula, *Twilight* or Buffy, you may count yourself lucky to have escaped.

If I have offended anyone in describing the Eucharist in this way, I am not altogether sorry. The words of Jesus at the Last Supper were, as the disciples discovered later, expressing the depth of his love for them, but they were also, at the time, profoundly unsettling: not only because Jesus spoke of his coming death, but because he told his disciples that they were to consider the bread his body and eat it, the wine his blood, and *drink it*. We who have grown used to the symbolism of this have separ-ated ourselves from the shock of these words. We need to reimagine it if we are to begin to understand the mystery of this atonement story.

To help jolt us into that unfamiliar way of thinking, pause for a moment to think about the strange mythology of the vampire. As a youngster I was always repelled by vampire stories and could not understand the fascination so many had with them, but what does intrigue me are the often undefined assumptions behind the myth. Why, for example, should vampires drink blood? And why, of all hideous mythological creatures, should vampires alone be damned and unable to enter hallowed ground? Many strange mythological ideas that are now completely divorced from Christian beliefs are nonetheless grounded in the same ancient stories. In Christianity, the stories about blood developed in life-giving ways, while vampire stories headed towards horror, but what they have in common at their source is – bizarre as it may seem – key to our understanding of sacrificial atonement.

All that follows will likely seem strange to you, but persevere. If we are going to talk routinely in our churches about Christ's blood, whether in hymns or scripture or Holy Communion, we need to understand what it is we're talking about, no matter how strange it feels at first. At the end of this block of chapters I will try to help you think about how we can understand it all today, but for now we need to start where the New Testament writers did: in their own scriptures.

The blood prohibition

There is one prohibition that runs through both Old and New Testaments, yet is routinely ignored by the majority of Christians. That is the prohibition against eating the blood of an animal killed for food. Instinctively, most of us relegate that teaching to undefined pre-Christian superstitions and the Law of Moses to which we are no longer bound: a set of beliefs that was superseded by Christ. Yet have a look at what were considered the bare minimum requirements for a new church in Acts 15.20:

> We should write to them to abstain only from things polluted by idols and from fornication and from whatever has been strangled and from blood.

Four prohibitions, and two of them are about consuming blood (strangling means that the blood is not drained from the animal as it is killed). Admittedly these were early days in Christian history, but it is interesting that of the four prohibitions so important to the early Church, we now only seem to be interested in the one that the Hebrew scriptures were least worried about. Idol worship and the evils of eating blood get far more biblical coverage than fornication.[1]

So what was the big deal about blood? It comes from the Hebrew understanding that blood was life (Leviticus 17.13–14). Whether we think that means that blood was a symbol of life, or that blood somehow carried life in its flow, or that blood *was* life in some mysterious way beyond our understanding, does not really matter. Even if it was only understood symbolically, that symbol was so strong that we will come closer to the original meaning of it to simply think: *blood is life.*

This is where the distasteful idea of vampires can help. The reason vampires drink blood is that by doing so they bring *life* into their otherwise dead bodies and reanimate them. That is how powerfully blood 'is' life even in modern re-tellings of these stories. The same idea can be seen reappearing in numerous fantasy books, where the dead or nearly dead are revived by the touch of blood.[2] In C. S. Lewis's *The Silver Chair*, when Eustace comes to Aslan's country and finds Caspian, who has died of old age, lying dead in a stream, Aslan asks Eustace to drive a thorn into Aslan's great paw. As the drops of blood fall into the stream, Caspian becomes younger and younger, and then leaps out, alive and vigorous.[3] We may no longer consciously think that 'blood is life', but when the belief appears in a fantasy guise we tend to accept it unquestioningly.

Stories like these that make no pretence of being factually true can nonetheless help us understand both the sense of the power that life-carrying blood holds in the Hebrew scriptures, and the depth of the abhorrence these scriptures show at the idea of eating meat that still has blood in it. To do so would involve eating the life of another, and that is hideous and wrong, even if the 'other' is an animal. For if blood is life, it is God's, and to take something that belongs to God is an unwise move. Only God can give life and take life away. The very first murderer, Cain, made the mistake of thinking that his brother's life was his to take, and his brother's blood cried out to God from the ground on which it was spilt (Gen. 4.10). Cain may have slain the body of Abel, but the life was still God's.

If we think of the Garden of Eden as a place where everything was as God wanted it to be, it seems that the original plan for humans according to the Bible was that they were to be vegetarian. It was only after the disastrous descent into violence which culminated in God wiping the world clean and starting again at the Flood that Noah was given new instructions. He's not given *many* instructions – God obviously had a good idea of humanity's capacity for following rules by now – but the ones he's given do two things. First, they reinforce the fun advice given to Adam and Eve ('Be fruitful and multiply'). Next, they bring in one set of restrictions:

Every moving thing that lives shall be food for you; and just as I gave you the green plants, I give you everything. Only, you shall not eat flesh with its life, that is, its blood. For your own lifeblood I will surely require a reckoning: from every animal I will require it and from human beings, each one for the blood of another, I will require a reckoning for human life. (Genesis 9.3–5)

And then he returns to the 'fruitful and multiply' theme. Life is sacred, holy, God's. Don't mess with it.

Later, these simple rules had to be spelled out in more detail and we get the 613 laws of the Hebrew scriptures.[4] They don't all apply directly to the 'blood prohibition' but, as we'll see soon, most are connected by some common themes.

It's worth noting here that while from Noah onwards animals are allowed to be eaten, that is not permission for random killing. Life is still sacred. While we may kill the body of an animal for good cause (survival or sacrifice), the life must be honoured and returned to God either by burial or through the sacrificial system:

And anyone of the people of Israel, or of the aliens who reside among them, who hunts down an animal or bird that may be eaten shall pour out its blood and cover it with earth. For the life of every creature – its blood is its life; therefore I have said to the people of Israel: You shall not eat the blood of any creature, for the life of every creature is its blood; whoever eats it shall be cut off. (Leviticus 17.13–14)

There are two key points here to remember. Blood is life, and it is God's and therefore holy. To treat it without reverence is not only wrong but dangerous, as with all holy things. But treat life with respect, and it is among God's greatest gifts.

Holiness gone bad

In Cassandra Clare's *Mortal Instruments* series, the 'instruments' in the title are three gifts given by the Angel Raziel to humanity to aid their battle against demons. They are the sword that God used to guard the entrance to Eden after banishing Adam and Eve; a chalice; and what is referred to as a mirror. These things are holy, and used well they give divine aid to demon hunters. However, a character who models himself on Lucifer steals the sword and chalice, and desecrates them by filling the chalice with the blood of those he has murdered and dipping the sword into it. From being a powerful instrument of holiness, the sword is now an equally powerful instrument of death, able to summon hoards of demons on command.[5]

This idea that holy things can be desecrated and their power turned from good to evil is an ancient one, and reappears in stories over the ages.[6] We have likely heard tales of satanic rituals involving upside-down crosses, or chalices full of human blood. In a similar vein, thriller writers routinely exploit the extra layer of horror we feel when something that should be innocent (like a child or clown or doll) is revealed to be evil.

Try now to get into the mind of those who wrote, read and lived the ancient Hebrew teachings in ancient times. Blood is life. It is God's gift, and it is holy. It thus holds power within it, and that power will remain, whatever the blood is used for. However, if it is desecrated, it will turn from the power of life to the power of death.

We see the truth of this early in Genesis, when the blood that had given life to Abel is spilt by Cain and brings death (infertility) to the land (Genesis 4.10–12). In fact, any murder has this effect: it does not only kill an individual, but also pollutes, desecrates the land. That means that righting the wrong of a murder involves cleansing the land as well as finding the murderer. Have a look at Deuteronomy 21.1–9 or Numbers 35.30–34 if you are interested in the detail of how that was done, but the key thing is that while blood, wrongly shed, polluted the land, it is also blood, used rightly, that can cleanse it. Nothing can defeat death but life.

Pollution and what to do about it

Before we look at how that works, you may be wondering why it matters if the land is polluted by sin (particularly since it is difficult for us in the twenty-first century to believe that it is). The obvious, practical, answer is that an infertile land cannot sustain a people. But, deeper than that are the beliefs that a land which is deeply desecrated and polluted by sin will eventually 'vomit out' its inhabitants (Leviticus 18.28),[7] and that an unholy land cannot be dwelt in by a holy God. It was vital that the land and the people within it be cleansed.

Nor is murder the only thing that affects the land, although it is the most extreme. All sin pollutes. As John Goldingay (who has written two mammoth commentaries on the Old Testament) graphically puts it:

The problem with sin in Leviticus is not that sin involves infidelity or disloyalty which makes God angry but that sin pollutes, stains, and spoils, and thus makes people or things repulsive; it is the u-u-u-ugh factor in our relationship with God.[8]

Every time something associated with desecration, death and illness enters the world, it pollutes the land and anything or anyone who comes in contact with it, creating an 'ughh' factor that needs to be set right.

Step away from anything that strikes you as magical or mythical about this, and we can still see their point. Possibly we are used to the idea that 'sin' is something one person has done and one person needs to repent of. An Old Testament understanding of sin is more like an oil spill. Someone could perhaps be blamed for the spill, but the pressing issue is to stop it spreading and killing everything in its path. 'Sin' is not just my wilful disobedience, but anything that is counter to life and holiness, and it does not stay attached to one person but impacts on the world.

Is this beginning to sound familiar? Think about the impact of our individual and collective greed on the climate, on the seas, on the atmosphere – on our world. We are daily witnessing the literally polluting power of sin. Or another example: the Covid-19 pandemic paralysed the world into lockdown. Every day each person had the choice of staying in isolation to protect others, or flouting the rules. Their choice to flout the rules would be partly driven by their own desires and thoughts, and be partly the result of the influence of others. That choice could, in turn, influence that of others, spread infection and potentially impact the whole country. There is no escaping the realization that what we do can pollute not only the lives of others, but the very earth on which we live.

To return to the Hebrew scriptures: we can think of their situation as two opposing sides in constant tension. On one side is God, holiness, life and health. This is God's design for God's world. But humans are constantly grappling with desecration, sin, death and illness – sometimes self-inflicted, other times apparently accidental or 'natural'.[9] God gives laws to the people of Israel that go some way towards preventing this ongoing pollution, but you can almost imagine him sighing as he does so. He's tried that a few times already. No matter how detailed these laws are, God will not force the people to obey them, nor can laws deal with those things that are beyond their control, but which still pollute the land. So God finds other ways to help.

The Temple

One of the problems about cleaning up a polluted land is that it is so *big*. Where do you start? Enter the Temple. In a wonderful commentary on Leviticus, Jacob Milgrom helps us understand this aspect of the role of the Temple through an analogy with *The Picture of Dorian Gray*.[10]

If you have not seen the film or read this novel by Oscar Wilde, it is the gothic story of a beautiful young man, Dorian, who 'sells his soul' for the right to remain young while a portrait of him ages. He then lives a life of increasing dissipation and crime, including murder, while remaining young and beautiful – but his portrait both ages and takes on Dorian's cynicism and evil. In a final scene, Dorian, horrified by the appearance of the portrait and what it says about his own life, stabs the picture and in doing so kills himself.

Not a cheerful tale, then. However, the image of the portrait somehow absorbing and taking on all that Dorian did in his life can help us imagine the role of the Temple. Whenever a sin (or death or illness) occurs in Israel, its impact is drawn into the Temple, polluting it while leaving the land unscathed.

Another author likens the Temple to a large magnet, drawing in the 'iron filings' of pollution from the land around it.[11] Once there, it can be dealt with in one place.

So, we now have a clean land and a thoroughly polluted Temple. But the Temple was the place where the Holy God was to meet God's people, so could not be allowed to *stay* polluted. To restore it, the people of Israel needed a weapon or cleanser of holiness and life that was stronger than the pollution of unholiness and death. They used blood: blood, which is life, which is God's, and which is holy.

We cannot understand the sacrificial system until we realize that it is not the death of the animal that is important in itself; it is the life-blood taken from the animal and used to conquer the death of sin that is important. Death is not defeated by death, but by Life.

How was this done? Individuals would come to the Temple with their animal, and lay their hand on the animal's head: identifying themselves with the creature. Then the life-blood of that creature – symbolically the person's own life-blood – would 'make atonement' for any way they had contributed to the pollution of the Temple, by soaking up death in life, unholiness in holiness. Think of blood as an ultra-strong detergent, a miraculous sponge, and you're close to the idea. Or, if this analogy works better for you, think, 'The life-force can undo, or cleanse, the death-force that is impurity. Expressed by analogy with electricity, we can say that blood carries a life-charge that neutralizes the negative charge of the pollution.'[12]

Let me highlight a few important points here as we move towards the New Testament. In this picture, blood achieves atonement by cleansing God's dwelling place and thus restoring God's relationship with the people, rather than by any payment or punishment. Using the blood of the animal is an act of vicarious cleansing, not an act of vicarious punishment. And within the whole act we see the belief that life is stronger than death.

There is one final, and vital, stage we need to look at in God's process of helping his people deal with sin. It is what we call in English the Day of Atonement.

The Day of Atonement

At the centre of the Temple, and separated from the rest of it by a curtain, was the Holy of Holies. Here was where heaven and earth intersected, where God was encountered in a particular, immediate way, and the holiness of this place meant that it needed to be approached with extreme care. It was, however, not immune from pollution. Inadvertent sins, sins that had been confessed and repented of, or unintentional uncleanness, could be cleansed from the outer temple. Deep, deliberate rebellions and transgressions, however, polluted the Holy of Holies, and the sacrifices brought by the people were not strong enough to deal with them. Stronger blood – stronger life and holiness – was needed.

Hence, once a year, after elaborate preparation, the high priest undertook the rituals of the Day of Atonement, where the blood used was not the vicarious blood of people, but of God.[13] Instead of a person laying their hands on the head of an animal to transfer their identity to it, two goats are brought before God and one is 'chosen' by God.[14] The priest, wearing the Name of God on his forehead, enters the Holy of Holies and cleanses it with the blood of the goat that God 'laid his hand on'. In other words, God's representative uses God's representative blood to clean the worst of humanity's sin: that which we could not clean even with our own lives.

With that, it is time to move to the next stage of this story.

Notes

1 Try doing a simple search on an online Bible app. The word we translate 'fornication' doesn't appear at all until the Apocrypha. 'Adultery' appears fewer than 50 times across the Bible, whereas 'blood' comes up closer to 500 times. Read through the Genesis appearances alone and you will see that it is a dangerous substance.

2 See, for example, Garth Nix, 2003, *Sabriel*, London: HarperCollins, p. 62. Blood is used to break the barrier between life and death and allow the dead to

return. Or see J. K. Rowling, 1998, *Harry Potter and the Philosopher's Stone*, London: Bloomsbury, pp. 187–9. Voldemort drinks unicorn blood in order to give his displaced soul substance.

3 C. S. Lewis, 1998, *The Silver Chair*, London: HarperCollins, pp. 216–17. Original edition 1953.

4 That's the total decided on in the Talmud.

5 Cassandra Clare, 2008, *City of Ashes*, *Mortal Instruments* series, London: Walker Books, p. 134.

6 This is the answer to why vampires, alone of monsters, are unable to enter holy ground. They have desecrated life itself, consumed something holy, and can no longer confront holiness.

7 The apparent evidence for this lay in the fact that from 597 BC there were a series of deportations of people from Judah to Babylon: the exile.

8 John Goldingay, 1995, 'Your Iniquities Have Made a Separation between You and Your God' in John Goldingay (ed.), *Atonement Today*, London: SPCK, p. 51.

9 Understanding 'sin' in this way helps to make sense of odd things in Old Testament laws like mould on the walls of houses being seen as needing religious cleansing. Mould is connected to death. Similarly, with skin diseases. Spilling menstrual blood or semen on the ground is again spilling life.

10 Jacob Milgrom, 2004, *Leviticus: A Book of Ritual and Ethics*, Continental Commentary, Minneapolis, MN: Fortress Press, p. 13.

11 Stephen Finlan, 2005, *Problems with Atonement*, Collegeville, MN: Liturgical Press, p. 15.

12 Finlan, *Problems with Atonement*, p. 13.

13 The blood is not universally understood in this way, but there are strong arguments for it and – as will be seen soon – it makes sense of much New Testament language. See Margaret Barker, 'Temple and Liturgy', a paper presented at Lambeth Palace, London, June 2009, p. 5.

14 The other, the 'scapegoat', is important in other atonement stories. Here we focus on the sacrificed one.

4

The New Testament

I realize that the sacrificial world of the Old Testament is very strange to us, but it is a story the New Testament writers grew up with. We have no hope of knowing whether what they are talking about is a shape-shifter or an otter unless we, too, know the story.

Once all the backstory is in place, however, understanding how the New Testament writers used the story to make sense of Christ's work is comparatively straightforward. Every year, the Hebrew people celebrated the Day of Atonement. Every year, for a time, the Holy of Holies was pure, the people were reconciled to God, sin was wiped out. Every year it was effective but temporary, partial, local.

But what if God were able to be there in reality, in material form – incarnated – rather than through the representation of the priest? What if the actual *blood of God* could soak up the sin, rather than the representative blood of a goat doing so? The real thing, of which the Temple rites had been only a shadow? Think of the wonder of the idea of this blood, of the infinite Life of God in liquid form. Material existence had never held something of such life and holiness before. Nothing of such power had ever been offered as a means of dealing with the deepest pollutions of the world. The Day of Atonement was the imprint of God's foot in the sand: now God was there in Jesus, offering his own Life-blood.

This offering would never need to be repeated, and nor was it local any more. The impact of this cleansing power swept through not the imitation or image of the world (that is, the Temple), but the world itself – pulling all the pollution of the sin of the world into itself and transforming it there:

But when Christ came as a high priest of the good things that have come, then through the greater and perfect tent (not made with hands, that is, not of this creation), he entered once for all into the Holy Place, not with the blood of goats and calves, but with his own blood, thus obtaining eternal redemption. (Hebrews 9.11–12)

The book of Hebrews is all about this. Go back and read it now, with this backstory in mind, and everything falls into place. Christ was the *true* High Priest, the one through whom atonement was made, and the Life-blood that he brought into the Holy of Holies was truly God's blood.[1] Everything in our backstory – the understanding of blood, the sacrificial system, the Day of Atonement – had been a foretaste of the reality that came to fulfilment in Christ.[2] What Christ did, he did 'once for all': nothing more is required.[3] The power of his life, poured out in love, was too strong for sin and even too strong for death: 'death has been swallowed up in victory'.[4]

That is the essential message of sacrificial atonement, and if you grasp that you have grasped enough. But the links with the Old Testament understanding of blood go even further.

The power of life in Jesus

The idea of following the footprints of Christ through the Old Testament into the New is what theologians call 'typology': the belief that events and ideas from the Old Testament were 'types' or 'imprints' or 'foot-prints' of the reality that was to come in Jesus. So it is not just the Day of Atonement where we find these prints, but scattered throughout our blood backstory.

Start with the Temple in its everyday use. As we saw in the previous chapter, the Temple was the place people came to cleanse themselves and their land from sin, desecration, illness and contact with death. They did so by using the holy, life-filled power of blood, which was somehow able to soak up pollution without being polluted itself. With that in mind, notice what Jesus did as he wandered the paths of Palestine. Wherever he went, people who were 'polluted' by sin, desecration (demons), illness and death came to him and were cleansed. It was as if Jesus was a mobile Temple!

The major difference with this Jesus-temple, however, was that the Life which could cleanse and heal the people was permanently available, per-manently poured out for those who met, asked or even simply touched him.[5] No sacrifices were necessary. Nor did any of this contact defile him, as it should have according to the Law. Jesus regularly touched those who were accepted as ritually unclean: lepers, the dead, a haemorrhaging woman, yet there is no sign that he had to undergo the Temple rituals such contact would normally require.[6] Uncleanness simply dissolved in his presence. This was Life on a different scale to anything known before.

Next, think about the blood prohibition itself. God prohibited murder and the 'consumption' of blood because we are not to 'take life' from another.[7] We can see how the whole language about Jesus, particularly in John's Gospel, paints a picture of one who does the exact opposite of taking life from others. Instead, Jesus has 'life in himself' for 'in him is life', and through him there is abundant and eternal life for *others*.[8] To their complete bemusement, the disciples and crowds are told to take Jesus' Life-blood into themselves and are assured that in doing so their own lives will flow into the excess of life that is 'eternal'.[9] Jesus' life was one that was ever flowing outwards to give life to others. Ideally, when we have Jesus' life within us we should have no need to metaphorically 'feed' on another, or build up our own lives at the expense of someone else. We are already being offered more 'fullness of life' than we could ever contain. And this is Life that is no longer at the mercy of death, but has flowed through the grave itself, soaking up its power and defeating it.

Jesus' life, poured out into the world, acts as life/blood always did in the Hebrew scriptures, but so much more. Just as blood made the Temple a place that God could inhabit, so Christ's blood prepares us, or the Church, for God to dwell in us, making peace between us.[10] But notice on what a different scale we're working now. Rather than annual redemption we have *eternal* redemption; rather than Israel being cleansed and reconciled to God we now have the reconciliation of *all* things on heaven and earth.[11] When we sing and speak of Christ's blood, it is this power of Life, sweeping across time and space and eternity and cleansing everything in its wake, that we are thinking of.

There is one final, and I think beautiful, image to take away from this. We have looked at how Jesus lived as a mobile Temple, and we know that Christ referred to himself in that way in John 2.19–21:

> Jesus answered them, 'Destroy this temple, and in three days I will raise it up.' The Jews then said, 'This temple has been under construction for forty-six years, and will you raise it up in three days?' But he was speaking of the temple of his body.

In the Gospels, the Temple, God's dwelling place on earth, the site of forgiveness and reconciliation and healing, is Jesus. That we have already discussed. But what happens after Christ's death, resurrection and ascension? Jesus comes, through the Holy Spirit, to dwell in his people, his 'body', his Church. The young Church thus saw itself as formed by the Spirit into the new Temple, both collectively (Ephesians 2.21) and individually: 'Don't you not know that you are God's temple and that

God's Spirit dwells in you?' (1 Corinthians 3.16). Now *we* are to be the site of God's dwelling among humanity; we are to be the site of forgiveness and healing and reconciliation. Isn't that a remarkable picture of the Church, and of each of our lives?

And if we ever forget that, every Communion, Eucharist, Mass should remind us. Think of what we do then. We take the blood – the Life – of Christ into ourselves, into that temple of our bodies, so that it can cleanse us as the holy power of life/blood always has, sweeping through the sin and pollution and failure of our lives and soaking it up in Life. That, I believe, is still good news.

Notes

1 Hebrews 5.1–6; 7.22—8.6; 9.11–28.

2 Hebrews 11.1–14.

3 Romans 6.10; Hebrews 9.27; 1 Peter 3.18.

4 1 Corinthians 15.54; cf. Hebrews 2.14.

5 For example, Luke 8.43–48.

6 For example, Matthew 8.3; Luke 7.14; Luke 8.43–48.

7 If any of you are familiar with the writings of René Girard or Slavoj Žižek, this will sound familiar.

8 John 5.26; John 1.4; John 5.24; 6.33; 10.10.

9 John 6.53; John 6.54.

10 Colossians 1.20; Ephesians 2.13–18; Acts 20.28.

11 Hebrews 9.12; Colossians 1.12; cf. Ephesians 2.14.

5

Good News (1): Looking at Sin in a Fresh Ancient Way

The essential 'good news' of the story of sacrificial atonement is the same now as it was 2,000 years ago, and I believe much of the last chapter is applicable today. But the richness of the story raises possibilities of good news for some particular bad news stories of our times, and this is what we will look at here.

First, a warning. If we are to use this story today, it is unwise to try to base it on a belief that blood is, literally, 'life'.[1] But if we are content to leave this idea as an element in a story in the way that the lion Aslan is an element of C. S. Lewis's Narnia story, we may get somewhere. Within the world of Narnia, Aslan is real and true, and countless young and not-so-young people have had the foundation for their love of Jesus prepared or strengthened through their imaginative relationship with Aslan. Within the world of the Old Testament, blood is life, and if we let it be so, it can help to prepare the imaginative foundation for understanding Christ's work. If we put aside for the moment the question of literal truth, we can use what it has to tell us of meaningful truth.

If we do so, we may find that the very strangeness of these ideas challenge and stretch our understandings of atonement in ways that more familiar and comfortable concepts would not.

Looking at sin in a 'fresh' ancient way

Let's start with what these stories tell us of sin: those things that needed 'cleaning up' by blood at the Temple. The first thing that strikes me is the sheer range of reasons people sought atonement. When we think of the sins Christ made atonement for, and which we bring to God in confession, what usually comes to mind are times that we deliberately or knowingly 'do wrong'. After all, why would you repent of something that was patently not your fault? But if you read through Leviticus, you'll find that people were told by God to bring sacrifices for things they had done accidentally (Leviticus 4—5), things that were a natural part of life (for example, childbirth, Leviticus 12), and things that happened to them (for example, skin diseases, Leviticus 13). If we think the issue here is solely one of blame, it's completely unfair. But that's the point: blame is not the primary issue.

The primary issue is that anything which in some way injures, decreases or wastes life needs to be touched and countered and cleansed *by* life (in this case, blood), regardless of how it happened.[2] God's main interest is not in catching out wrongdoers and punishing them, as if he were a sadistic nineteenth-century school teacher getting a sick satisfaction out of whipping small children. God's main interest is clearing up the mess his beloved children create at the end of each day: teaching them to put their toys back in the box; teaching them that, yes, that does make a bad stain in the carpet; that the biscuits are meant to be shared evenly; that hitting your brother over the head with a toy train has consequences for you as well as him. Or, if you like, that our contribution to the state of the world affects everyone; that every spark of life is sacred and needs to be treated as such; that disease and misery and death are not of God.

If this is what atonement is about, it is a far, far bigger picture than the one we have communicated for centuries. It is a far, far bigger picture than my petty acts of selfishness (although it includes them). It is even a bigger picture than what we term 'morality', for it includes anything that is on the side of death over life.[3] Animate or inanimate, deliberate or accidental: all are God's concern, all come under the atoning power of Christ. If this is so, we have some work to do in broadening the scope of the good news we proclaim, both to ourselves individually and to ourselves as we are interconnected with our world.

Shame and failure

To begin with, what if that life-giving act of Christ could not only lift from us the guilt of our wrongdoing, but also the weight of shame we feel for our inadequacies and failures, the paralysing fear of disappointing others – all those things that shrink our lives? Over the past few years I have asked (and recruited school chaplains to ask) groups of young people what their 'bad news' is, and what 'good news' would look like to them. The majority of 'bad news' responses were about the weight of pressure they felt from the expectations laid on them from multiple sources (including themselves). 'Good news' would be knowing they were accepted exactly as they were.

The evident anxiety underlying these responses was one element that the 2019 Barna Report on 'The Connected Generation' surveyed in young people across the world. They found:

> On average, one in five 18–35-year-olds around the globe identifies with feelings related to anxiety – specifically, they report feeling at least three of the four following emotions: anxiety about important decisions, sadness or depression, fear of failure and insecurity in themselves.[4]

What is bizarre about this is that the level of anxiety found in young people in the UK, New Zealand and Australia was higher than in any other country surveyed except Taiwan. As a comparison, 29 per cent of young people in the UK and New Zealand indicated that they felt this anxiety, whereas only 9 per cent of those in Ghana did.[5]

The complex question of why anxiety should be higher in these countries with relatively adequate social security, no immediate threat of war, and *comparatively* low levels of poverty, occupies sociologists, psychologists and theologians alike, and naturally each will view the problem – and therefore the solution – differently. It is possible, though, that our atonement stories could play a vital role here.

Christianity has both a very high view of humanity, and what many would see to be a pessimistic one. It is high because we are made in God's image (and it couldn't get much higher than that); we are known by and 'chosen' by God in our mothers' wombs; we are not accidental; we are breathed into life by the breath, the Spirit, of God and, as we have seen, that Life lives in us making every single life holy. Whether we are extremely important in the world's eyes, or someone society has decided is not worthy of being born, does not change the holiness of the Life within us or make any difference to our importance to God.

On the other hand, Christianity does not have the optimistic view of human *behaviour* that humanists do. Christians, whose hope is based in God, not themselves, can face the fallibility of humanity unflinchingly. The basis of hope for the humanist, however, is the ability of individuals and humanity as a whole to 'evolve' in morality and virtue. In order to maintain that belief, our society works hard to protect people from having to face their fallibility, from experiencing failure and shame. 'Just think positively and you can do anything' has to be one of the most patently false pieces of life advice ever perpetuated. Yes, we will achieve more by thinking positively than negatively, but there will always come a point where we fail, or we reach our limits. If we do not build that fact into our understanding of life, we will find ourselves carrying the weight of impossible expectations.

We will also find that failure itself becomes even more of a monster to be feared. We in the largely secular West are taught that we *should* be able to achieve anything we set our mind to, so failure is entirely our fault and the shame is entirely ours. For some, fear of failure can drive them to frantic overwork; for others, it paralyses. Think of how people respond if they are hunted: some endure unspeakable hardships rather than be caught, while others freeze and give themselves up. Neither is what we want for ourselves or those we care for.

Nadia Bolz-Weber, writing in response to the Covid-19 pandemic, wondered if the opposite of fear was love.[6] We will not lift anxiety long-term through bolstering ourselves, positive thinking, or a 'can-do' attitude alone, because these turn out to feed the monster of failure: failure that constantly threatens to expose our weaknesses and undermine our most positive facades. We have been trying this path since the 1950s and anxiety levels have only grown. Perhaps what will lessen the fear of failure and shame is not avoiding it at all costs, but knowing that we are loved regardless.

We have a way of directly addressing the weight of expectations and fear of failure that haunt so many young people. It is the love of God who knows our failures perfectly well, loves us anyway, and offers to wipe them clean.

A school chaplain told me about a teenage girl who came to see her in tears, certain that she 'wasn't good enough' for anything – not for her academic work, nor for sport, not for her friends, not for her family. Understandably, the chaplain wisely helped her see her strengths and how much she was loved. But when we discussed it later, we realized there was another thing she could have said. She could have said, 'No, maybe you're not good enough for all these things. Neither am I. And that's OK. Here's why ...' We don't have to run from the monster of failure. We can face it, because we know it has been cut off at the knees. We know that if it destroys our wobbly foundation of self-expectations, we have an immovable foundation of God's love to build on instead. And – vitally – God has done something about it. The God we build on is one who knows us perfectly well, and who loves us so deeply that he poured out his life so that our embarrassing, crippling failures and shame, along with everything that is counter to life, could be gathered up and filled with life.

Anglicans and Catholics regularly confess 'the wrong we have done, and the good we have left undone', believing that Christ's atonement was strong enough to wipe 'sins of commission and sins of omission' clean.[7] How about our toe-curlingly embarrassing failures? How about the dreams we worked towards and never reached? How about the dreams our parents dreamed about for us that were not fulfilled? Is Christ's atonement strong enough to set us free from the failures and shame that pollute our lives? This story says it is, and this is good news that those of us drenched in a secular worldview are crying out to hear.

Notes

1 This isn't to say that it was 'literally' understood as 'life' in the Hebrew scriptures. We cannot divide their understanding of beliefs like that into clear-cut terms like 'literal' and 'figurative': it was likely far more nuanced than that.

2 In the case of childbirth, it's not the production of the new life of the child that is the problem, but all the spilt blood it involves.

3 We particularly need to realize this in a world where many outside the Church think we equate sin with sexual immorality.

4 Barna Group, 2019, *The Connected Generation*, Ventura, CA: Barna, p. 52.

5 Barna Group, *The Connected Generation*. The figure for Australia was 28 per cent.

6 Nadia Bolz-Weber, 2020, 'Be Not Afraid', *The Corners by Nadia Bolz-Weber*, 19 March, https://nadiabolzweber.substack.com/p/be-not-afraid-um-yeahok?r=3dw94 &utm_campaign=post&utm_medium=web&utm_source=copy&fbclid=I-wARo2biCFWZ8KlCdlWItkd_ehToqeY4ejbf4pDX9NPE-_pvrIkZ65SIsdWg4 (accessed 18.09.2022).

7 Anglican Church in Aotearoa New Zealand and Polynesia, 1989, *A New Zealand Prayer Book – He Karakia Mihinare o Aotearoa*, Christchurch, NZ: Genesis, p. 407.

6

Good News (2): Looking at Connections in a Fresh Ancient Way

Most of us who preach suspect that our sermons drift in and out of people's minds without making any lasting impression. We would be pleasantly surprised to find they were remembered a week later, let alone quoted almost 400 years after they were delivered. But one passage from a 1624 sermon of John Donne's is known in part even by many who have no clue where it came from:

> No man is an island entire of itself; every man
> is a piece of the continent, a part of the main;
> if a clod be washed away by the sea, Europe
> is the less, as well as if a promontory were, as
> well as any manor of thy friends or of thine
> own were; any man's death diminishes me,
> because I am involved in mankind.[1]

No one is an island. We are all connected inextricably with one another, and what one of us does, or what happens to one of us, will affect us all. Donne has given us a beautiful depiction of one of the main assumptions behind the rites at the Temple. Everything we do affects one another and creation itself: humanity is not an archipelago but a continent. As a result, atonement was a communal as well as individual responsibility. Believers were to clean up the pollution caused by sin together as they had caused it together. Being connected with one another, with creation and with God is not something we choose or discard, but is simply how things are. If there is truth in this, why then is one of the main 'bad news' issues today in the West one of isolation and loneliness?

The Barna Group's report I quoted in the last chapter with regard to anxiety was specifically looking at the sense of connectedness among young people across the globe, and the results are daunting for Western countries:

The U.S. and Australia top the list in reporting frequent loneliness and isolation (34%), followed by the UK and New Zealand (31% each) – all very Westernized contexts. On the other end of the spectrum, young adults in countries like Indonesia (11%), Kenya (12%), Mexico (13%) and Romania (13%) less often report this kind of detachment.[2]

Years earlier, Mother Teresa warned us of the same thing. In 1975 she was interviewed by an American journalist, Dan Wooding, who later said that it was the interview that had impacted him most in his career. He wrote of this conversation:

'The spiritual poverty of the Western World is much greater than the physical poverty of our people,' she told me, as the fan whirred above us, trying to alleviate the unbearable heat of that Indian city ... 'You, in the West, have millions of people who suffer such terrible loneliness and emptiness. They feel unloved and unwanted. These people are not hungry in the physical sense, but they are in another way. They know they need something more than money, yet they don't know what it is. What they are missing, really, is a living relationship with God.'[3]

Although not everyone around us would agree with her conclusion, we are all well aware that the poverty of isolation and loneliness is a problem. Solitary confinement is a particularly debilitating form of punishment, yet we have countless people – particularly the aged – living alone with minimal social interaction. The Covid-19 pandemic gave us all a taste of the mental and physical impact of long-term isolation, and our attempts over that time to imitate relationship through video conferencing were a bit like trying to survive on water rather than a hearty meal, leaving most of us exhausted and drained. Yet we have created a world where most of the 'connections' we and our children have are virtual. Our societies have recognized the need for community, connections and belonging, and everyone from teachers to sociologists to advertisers are working to promote them – yet here we are, still topping the list worldwide for lonely young people.

Perhaps our problem is that our entire worldview is light years away from the one the Hebrew people held. Our attempts to create community are like painting a layer of very thin gold plate over a brass candlestick: it doesn't take much wear for the foundational metal to show through. We can decide to add connectedness on to our lives, but for the Hebrews it was a 'given'. One person might choose to ignore their connection to the land, but their sin still polluted it. Another could choose to separate themselves from their people, but that was rather like separating themselves from food: it is possible, but is not good for long-term health. We do not know how overtly the Hebrew people were taught that their actions affected one another and the land. It seems that they simply knew it; it was part of their understanding of the world. The issue was what to do about it.

What we in the West need are new foundational stories or, if you like, corrective lenses that can begin to alter our very worldview. I believe that digging a little deeper into this atonement thread will offer one such story, one that challenges our heroic individualism with news that is good if only we can accept it: we are not alone. We are always in relationship, not only with one another, but with our world and especially with God. What we took to be brass under that layer of gold plate turns out to have been solid gold all along.

A new pair of glasses

I am in the process of trying to learn the basics of the Māori language: *te Reo Māori*. My infinitely patient teacher not only wants to help me understand and pronounce the words, but – more importantly – understand the worldview behind them: the lens through which I need to view the world they speak of. Despite having only taken a few hesitant glances through this lens, I am already fascinated by how everything shifts and changes focus. One example: my teacher explained how in *te Reo* there are no possessives ('my', 'your', etc.). There are words English speakers translate and understand as possessives, but they are really terms of relationship. They do not denote possessing something as much as being in relationship with something. The quality and type of relationships differ from one relationship to another (I am in a different relationship with the song I write than I am to the song another writes for me, and my relationships could be personal, established or future), but they are never something I pick up from 'over there' and make 'mine'. I am in relationship with the earth I walk on (and therefore address her by name, *Papatuanuku*). I am in relationship with the mountain my people live on, with the one who gave birth to me, with the keyboard I am typing on.

This is not unique to te *Reo Māori*. Yet think of how different this lens is to the dominant one of the West, a consumerist lens, where we are encouraged to take us much as possible from 'over there' and bring it into the fiercely guarded, carefully nurtured cell we call 'mine'. Is it any wonder that these consumerist societies are filled with loneliness?

This is a glimpse of the world through a lens that brings us much closer to a Hebrew worldview. Yet even with this to help, and the back-story we have already covered, the final element of the blood-atonement story I want to explore now will seem a little odd. Christ's atonement – at-one-ment – is something that went further than the accepted levels of connection, even in a Hebrew or Māori worldview. Somehow, something new happened, primarily in terms of our relationship with God. In Christ, God went to the inconceivable lengths of taking on human blood and flesh and thus embedded himself into connectedness with humanity in a new and bizarre way. It was this act – the incarnation – and the new quality of connectedness that it brought about, which gives us one more insight into the good news of the story of sacrificial atonement.

Taking on blood and flesh

Followers of Jesus have wrestled with what the incarnation meant since his earliest bewildered disciples first tried to make sense of the gap between what they knew was logically possible and what their senses were telling them was happening. We must admire the brilliance of theologians who battled with words (and one another) in order to express this wonder in the spare, clear, open statements of our creeds. Their wisdom has guided the Church ever since, and however much I may encourage you to use your imagination, it is always wise to keep one foot in the creeds and another in the scriptures while our minds reach up to the clouds. But it is also good to do that cloud-reaching exercise, if only to remind ourselves of the vast uncaptured wildness of what is.

So as we venture to link the incarnation with atonement, here are two more imaginative pictures to start us off. If we go back to the *Mortal Instruments* series we dipped into in Chapter 3, we are in a world where there are vampires and werewolves, but also 'Nephilim': humans with a strain of angelic blood in them. For complicated reasons, the hero, Jace, has far more angelic blood in him than most Nephilim. At one point another key character, Simon, who has become a vampire, has been attacked and is dying. Jace calmly slices his own arm, gives him his blood to drink, and watches as his blood fills up Simon's veins, bringing him back to life.[4] But an even more remarkable thing follows. As in other vampire stories, these vampires cannot survive sunlight, and as Simon and Jace escape and race home in a boat, the sun rises. Simon expects to die, but finds the sunlight no longer affects him. Jace's angelic blood has cleansed the demonic taint from Simon and he is no longer forced to be a creature of the night.

As the Harry Potter series starts, we learn that Harry's mother has died protecting Harry: giving her life for his. By the end of the first book we have discovered that in doing so her life entered Harry's very blood and lingers there. The power of the sacrificial love carried in that life is of such goodness that Voldemort, filled with pure evil, cannot physically touch Harry, let alone kill him.[5] Voldemort's skin is burned by contact with the fiery holiness of such love-filled life.[6] In the final book (semi-spoiler alert), a key character willingly offers his own life for those of his friends, and by doing so covers all of them in a similar protection.[7] How does all this happen?

What these and other stories have in common is the idea that life can be passed from one person to another through their blood. Admittedly, that is logically impossible, but it is made to make imaginative sense within fantasy worlds. And that same imaginative picture can help us to grasp the beyond-logic sense of the centrality of the incarnation to atonement. When the American theologian Luke Timothy Johnson wrote a commentary on Hebrews, he acknowledged how difficult it is for us to comprehend the Hebrew understanding of life, but described it as a gift of God in which all of us 'participate': rather like a river of life-blood flowing through all of us.[8]

With that picture in mind, we can see Lily Potter's love-filled life-blood flowing from her into her son and protecting him, Jace's angel-touched blood flowing through Simon and cleansing him.[9] But we can also imagine how our own choices and actions and self-sacrifices might be flowing into the life of others, and how, even if we find ourselves alone, those connections remain. The prayers we mumble in our bedrooms, the quiet, unseen acts of love or self-sacrifice we make are not lost, but flow into the life of others. What we make of our lives does not only affect us, but humanity as a whole.[10] We are that deeply connected.

Most of all, though, this imaginative picture can give us a way of understanding that remarkable verse, 'As in Adam, all died, so in Christ shall all be made alive.'[11] How? *How* can we understand being 'in Adam' or 'in Christ', and how can we think of being 'made alive' through them? Only through the incarnation. In becoming human, Christ took on blood and flesh, and in doing so God's Life joined our shared river of mortal life.[12] That is perhaps the greatest wonder of our faith. Then, by dying, God was able to pour that all-powerful, love-filled, sacrificial Life of Christ into the shared river of life to bring Life to all: protecting, cleansing away sin, failure, shame and evil, healing as Jesus always healed, and conquering death itself.

Notes

1 John Donne, 1997, 'Meditation XVII' in *No Man is an Island: A Selection from the Prose of John Donne*, London: Folio Society, p. 75.

2 Barna Group, 2019, *The Connected Generation*, Ventura, CA: Barna, p. 46.

3 Dan Wooding, 2013, 'The Day Mother Teresa Told Me, "Your Poverty Is Greater than Ours"', *Patch*, 6 April, https://patch.com/california/lakeforest-ca/bp--the-day-mother-teresa-told-me-your-poverty-is-gree85a671097 (accessed 18.09.2022).

4 Cassandra Clare, 2008, *City of Ashes*, London: Walker Books, p. 377.

5 Think again of how vampires cannot enter hallowed ground.

6 J. K. Rowling, 1998, *Harry Potter and the Philosopher's Stone*, London: Bloomsbury, pp. 213–14. It is not precisely Voldemort's skin here but the skin of the man he is possessing. The outcome is the same.

7 J. K. Rowling, 2007, *Harry Potter and the Deathly Hallows*, London: Bloomsbury, p. 591.

8 Luke Timothy Johnson, 2006, *Hebrews: A Commentary*, Louisville, KY: Westminster John Knox Press, p. 26.

9 John 15.13.

10 You may have noticed that I have not addressed our connection with creation much in these chapters, despite climate change being a huge 'bad news' item. Don't worry – it will come up in a later chapter.

11 1 Corinthians 15.22.

12 Hebrews 2.14.

PART 3

Candles in the Darkness

The Story of Victorious Atonement

7

The Backstory: War and Victory

The second atonement story we are going to tackle is what has traditionally been called 'Christus Victor' or 'victorious atonement'; this means understanding Christ's work in terms of conquering the forces of evil. Like it or not, this is a story filled with imagery of war and power struggles and things that many Christians, understandably, want to keep a safe distance from their faith. But there are surprises lurking beneath the dust that has accumulated around this tale. As we look carefully we will find that far from glorifying violence, this story challenges it and turns our normal paths to victory upside down. Yet, ironically, the challenges to violence it issues would lose much of their impact if we separated them from their clothing of battle imagery.

It is to that imagery, then, that we turn now: imagery of victory and defeat, of war and ongoing battles, of enemies and allies. As is the case with all imagery, we need to start with what is familiar to us before we can understand the less familiar world it evokes; therefore we will begin by looking at some aspects of victory in earth-based war which will help us find our way as we venture into the strange other-world of Satan and his minions.

On 23 October 1956, 100,000 people descended on a statue of Stalin in Budapest and tore it down, destroying everything except the boots, into which they planted a Hungarian flag.[1]

A German Jew who had found refuge in the UK tells of hearing that Hitler had died: 'I felt total relief because [Hitler] had ruined my life ... The whole building cheered. We realized how important it was. It meant the end of the war against Germany.'[2]

On 2 May 2011, President Obama announced that Osama Bin Laden had been killed: 'A terrorist responsible for the murder of thousands of men, women and children.'[3]

Similar stories could be pulled out of any era of human history. Whenever we think of regimes of oppression and devastation, almost invariably there is one name that comes to mind: one central figure who somehow epitomizes the evil, and whose end marks the end of that evil's reign (for now, at least). It makes sense to think that way. It did take someone of Hitler's charisma and single-minded certainty of being right to lead the Nazi movement into the atrocities it committed, just as it took the particular personalities of Stalin and Bin Laden to rally their own powerful movements. But the leader is obviously not the whole story. Without a people with an ideology primed to accept them, they would have been powerless. Stalin rode on a wave of corrupt communism, Bin Laden on a wave of corrupt Islam, Hitler on a wave of corrupt humanism, and (in case we start feeling complacent) countless past leaders in Western history on waves of corrupt Christianity.

Two major elements appear to be necessary for evil to reign in such a way that we sit up and take notice of it: a charismatic leader, and a corrupted worldview. Corrupted worldviews may pave the way by working slowly and insidiously in the background for years, but for them to be brought spectacularly to the fore, you need a charismatic leader.

Take the example of Hitler and eugenics. It so happened that both worldview and leader came together in Germany at that time, but a party with much in common with the Nazis could have easily formed in the UK or the USA instead. The eugenics that so horrified the world when carried out on a widespread scale in Germany on Jews, gypsies, homosexuals, Catholics and the disabled had for decades been a popular way of thinking in the UK and the USA. The word 'eugenics' was actually invented in 1883 by an Englishman, Francis Galton, who was a cousin of Charles Darwin, and the ideology of eugenics grew from the popularity of Darwin's work.[4] Interest in eugenics spread across both sides of politics, on both sides of the Atlantic, and was considered seriously by influential people from George Bernard Shaw to Winston Churchill. The fire was being laid ready in many countries, and it was not until they witnessed the size of the conflagration emanating from Germany that the Allies dampened the ideological coals in their own grates.

Victory over Hitler meant the war with Germany was won. That was the first part of the problem solved. The Nazi ideology, too, has been determinedly suppressed in postwar German policy, which valiantly refuses to let itself forget the atrocities committed under its name. But those dampened coals around the world have never completely gone out, and victory over the creeping power of the worldview that put Hitler in power has never been complete. Elements of fascism keep rising up across the globe. The ideology of eugenics has never stopped growing quietly in the background of Western society, with presentable forms of it being accepted as calmly by many of us today as early eugenic theories were by decent people in the early 1900s. I am aware that this is an uncomfortable and possibly controversial statement, but we will unpack it more in Chapter 23. For now here is the key point: victory in 1945, or at any time in our history, was both complete in terms of defeating the leader, and partial in terms of defeating the worldview that gave him power.

These two elements, the charismatic leader and the underlying worldview or ideology that put the leader in power, are important to keep in mind as we move to consider the cosmic war that underlies the victorious theory of atonement. In this story, too, there is both a charismatic leader and an underlying corrupted worldview to deal with. The Old Testament is the story of a brave struggle to stop this corruption gaining the upper hand, but eventually, inexorably, Satan emerges: a leader who both epitomizes that evil and galvanizes others into following him. By the time we reach the birth of Jesus, Satan is a well-established reality impacting daily life, and a cosmic war is underway. The 'victory' we speak of Christ achieving, then, as in all our experiences of victory in war, involved both an initial triumph over the evil leader, and an ongoing battle to defeat the insidious tendrils of the worldview that had put Satan in power. It is a battle we are still waging.

Fortunately, we are neither alone nor unarmed in this strange, utterly non-violent, already-won-yet-ongoing war we are invited into. But if we are somehow to be a part of the Resistance, it is important we understand a little more of what it is all about.

So let's start with the strangest part of it. Where did this leader, Satan, appear from?

The emergence of Satan

Whether we 'believe in' the devil or not, we are well accustomed to his presence in religious talk. It is a little odd, then, to discover how unimportant he is in the Hebrew scriptures. Most of us, whether or not we realize it, have grown up with an understanding of Satan shaped more by John Milton's depiction of him in *Paradise Lost* than by his appearances in the Hebrew scriptures. That is not surprising: Milton's Satan is far more interesting, and his story caught the imagination of countless artists and writers who came after him. They, in turn, shaped the popular understanding that influences us. But while, if you are game, it is always worth reading *Paradise Lost*, here we need to turn to Satan's less picturesque appearances in scripture.

There we find the word 'satan' generally used as a common noun referring to a range of characters – even God. It was the equivalent of saying, 'the person acting as a tempter'.[5] A distinct Satan figure (one we would give an 'S' rather than an 's' to) appears in a grand total of *two* places before Matthew's Gospel in our Bible. He has a starring role in the folk-tale-style book of Job and appears for two visionary verses in Zechariah 3.1–2 where he tries to accuse the high priest Joshua and is rebuked by God. And that's it.[6]

He didn't appear in the garden of Eden in the form of a snake – or, if he did, it isn't mentioned. As far as that story goes, the snake was a snake. Maybe it was Satan that Isaiah was speaking of when he wrote, 'How you are fallen from heaven, O Day Star, son of Dawn!' but when you read on it sounds more like the story of an earthly leader who aimed too high.[7] We are not told it is Satan. So, essentially, his appearances in Job and Zechariah are it.

Yet by the time Satan appears in the New Testament he is ruling over countless demons, he is 'prince of this world', and he claims that all the nations of the world are his to grant Jesus if he will bow down and worship him.[8] A lot seems to have happened between Old and New Testaments.

It did. But in order to understand these changes and developments, we need to look even further back than Satan's first appearances. We need to go to the foundational issue that lies behind all our atonement stories: the origin of evil. And we need to tackle the hoary question that always arrives when we start investigating this issue: how can an all-powerful, all-good God let bad things happen? We will have all heard this trotted out as a knock-down argument against God's existence by people who assume they've caught us in a whole new dilemma. They haven't. It's been causing followers of the One God headaches for at least 2,500 years. I would love to be able to tell you that if we read the Hebrew scriptures correctly, we can answer it, but no such luck. What happens when we read the Hebrew scriptures is that we accompany generations of believers as they try, with limited success, to reach a foolproof answer themselves. Along the way, however, they come up with some interesting ideas, and Satan is one of them.

Evil and God: let's start at the very beginning

In Rick Riordan's series of young adult books based around Egyptian mythology, the modern hero and heroine must fight against the ancient god of chaos, the snake Apophis, before he once again rises to swallow the sun. Poor old Ra, the sun god, is decrepit and senile, and it takes several books before the teenagers and their divine and semi-divine companions win through, conquer Apophis, and allow the world to return to its state of *ma'at* (harmony, balance, peace) in which life can exist.[9]

As with all Riordan's delightful books, he is faithful to the essence of the mythologies he uses. In the stories of ancient Egypt, not only did Apophis have to be defeated for life to exist, but each night he had to be fought by Ra, with the support of priests and laity, so that the sun could rise in the morning. This idea – that the threat of chaos needs to be overcome in order for life to survive – is a common theme of the time. If you look at the Mesopotamian, Akkadian, Egyptian or even Greek stories about the dawn of time, they are full of battles between gods, and usually feature a god or goddess of chaos who must be overcome at great cost to all involved.

But then we come to the beginning of our scriptures:

> When God began to create heaven and earth, and the earth was then welter and waste and darkness over the deep and God's breath was hovering over the waters, God said, 'Let there be light.' And there was light. (Genesis 1.1–2)[10]

This first chapter of Genesis takes every opportunity to thumb its nose at the religions of neighbouring cultures, starting right at the opening sentences. What it is describing here is God's complete control over chaos ('welter and waste and darkness'): God's 'victory over chaos' which is achieved not by the heated battles found in creation stories of surrounding cultures, but by dropping two words into space.[11] Serene, controlled, rhythmic. Absolute and unrivalled authority speaking light and life into being, controlling darkness and the swirling waters with the simple power of a divine word. Later, Leviathan, who appears first as a terrifying chaos monster in Mesopotamian mythology, is said by the psalmist to have been created by God to frolic in the sea.[12] Imagine a ferocious dragon who has been terrorizing villages rolling over to have his tummy tickled, and you've got the idea.

The point was that unlike the gods of surrounding cultures, the One God of the Hebrews was Almighty. God had no rivals. Everything was beneath God, created by God. There were beings that humanity referred to as 'gods'; there were 'angels', 'sons of God', 'principalities and powers', 'daemons', depending on what translation you are reading, but these were all secondary powers and completely under the control of God.

Christians, Jews and Muslims would agree with this wholeheartedly. But there is a problem. In that case, where does evil fit in? If God created and controls everything, did God create and control evil? For large portions of the Hebrew scriptures, the answer to that is 'yes'.

> I form light and create darkness,
> I make weal and create woe;
> I the LORD do all these things. (Isaiah 45.7)

Perhaps that is why the Hebrew scriptures give us so many confusing and, to be honest, unpleasant depictions of a God who has to be talked into mercy by Abraham or Moses,[13] or who hardens not only Pharaoh's heart so that he can punish the Egyptians and show his glory,[14] but also the hearts of the Canaanites so that they may be slaughtered by the Israelites.[15] If you are determined that absolutely everything in the world is controlled by the one God – and, surrounded by polytheistic cultures, it took determination to hold by that – what other options do you have than to attribute all that happens to his will?

But if you're also determined that your One God is good, you have to find some other options in order to make sense of the world. Maybe it is humanity's fault. What God created was perfect (Eden), but in giving humans the chance to disobey he also gave them the chance to let chaos back into the world. This idea, and the accompanying story of God's attempts to work with humanity to control chaos again through covenants, will be important when we look later at covenantal atonement.

But, as Jeffrey Burton Russell points out in his excellent book about the devil, even with the recognition that humanity was to some extent to blame, the Hebrew people clearly puzzled over the *degree* of suffering they experienced as God's chosen people. Surely the scale of evil in the world was too great to attribute to the sins of puny humans?[16] There had to be something more happening here, and given the cosmic nature of the catastrophes that hit the world, perhaps that 'something more' also worked on a cosmic level. If so, we must be looking at some form of rebellion against God on the part of those lower-than-God beings mentioned earlier.[17]

This idea is not plucked out of nowhere. There are a few tantalizing references in the Hebrew scriptures to there being more going on in God's heavenly household than we generally imagine, and in Deuteronomy 32.8–9 and Psalm 82 we find hints that at least some of the world's ills could be the fault of those 'sons of God', daemons, principalities and powers. In the book of Deuteronomy we read that God assigned all nations except Israel to 'the gods', keeping Israel alone under his direct care.

When the Most High apportioned the nations,
when he divided humankind,
he fixed the boundaries of the peoples
according to the number of the gods;
the LORD's own portion was his people,
Jacob his allotted share. (Deuteronomy 32.8–9)

Psalm 82 tells us that these gods 'judged unjustly' and 'showed partiality to the wicked' so that God was forced to demote them, let them 'fall like any prince'. It appears that the sons of God can go wrong and, when they do, the nations go with them.

This is, perhaps, a rather thin basis on which to build a theory of evil. However, when we come to that body of literature written between the testaments and overlapping with them, the stories grow, multiply and make space for Satan to establish his position.

Dipping our toes in the Pseudepigrapha

Nestled into the introduction to the story of Noah is another fascinating little verse:

The Nephilim were then on the earth, and afterwards as well, the sons of God having come to bed with the daughters of man who bore them children: these are the heroes of yore, the men of renown. (Genesis 6.4)[18]

There is no further explanation, no further references to this bizarre little tale in the rest of scripture. That's it. But as later writers continued to wrestle with the problem of evil, this one verse seeded a rich set of stories. None (understandably) was deemed worthy to be sacred scripture (you won't find them in any Bible), but they make great reading and it is rather surprising that no one has based a film on them yet. They are collected under the heading of Pseudepigrapha, meaning that most are written under the pseudonym of some famous biblical character (Enoch, the Twelve Patriarchs, etc.).

1 Enoch tells the story of the angel Semyaz (later called Satan) being granted a position of leadership by God, which he promptly abuses. He talks 200 angels into binding themselves together by a curse of disobedience, and together they descend to earth to choose wives and beget children.[19] Once there, the angel Azazel teaches the people war and

vanity, while others teach them magic, and the faithful among the people cry out to God for help.[20] The good angels Michael, Surafel and Gabriel hear the complaint and take it to God, who makes a pit in the desert, binds Azazel hand and foot and throws him into it, 'writing upon him all sin'.[21] The other fallen angels are also cast down and bound, ready for later punishment.[22]

Even in their bound state, however, these fallen angels are not powerless. The book of Jubilees tells how they send out spirits or demon-children to torment Noah and his family.[23] Poor Noah, having already gone through unusual levels of trauma in his life, cries out to God to be relieved of these spirits, but Mastema, the chief of the demons, argues that at least some of them should be allowed to stay and torment humanity. After all, humanity deserves it. God compromises, binding nine-tenths of the demons, and leaving one-tenth on earth – under the control of Satan. Noah is comforted by being shown how to heal the torments they cause but, very significantly, Satan now has his own little 'army' on earth.[24] The stage is set for Satan to establish his own kingdom: the kingdom of darkness.

The kingdoms of light and darkness

Imagine that you are standing in front of two tunnels with everyone you have met on earth standing behind you. One tunnel is pitch black. You have no idea where it goes. The other is filled with a blazing light. You are told that there is goodness and life at the end of it, but were you to walk down it your entire life would be played out at the entrance way for everyone behind you to see. Your *entire* life – not just the parts others know about, but everything you have carefully kept hidden. You can choose which tunnel to walk down, but you must choose one.

A scenario something like that was once outlined to me as a picture of what judgement is like. I was young at the time and the lit tunnel did not seem a big deal. The older I get, the more excruciating such an idea seems and I deeply hope that judgement is *not* like that. But the picture does help us to understand why darkness could seem appealing. As John writes, 'And this is the judgement, that the light has come into the world, and people loved darkness rather than light because their deeds were evil.'[25] Light exposes us, forces honesty on us, and there are times in all our lives when we would rather hide in the shade. We are only playing with our faith if we do not sometimes quail at facing the blazing light of God. After all, 'It is a fearful thing to fall into the hands of the living God.'[26] If you have read the Narnia books, think of Eustace's encounter with the Lion when Eustace has been turned into a dragon. Eustace had been trying unsuccessfully to return to his human self by peeling off layer upon layer of dragon skin, but it is not until he offers himself, completely vulnerable, to the deeply penetrating and painful claws of the Lion that he is restored.[27] If we are honest, remaining curled up around our dragon gold – putting off the painful encounter indefinitely – is a genuine temptation.

It is precisely this that Satan is said to play on. His kingdom is portrayed as a safe hiding place of darkness. What we conveniently forget is that the centre of his power, the centre of the kingdom of darkness, is death.

Those who wrote between the Testaments became increasingly certain that death was Satan's fault, Satan's weapon, and the heart of his kingdom.[28] Yet both angels and humans continued to respond to the allure of comforting darkness. The 'Testament of Levi' tells how since the time of those pesky spirits tormenting Noah there have been two types of spirit on earth: those guided by God, and those led by Satan with the sole aim of leading humanity astray. The result is that humanity is given a choice of allegiance: 'And now, my children, you have heard all: choose therefore for yourselves either the light or the darkness, either the law of the Lord or the works of Beliar.'[29] Or, as the writings of Qumran claim, they must choose to fight in the cosmic war either on the side of the kingdom of light or on the side of the kingdom of darkness.[30]

This, then, is some of the background to the Satan who appears boldly and repeatedly on the pages of the New Testament. I have catapulted you through numerous snippets of story from numerous sources, so before we move on let's try to pull them together in simplified form.

There has been a rebellion among the angels: those placed in charge of the nations, and those given other positions of responsibility. Those in charge of the nations drew the nations with them in their rebellion. Those cast down to earth drew individual humans into the darkness of their kingdom. Satan, who emerges as the leader of this kingdom, has built a cosmic and earthly army of those who have chosen to side with his kingdom of darkness over God's kingdom of light, and this army is taking over the world. We have reached the point where the problem facing God is therefore twofold, and familiar to all of us who have seen similar problems on earth: a charismatic, plausible 'dark' leader, and the allure of darkness as a way of living.

At last we are ready to step into the more familiar air of the New Testament world.

Notes

1 Wikipedia, 'Stalin Monument (Budapest)', Wikipedia, https://en.wikipedia. org/wiki/Stalin_Monument_(Budapest) (accessed 23.04.2021).

2 Martin Vennard, 2018, 'Death of Hitler: How the world found out from the BBC', *BBC News*, 20 May, https://www.bbc.com/news/world-europe-44131106 (accessed 23.04.2021).

3 Macon Phillips, 2011, 'Osama Bin Laden Dead', White House, 2 May, https://obamawhitehouse.archives.gov/blog/2011/05/02/osama-bin-laden-dead (accessed 23.04.2021).

4 If evolution depends on the survival of the fittest, they argued, what are we doing letting the unfit live? Charles Darwin wrote in *The Descent of Man* that, 'We civilised men … do our utmost to check the process of elimination; we build asylums for the imbecile, the maimed and the sick … Thus the weak members of society propagate their kind.' Available from *Classics in the History of Psychology*, https:// psychclassics.yorku.ca/Darwin/Descent/descent5.htm (accessed 18.09.2022).

5 Gerald Morris, a friend and Old Testament scholar, pointed out that in 1 Kings 11.14, the 23 'satans' aren't so much tempters as 'pains in the backside'. You won't find that in many commentaries, but feel free to use it as a scholarly interpretation.

6 1 Chronicles 21.1 talks of Satan inciting the people, but the same story told in 2 Samuel 24.1 says that God incited the people, so that's a tricky verse to use. He also appears in the Apocrypha, but Protestants do not recognize that as part of the biblical canon.

7 Isaiah 14.12.

8 Luke 4.6.

9 Rick Riordan, 2010–12, *The Kane Chronicles*, New York: Hyperion Books.

10 Translation by Robert Alter, 2019, *The Hebrew Bible*, Vol. 1, New York: Norton, p. 11.

11 'Let there be light' is two words in Hebrew.

12 Psalm 104.26.

13 Genesis 18.25; Exodus 32.11–14.

14 Exodus 4.21; Joshua 11.

15 Job 11.20.

16 Jeffrey Burton Russell, 1977, *The Devil: Perceptions of Evil from Antiquity to Primitive Christianity*, Ithaca and London: Cornell University Press, pp. 181–3. I am indebted to Russell for many of the trains of thought in this chapter, and recommend his book highly.

17 Martin Parsons, 2007, 'Binding the Strong Man: The Flaw of the Excluded Middle' in Peter G. Riddell and Beverley Smith Riddell (eds), *Angels and Demons*, Nottingham: Apollos, pp. 106–7. The terms 'daemons' and 'authorities, principalities and powers' came from the Greek translation of the Hebrew scriptures, the Septuagint, which translated 'hosts' and 'angels' and 'spirits' with these more abstract terms. The New Testament writers were clearly familiar with the Septuagint: hence those passages in the epistles that refer to them in this way. For example, Romans 8.38; Ephesians 6.12; 1 Peter 3.22.

18 Robert Alter, 1981, *The Art of Biblical Narrative*, New York: HarperCollins, p. 25.

19 Written sometime during the first two centuries BC. 1 Enoch 6.1–5; 9.7.

20 1 Enoch 8.1–3.

21 1 Enoch 10.8. When the scapegoat is sent out during the rite of the Day of Atonement, he is sent 'to Azazel' (Leviticus 16.8–10) so something like this story must surely have been around when Leviticus was written.

22 1 Enoch 55.3; 54.6.

23 Jubilees 10.1–6.

24 Jubilees 10.11.

25 John 3.19.

26 Hebrews 10.31.

27 C. S. Lewis, 1980, *The Voyage of the Dawn Treader*, Chronicles of Narnia, London: HarperCollins, pp. 103–4. Original edition 1952.

28 Proverbs 2.12–13; Job 10.21; Wisdom 17.2, 7; 1.13; 2.23–24.

29 Testament of Levi, p. 19. 'Beliar' and 'Satan' seem to be used interchangeably in this book.

30 Florentino Garcia Martinez, 1996, *The Dead Sea Scrolls Translated*, Wilfred G. E. Watson (trans.), English edition, Leiden: E. J. Brill. The 'War Scrolls' concerning the battle between kingdoms of light and darkness go from p. 95 to p. 125.

8

The New Testament and Beyond

Imagine the world under the rule of the kingdom of darkness. Satan governs all the nations and can grant them to another if he wishes.[1] Individual lights have flickered in the darkness over the ages but were always extinguished by the living darkness that surrounded them or, eventually, by the darkness of death.

Into this dark world comes one unconquerable shard of light: the kingdom of Light incarnate. *The true Light, which enlightens everyone, was coming into the world.*[2] This is a Light that all the efforts of darkness cannot put out. *The Light shines in the darkness, and the darkness did not overcome it.*[3] The Light moves among the darkness on earth, and wherever He goes, the darkness is pushed back and the space is filled with light: illness becomes health, rejection becomes acceptance, death becomes life, demons flee. Wherever He goes he tells people 'Look! The kingdom of God is here, among you. This is what it looks like!' but still people cannot recognize it. *He was in the world, and the world came into being through him, yet the world did not know him.*[4]

Eventually, the Light is drawn into the very stronghold of Satan itself: death. But even there the Light cannot be extinguished. Instead, He bursts through the gates of Hades, rises to life again, and defeats the worst that the prince of darkness could bring against him.[5] Once He returns to the heart of the kingdom of Light, no longer restricted to a human body, He sends the Light to burn on the heads of each of His followers at Pentecost, turning them into human candles. Why? Satan was defeated, but the lure of the kingdom of darkness continued in the world. Each follower of the Light became an ambassador for the kingdom of Light, a part of the *resistance*, a bearer of unquenchable Light, and was sent to bring that Light to the dark places of the world:

The people who sat in darkness
Have seen a great light,
And for those who sat in the region and shadow of death,
Light has dawned. (Matthew 4.16; Isaiah 9.2)

He came, and sends us:
To give light to those who sit in darkness and the shadow of death
To guide our feet into the way of peace. (Luke 1.79)

I do not believe any analysis of the 'how' of Christ's victory can bring us closer to the sense of what he achieved more powerfully than sitting with this simple story of Light entering and conquering darkness. However, we humans have an insatiable need to explain things, to feel that we can 'grasp' and thus, to some extent, control them. I cannot, therefore, leave it here as I would like to. Too many ideas have grown around this story since New Testament times, and too much of our accepted theology is based on those ideas for us to stop here. Doctrines as contrasting as the Eastern idea of *theosis* and the Western idea of the penal substitutionary theory of atonement grew from this same story, and it is important that we understand something of what lies behind the differences. So, briefly, here are some of the ways we have sought to explain the 'how' of this victory by turning story into analysis.

Recapitulation

This is a theory associated with an early follower of Christ, Irenaeus (b. AD 130). His idea is that Jesus, in his life, 'recapitulated' or 're-lived' all the failures of humanity, and lived them correctly. Think of a long polluted river being cleaned up metre by metre, right back to the source. Think of Jesus bringing everything that made up humanity into himself, filling the darkness with his light. Or, in Irenaeus' words, Jesus 'comprised in himself that original man out of whom the woman was fashioned ... in order that, as our species went down to death through a vanquished man, so we may ascend to life again through a victorious one'.[6] This became the foundation for the atonement theory of '*theosis*' or 'divinization' which we will dig into later in this book.

It can be fun finding all the 'repeats' between Jesus' life and the life of Israel, all the ways in which he cleaned things up or brought light into a dark part of history. The most obvious is Jesus' 40 days in the desert, in which he faced all the temptations that Israel had succumbed to over their 40 years in the desert, and resisted them. Everything we discussed in previous chapters about the fulfilment of the role of the Temple in the life of Christ could come under this heading, and it is possible to explore beautiful little details such as the parallels between the burial slab Jesus was laid on, which his followers found with an angel seated at either end, and the Ark of the Covenant which also had cherubim at the head and foot.[7] The most important point, however, is that where Adam unleashed disobedience and therefore death and darkness on the world, Christ unleashed obedience, life and light.[8]

This is an appealing understanding of 'victory' because there is no sense of violence involved. Christ's victory came about simply by progressively bringing light into more and more of the darkness which surrounded and filled us and our history.

Christ the Redeemer

The second theory looks very different, at least at first. The Old Testament is full of references to God *redeeming* his people from slavery, exile or the rule of other nations. In these stories, victory through 'redemption' is understood as God coming in with his great power and defeating these lesser powers in order to set his people free. The New Testament writers continue this imagery, but now it is Christ who comes in as the powerful redeemer. Christ defeats the ruler who has kept humanity enslaved and bound, 'binding' the 'strong man' so that he can 'plunder' his house and set us free.[9]

This imagery is all rather violent, and feels a little odd in contrast to the radically non-violent life of Jesus. When we read of God redeeming Israel in the Hebrew scriptures the descriptions are full of broken dragons' heads, and God's 'cruel and great and strong sword' winning his people's freedom.[10] There's definitely something that jars there.

But when we look closer, we can see the transformation that takes place in the imagery of warfare when it reaches the New Testament. The followers of Christ are told to put on 'the armour of *light*' – and look closely at what that armour is.[11] It is the 'breastplate of faith and love' and 'the helmet of the hope of salvation' and is only available to them because they are 'children of the light and children of the day', not 'children of the night or of darkness'.[12] This armour of light has completely abandoned the weapons of 'vengeance' and 'fury' that had been a part of the Divine Warrior's armour in Isaiah 59.16–19. Instead, we take up 'weapons' of faith, hope and love. More than that, this armour is not to be used against peoples of any nation, or 'enemies of blood and flesh', but solely in our 'struggle against ... rulers, against the authorities, against the cosmic powers of this present darkness, against the spiritual forces of evil in the heavenly places'.[13] When Paul writes of rulers, authorities, principalities and powers it is the Septuagint translation of those 'middle-layer' spiritual beings he is referring to. People are not our enemies. It is the darkness that is our enemy.

The war is over, but the battle against the worldview offered by the darkness continues. The weapons we are given to fight with are not weapons of violence to be wielded against humanity, but weapons of faith, hope and love with which to defeat the allure of darkness. These are the weapons of the Christ who emptied himself of power and died for the love of us all.[14]

Ransom

This is, perhaps, the most complicated of the victory motifs, yet it should be the simplest. It has certainly had the most enduring impact on Protestant theology. On four occasions the New Testament refers to Jesus offering his life as a 'ransom' to set free those imprisoned by Satan.[15] This is completely different to the imagery of the Divine Redeemer coming in with force. There is no war here. Instead, this imagery evokes the idea of a people enslaved to Satan, captured by the kingdom of darkness, whose freedom can be bought if the ransom paid is high enough.[16]

So, Jesus paid the ransom with the highest price possible: God's Life, and won the right to free his people. The story seems simple, clear and beautiful.

Unfortunately not. You see, the New Testament never actually states to whom the ransom is paid. You might think something as obvious as that should not need to be spelled out. It must have been paid to the one who had the people enslaved, since that is how ransoms work. As Irenaeus, again, wrote, 'the ransom is always regarded as paid to the powers of evil, to death, or to the devil: by its means they are overcome and their power over men is brought to an end'.[17] But very quickly, Christians became more conscious of God's dignity than God seems to be, and felt uncomfortable with the idea that God should have to *pay Satan* in order to free us. In fact, within a few short centuries they became uncomfortable with the idea of a force like Satan having any influence on God's actions at all and tended to leave him out of the story completely.

Who was left, then, to pay the ransom to? Well, God seemed the only option. Why would God need a ransom paid to him when he didn't have people enslaved? That was a poser, but since maintaining God's dignity was more important than preserving the story of slavery that this imagery came from, they had to think of something. It must be that sin offended God, or that unpunished sin was a slur on God's righteousness. So, from the writings of Anselm through to the teachings of the Reformation, the victory Christ wins by giving his life as a ransom is not over Satan and the kingdom of darkness, but over the demands of God's honour and justice.

Can you see the tragic irony here? A story that was one of God, in love, paying with his life to set his people free, becomes one of God *demanding payment* to satisfy his justice. Yet this belief has shaped the theology of many Western churches for centuries.[18]

Victory and allegiance

I want to suggest another simple way we can understand this victory brought about through Christ's atonement. Think back to the discussion with which we started this section on the two stages of any victory. The first stage is defeating the leader. Do we have any reason to believe that Satan was defeated? That is tricky when we are talking about some cosmic, invisible power. How do we know? The evidence of Satan's defeat is that his power-base was destroyed. Any *Star Wars* fans will remember that for the Alliance in the original *Star Wars* trilogy, the sign that the Dark Side had been defeated was not just that Darth Vader died, but that the centre of the Dark power, the Death Star, had been blown up. For us, the sign that Satan was defeated is Jesus' glorious destruction, even 'blowing up', of death itself, Satan's power-base. That is a victory we could never have won ourselves and is mindblowingly good news. We will think about it more in the next chapter.[19]

The second stage of any victory involves the ongoing battle against the beliefs and ideologies that put that leader in power: in this case a battle for humanity's allegiance to God's kingdom of Light. This stage, too, Jesus will win, but it will be a different kind of victory.

Nowhere in Old or New Testaments, nor in any writings in between, is Satan seen as a power equal to God. There are hints in the New Testament that Satan is almost completely independent from God and has established himself as the world's ruler or surrogate god.[20] But Satan is still used by God to discipline church members or to stop Paul from being 'too elated',[21] and all his machinations during the Passion week seem to be unwittingly playing into God's hands. In what way does Satan really pose a threat to God, then? He is a mere angel. His powers are negligible in comparison to God's.

When it came to a direct confrontation between Satan and Jesus, this drastic difference in power was obvious. In the same way that God controlled primeval chaos, Jesus controlled the chaos of disease and possession and death with no more than a word. When it came to defeating death, Christ's victory was complete and utter. But when it comes to the second stage of the battle, there are other factors at play. Satan has powers God would never use: powers of deception, of lies, of blinding the minds of unbelievers, of instigating sin and binding people to it.[22] These powers *are* negligible on a cosmic scale compared to God's, but are highly effective when working on the weaknesses of humanity. Allegiance – faith, trust, dedication – cannot be forced, so if God is to win back his people from the lure of ongoing darkness, a different sort of power needs to be at work here to the one that blew death apart, and a different strategy employed.

For some reason God has chosen a strategy of equipping an 'army' of candle-bearers with the power of his Spirit to gradually, haltingly, but persistently, permeate the darkness. To paraphrase Jesus' summary of his own calling:

> The Spirit of the Lord is upon me, because he has anointed me
> to bring the Light of the Good News into the darkness of poverty;
> the Light of Freedom to the darkness of imprisonment;
> the Light of Sight to the darkness of blindness;
> the Light of God's Grace to the darkness of condemnation.[23]

As Christians, that is our calling and our reason for being: to be people whose allegiance is solely to the kingdom of Light, and who bring that Light into every area of darkness in our world. That is our part in the great resistance.

So with that in mind, let's look more closely at two ways in which victorious atonement may help us to spread that Light in our still-dark world.

Notes

1 Luke 4.6.

2 John 1.9. Italics mine.

3 John 1.5. Italics mine.

4 John 1.10. Italics mine.

5 1 Peter 3.18–20. In the Orthodox Church they interpret these verses to have Jesus standing on the trampled gates of hell, opening the way for all inside to come out to the light. I'll come back to this when we consider *theosis* in a later section.

6 Irenaeus, 'Adversus Haereses' 5.21.1, http://www.earlychurchtexts.com/pub lic/irenaeus_on_recapitulation_in_christ.htm (accessed 20.06.2021).

7 John 20.12; Exodus 25.17–22. For more on this, see Nicholas P. Lunn, 'Jesus, the Ark and the Day of Atonement,' *JETS (Journal of the Evangelical Theological Society)*, 52.4 (2009), pp. 731–46.

8 Romans 5.12–21.

9 Mark 3.27.

10 Psalm 74.13; Isaiah 27.1.

11 Romans 13.12, 14.

12 1 Thessalonians 8; 1 Thessalonians 5.4.

13 Ephesians 6.12.

14 Philippians 2.5–8.

15 Mark 10.45; 1 Timothy 2.6; 1 Peter 1.18; Revelation 5.9.

16 See Leviticus 19.20.

17 Gustaf Aulen, 1970, *Christus Victor*, London: SPCK, p. 30.

18 The Eastern Church rejects this theory. They followed the idea of 'recapitulation' which became a key part of the atonement theory of *theosis* (see the final section of the book).

19 This is one of countless reasons why the resurrection is central to our faith.

20 John 12.31, 14.30, 16.1; 2 Corinthians 4.4.

21 1 Corinthians 5.5; 2 Corinthians 12.17.

22 2 Corinthians 4.4; 1 Thessalonians 2.5; Luke 13.16. In the opening chapter of *Harry Potter and the Philosopher's Stone*, Dumbledore, the most powerful wizard of his day, claims that Voldemort, the epitome of darkness, has powers that Dumbledore has never had. His colleague points out that Dumbledore is easily capable of those powers but is too 'noble' to use them. Evil may be weaker than goodness but still has powers that goodness will never claim. J. K. Rowling, 1998, *Harry Potter and the Philosopher's Stone*, London: Bloomsbury, p. 14.

23 Paraphrase of Luke 4.18–19; Isaiah 61.1.

9

Victorious Good News (1):
Defeating the Dragon

> The baby has known the dragon intimately ever since he had an imagin-
> ation. What the fairy tale provides for him is a St. George to kill the
> dragon. Exactly what the fairy tale does is this: it accustoms him for a
> series of clear pictures to the idea that these limitless terrors had a limit,
> that these shapeless enemies have enemies in the knights of God, that
> there is something in the universe more mystical than darkness, and
> stronger than strong fear. (G. K. Chesterton)[1]

You may have thought that stories of blood and sacrifice were tricky to
translate into the present day, and you could now be wondering what
on earth we 'do' with demons and cosmic wars. It's no surprise that the
most common story we use to explain Christ's work is in terms of the
penal substitutionary theory of atonement, which involves something like
a court of law: it is so nicely logical and normal and unembarrassing and
earthy. None of which describes the stories of the victorious theory of
atonement. However, it may not be as tricky as it seems.

We do not need to believe that the biblical writers had an intimate and
accurate knowledge of the politics of heaven for the stories of victorious
atonement to speak truth to us. Just as the story of St George and the
Dragon in Chesterton's quote, above, shapes in children's minds the idea
that the dragons they already believe in can be conquered, so our stories
of Christ's victory over Satan create in our minds an assurance that the
darkness we are all well aware of is not the ultimate power. It is no
prerequisite for salvation that we believe in warring angels and a fallen
Satan, but we do believe that Christ, the Light of the World, defeated
death and darkness and gave us a mission to follow him.

What the stories of victorious atonement provide are images rich
enough to help us grasp the wonder of it all, and I do not believe their
obviously mythic quality should put us off. Our world is increasingly
postmodern and has begun to question the centuries-old assumption that

dissection is the only valid path to understanding truth. Let's be bold and instead entertain the possibility that there is 'more out there' than we can see; in other words, to explore the delightful idea that the angels who keep cropping up in the pages of our scriptures are real, that there is a spiritual world beyond our ken.

Admittedly, we must be careful when giving too much attention to the possibility of demons, as a fascination down those lines tends to threaten our spiritual sanity. Nonetheless, leaving Satan out of our theology many centuries ago led to his demands for a ransom being attributed to God, and it is possible that leaving the reality of a dark spiritual world out of our own understanding can lead us mistakenly to believe that our 'war' is against other humans. It is the darkness we are sent to defeat with the Light of Christ, not those who are trapped within it.

Even if we accept, however, that there may be few more vivid ways to communicate the story of victorious atonement than that provided by the Bible, we must nevertheless ask how this mythic imagery translates into the reality of our lives. The paradoxical non-violence of Christ's victory provides one path of light we can follow, and I will explore that in the next chapter. There is also one 'dragon' who impacts on all our lives in an all-too-real way: death. The story of victorious atonement tells us that this, perhaps the dragon we fear most, is defeated. If so, that is news which is as good now as it ever was.

The biggest dragon

A few years ago I began planning a new set of resources for middle-school students, and in preparation for it sent a number of classes two pages of fairly random questions: anything from, 'Who would you rather share a room with, a ghost or a snake?' to 'Is God male?' I asked students to say where each question lay on a scale from 1 (boring) to 5 (I'd really like to talk about this). The question that drew by far the highest number of 5s was, 'What happens after I die?'

This intrigued me, since our own death is something we so rarely talk about. We absorb the news of other, distant people's deaths daily, and most of us know the unutterable grief of someone we love dying, yet still we rarely discuss it. There are almost certainly hidden and complex reasons for this silence which I will leave to sociologists and psychologists, but the simplest explanation for avoiding the topic is surely fear. The thought of someone we love dying is too appalling to dwell on. Part of us finds the thought of dying ourselves somehow incomprehensible even as another part of us knows it is inevitable. It is something beyond our control, and we like being in control. It is a complete unknown, and we like being able to know and plan. Most of all, the thought of simply ceasing to be and of others we love ceasing to be can be almost unendurable.

Why, then, are many in the Church so often shy about talking about death? If Christ's atonement was real, the great dragons he overcame were sin, death and the devil. We have never been shy about discussing sin, and our reluctance to discuss the devil is understandable since we are unlikely to agree across the board on his literal or metaphorical existence. But there is no doubt about the reality and inevitability of death. There is also no doubt that if what we are told about Christ's atonement is true, we have news that blazes out its goodness: goodness that does not rely on any worldview or era to be good, but is good across all time and across all people.

Christ's victory over death did not just mean defeating it, but destroying it:

> This grace was given to us in Christ Jesus before the ages began, but it has now been revealed through the appearing of our Saviour Christ Jesus, who abolished death and brought life and immortality to light through the gospel. (2 Timothy 1.9–10)

> Where, O death, is your victory? Where, O death, is your sting? (1 Corinthians 15.55)

If this is true – if death truly is defeated, and if what awaits us on the other side of what we perceive as death is truly the resurrected life that the New Testament describes – there could be no better news. If it is *not* true, then, as Paul argued, what are we doing bothering with Christianity?

> For if the dead are not raised, then Christ has not been raised. If Christ has not been raised, your faith is futile and you are still in your sins. Then those also who have died in Christ have perished. If for this life only we have hoped in Christ, we are of all people most to be pitied. (1 Corinthians 15.16–19)

Yet Paul does not leave it there. He goes on with a glorious 'but': '*But* in fact Christ *has* been raised from the dead, the first fruits of those who have died.'[2] Paul knows it, because he met the risen Christ. Jesus' disciples knew it, because they met the man they had loved and followed and grieved for, risen, enjoying a meal of barbecued fish, and most definitely alive. It was that and only that which gave them, and the early Christian martyrs, the almost blasé attitude to dying for their faith that we read and hear about in the Bible and beyond. They would not have been human if they had not feared the physical pain associated with being killed, but death itself held no fear for them.

Don't misunderstand me: believing in the resurrection does not stop us grieving. Being separated from someone we love – having sudden silence and emptiness where there was once vibrant, warm life – is perhaps the deepest grief we can experience. I am so grateful to Jesus for weeping at Lazarus' tomb minutes before raising him from death. If Jesus, with his sure and certain knowledge that death is not the end, still grieved, of course we will when someone we love dies. Death is wrong and it is appalling. But our grief takes on a different quality if our fear can be removed. Fear of this being final, hopeless, the last word. Fear that can unconsciously haunt us throughout our lives, shaping and restricting us.

Think about the liberation that would result from no longer fearing death. We may have difficulty understanding what it means to be 'in slavery to Satan' but it is not so difficult to understand the slavery of fear:

> Since, therefore, the children share flesh and blood, he himself likewise shared the same things, so that through death he might destroy the one who has the power of death, that is, the devil, and free those who all their lives were held in slavery by the fear of death. (Hebrews 2.14)

Jesus has achieved a victory which should make that fear groundless now, which should cut its bonds around us completely. Imagine if death held no fear for you. What could you dare to do, dare to be, if that were true?

Daring to believe

We have no greater news to give. Let's see if we can believe it. Earlier on I talked about the difficulty the disciples had in accepting the evidence of their senses when the risen Jesus appeared, because 'in their joy they were disbelieving', and I suspect this is an ongoing problem for many Christians.[3] We don't dare believe Christ's victory over death was *really* complete, because surely it is too good to be true? So we clothe our claims in more modest and acceptable guises, and feel that since we're not wishing for the moon our beliefs are more credible. Let's not do that. Let's try to avoid watering down our understanding of what happens after we die into sweet poems about living on in the stream and wind and memories of our friends. Let's avoid the idea we inherited from Plato, not Jesus, that our disembodied souls float upwards and essentially merge into one. That is not the good news of this atonement story.

When we dream hopefully of some vague and insubstantial future existence, we aim too low. Jesus' victory was far more complete than that. He did not concede that death could take our bodies and all that gives us particularity and individuality – personhood – while leaving Jesus our wafting and formless spirits. This is important: Jesus did not concede anything at all. He was victorious. He destroyed death and claimed life for us in all its complex, particular, physical, emotional and spiritual fullness.

One of my all-time favourite analogies was one I heard John Polkinghorne give in a talk in Grafton Cathedral, New South Wales, during a Science, Philosophy and Theology Festival in the 1990s.[4] Polkinghorne was Professor of Mathematical Physics at Cambridge, and an Anglican priest. With the help of a jug, a bowl and a stone, he asked us:

Does a stone pass through water, or does water pass through a stone? *Clearly the first.*
If I pour this water out, is it passing through the air or is the air halting it? *Clearly it passes through.*
Which is more dense, water or the stone? *The stone.*
Which is more dense, water or air? *Water.*
So in every case, the more dense material passes through the less dense material.

Therefore, if the risen Jesus passed through the walls of the room where his disciples were hiding with the doors locked, he must have been made of something more dense than the walls.

Polkinghorne wasn't making any scientific claims here at all: it was simply a quirky, fun way of shaking our assumptions about the resurrected body. He was encouraging us to throw away any ideas of our being reduced to something insubstantial, or that the risen Jesus took on some ghostly form. He was encouraging us to refuse to believe that Jesus compromised with death. Christ's victory over this dragon was complete, and whatever the resurrected life will be, it will be somehow *more* real, *more* substantial than life here. After all, when Paul writes of the life to come, he does not use the image of a block of ice turning to steam but of an insignificant seed turning into a tree: something infinitely more, not less, than it was before.[5]

This is the ultimate good news. Let's talk about it more, let's explore it more, let's seize our freedom to face death with grief, yes, but also hope and faith and even (do we dare?) joyful anticipation – when it comes.

In the meantime, however, we have a job to do that, if we are to be part of the resistance fighting the darkness, we cannot discard at will. Even Paul, who clearly had no difficulty looking forward to dying and being with Jesus, knew that in the meantime he had much more to do on earth.[6] If he could know that from his prison cell, we can know it from wherever we are: whether we are fighting on the medical frontline of a global pandemic, or restricted by age and infirmity to a single chair in a single room. We are still part of God's peace-filled battle against darkness, and every candle counts.

Notes

1 G. K. Chesterton, 2011, 'The Red Angel' in *Tremendous Trifles*, Overland Park: Digireads, p. 36. Original edition 1909.

2 1 Corinthians 15.20. Italics mine.

3 Luke 24.41.

4 For an overview of John Polkinghorne's life and work, see https://royalsociety publishing.org/doi/10.1098/rsbm.2021.0044 (accessed 27.10.2023).

5 1 Corinthians 15.

6 2 Corinthians 5.2–21.

10

Victorious Good News (2):
Candle-bearers

Shortly after a treaty was signed in New Zealand, promising Māori sovereignty over their land, a combination of commercial and government interests led to widespread confiscation of that same Māori land. A region called Taranaki was particularly promising land for farming, but held by the village of Parihaka which had by the 1870s become the largest Māori village in New Zealand, and was led by two remarkable people: Te Whiti and Tohu. Both were Christians who modelled their lives and that of their people on three principles:

Glory to God on high
Peace
And goodwill to people on earth.

These were far from being fine-sounding but meaningless ideals on an otherwise ignored strategic plan. The people lived them and, as it turned out, were willing to die for them. As the settlers' greed grew, Te Whiti and Tohu led their people through a series of acts of non-violent resistance (ploughing and fencing confiscated land), instructing them: 'Go, put your hands to the plough. Look not back. If any come with guns, be not afraid. If they smite you, smite not in return. If they rend you, be not discouraged. Another will take up the good work.'[1]

The 'ploughers' were captured and sent to Dunedin, at the far end of the country, as slave labour for two years. On their return to Parihaka, the non-violent resistance continued:

So it was, on the morning of 5th November, 1881, that an invasion force led by two Members of Parliament, both Cabinet Ministers, arrived at Parikaha. In accounts of that day, some 200 young boys performed a haka; followed by a group of young girls skipping. Around 2500 adults had been sitting in silence since midnight, bracing for the attack. More than 500 loaves of bread had been baked to feed the militia. The Riot Act was read, Te Whiti and Tohu were arrested and taken away, leaving their people sitting in silence, in passive resistance.

Next day the troops returned and began destroying the town and forcibly dispersing some 1600 people. Houses and crops were destroyed, and thousands of cattle, pigs and horses were slaughtered. Women and girls were raped, leading to an outbreak of syphilis in their community. Meanwhile many men and youths imprisoned in the South never returned, as they died on average at one man every two weeks from the cold or malnutrition.

Throughout this long, bitter invasion on the people the spirit of non-violence prevailed. Te Whiti and Tohu themselves were held without trial for almost two years. And yet at the end of his life, Te Whiti remained true to his cause, stating: 'It is not my wish that evil should come to the two races. My wish is for the whole of us to live peaceably and happily on this land.'[2]

It is one of the most shameful stories of New Zealand *Pakeha* (non-Māori) history. It is also one of the most inspirational stories of this land. The establishment of Parihaka on principles of non-violence in 1866 predated Gandhi's first act of non-violence by 50 years and Martin Luther King's assassination by a century.

In 1987, descendants of the prisoners from Parihaka came to Dunedin, where their ancestors had been sent as slave labour, and set up a memorial stone. On one side of the stone is the shape of a *koru*, the uncurling fern frond that symbolizes new life, eroded there by the sea and sand. On another side they engraved the word *rongo*: peace. After all the injustices, all the reasons for anger and pain and revenge these people could have felt, this was their response.

Here, in this story, is the challenge and the promise of what it might mean to take a candle into the darkness. We, too, are charged with proclaiming the good news of *Glory to God on high! Peace, goodwill to God's people on earth*, but that brings with it no guarantee of personal safety. This is darkness we are dealing with. We, too, could take on Te Whiti's words: 'Go, put your hands to the plough. Look not back. If any come with guns, be not afraid. If they smite you, smite not in return. If they rend you, be not discouraged. Another will take up the good work.'

We are part of a much bigger story, one that starts and finishes with Christ.

Forging a non-violent path to victory

I started with this remarkable story because the most common objection to the idea of victorious atonement is that it is difficult to dissociate violence from victory. Any hint of religious violence is an immediate stumbling block today, and rightly so. When we hear terms like 'conquer' or 'defeat' used in a Christian context, we are painfully aware of the countless times in Christian history that violence, persecution and genocide have been perpetrated supposedly in the name of the Christ who told us to love others as ourselves. Australia, New Zealand, the USA, South Africa and any colonized country you choose to name will all have stories of physical and cultural violence inflicted on indigenous people in the misguided belief that this would somehow be interpreted as good news.

Add demons into the mix and you can cook up justifications for accusing people of being instruments of Satan, or every leader you disagree with of being the Antichrist, thus providing a satisfying excuse to treat them as less than human. We are right to be extremely careful in the language we use here.

But if a broken leg has been set incorrectly, do you amputate it or operate to set it right? If the wealth of imagery surrounding Christ's victory over sin, death and the devil has been misused for so long, do we cut it off from our understanding of atonement or set it right? It is debatable. Some would say it is beyond repair, and amputation is the only option left. I am putting in a vote here to give these stories another chance. The evil that needs 'defeating' is real. We are in need of stories that not only tell us the dragons *can* be conquered, but offer a non-violent path to that victory. We are in need of stories that show clearly that darkness cannot be defeated by further darkness. The transformation of the Divine Redeemer's armour from vengeance to love is not accidental; the imagery of a light illuminating darkness did not become central to this story by chance. Archbishop Tutu encapsulates the heart of this atonement story in his *An African Prayer Book*:

Goodness is stronger than evil;
Love is stronger than hate;
Light is stronger than darkness;
Life is stronger than death;
Victory is ours through Him who loves us.[3]

The weapons we are given, and are allowed to contemplate using, are goodness, love, light, life and the faith that rings through this acclamation. Violence does not get a look-in.

It is bizarre that we have ever thought it should.

Jesus is our model, our Head, God-made-visible, and Jesus did the impossible by emptying himself of divine power in order to become as vulnerable as soft-skinned, bleeding humanity. Somehow, God brought about victory through vulnerability.

Jesus called us to turn the other cheek when we are slapped, to give more than we are asked for, to love our enemies, and he showed us this in action by praying for those torturing and killing him. Somehow, God brought about victory through loving those who hate.

Jesus could have called on legions of angels when the crowds came to arrest him. Instead, he healed the ear of his enemy when his too-ardent follower sliced it off.[4] Somehow, God brought about victory through non-violence.

What don't we understand about all this? In a world that is sickened by past and present violence but often cannot see any choice when evil looms, Christ's atonement offers a non-violent alternative. It is good news.

But here is the challenge: our own non-violence is no guarantee of the non-violence of others. Non-violent peacemakers, like Jesus, often end up violently dead. It is not only the story of Parihaka, but of Gandhi, Archbishop Romero, Martin Luther King. Their non-violent lives were cut off by deliberate and cruel violence – but were they truly defeated? Who can measure how the light of their candles has spread through the darkness? Can you even remember the names of those who assassinated those men?

Not that fame is a measure of the spread of light. There are countless light-bearing peacemakers who have lost their lives just as violently and no one knows their names. It would be extremely foolish to risk a path of peace and non-violence in the hope of making a name for yourself. But that is the point. That is the glorious, foolish, counter-cultural, challenging and inspiring thing about seeking to spread the peace-bringing light of Christ. We don't do it for fame or progress or even because it invariably 'works' – frequently it appears to fail. We don't do it for any of the accepted reasons that our culture offers us. We do it because the God who created us and redeemed us lived an incarnated life of non-violence and peacemaking, and we are his children.[5] We do it because we believe in Christ's victory, and with that comes the belief that even if our own light is quenched, we are part of a much bigger story of Light which will never be quenched.

I suspect that a challenge as audacious as this one is exactly what many people are hungering for. After decades of encouragement to put our-selves and our well-being and our self-esteem first in our lives, our young people are still seeking something bigger than their lonely selves, worthy of pouring their lives into. Causes, gangs, nationalism, extremism all play on this need. The problem is that many of these paths add to the dark-ness, and many others provide challenge without an ultimate hope to carry them through inevitable disappointments. Our Christ-given pur-pose is not simply one choice among many we could invent or discover, but one given by the eternal God: one in which each of us has a vital part, but which does not stand or fall on any of us. The risks in following this purpose are real, but Christ has already won the victory and it is Christ's Light, not our own, we carry.

Before dawn on Easter morning many churches follow our most ancient liturgy, the Easter Vigil. The people gather around a 'new fire' outside the church in the darkness. From that fire, the Christ Candle is lit and the deacon leads the people into the dark church. Three times the deacon pauses, lifts the candle and chants, 'The Light of Christ', to which the people respond, 'Thanks be to God'. The candle is carried through the heart of the darkness to the east end, and then each person there lights their own candle from the Christ Candle or from the candles of others. Gradually the light spreads out through the darkness, passed from person to person, until the darkness is filled with glimmering sparks of light. Those candles are held faithfully through prayers and songs until, at last, the sun rises and light floods even the darkest corners of the building. Thus the story of victorious atonement, and the story of our place within it, is enacted, year by year.

We are called, we are given a commission, to bring the light of peace into the darkness, and that is good news. We are not alone in our 'battle' against that very real darkness, and that is good news. The Light will win, and that is the best news of all.

Notes

1 Tariana Turia, 2011, 'Parihaka – A Legacy of Non-Violence', *Catholic Worker*, http://catholicworker.org.nz/the-common-good/parihaka-a-legacy-of-non-violence/ (accessed 03.10.2022).

2 Turia, 'Parihaka'.

3 Desmond Tutu, 1995, *An African Prayer Book*, New York: Doubleday, p. 80.

4 Matthew 26.51–54.

5 'Blessed are the peacemakers, for they shall be called children of God' (Matthew 5.9).

PART 4

The Bonds that Hold Chaos at Bay

The Story of Covenantal Atonement

11

The Backstory (1):
Covenant and Creation

While they were eating, Jesus took a loaf of bread, and after blessing it he broke it, gave it to the disciples, and said, 'Take, eat; this is my body.' Then he took a cup, and after giving thanks he gave it to them, saying, 'Drink from it, all of you; for this is my blood of the new covenant, which is poured out for many for the forgiveness of sins.' (Matthew 26.26–28)

Try this experiment sometime. Ask the nearest priest or minister (which may, of course, be yourself) what precisely Jesus meant when he said at the Last Supper, 'This is my blood of the new covenant.' Then follow it up by asking what that has to do with atonement. Don't be fobbed off with generalities: dig for a specific meaning and see if they have one to offer. The words of Jesus over the bread and wine are the one direct clue he gives us as to what is going on with his death, and since we believe that what is going on is 'atonement' these words must be central to our under-standing of it. Yes, he has referred to his death several times already in the gospel story, but on those occasions he doesn't explain *why*. It is only when that death is looming and he has one last chance to communicate the heart – the purpose – of it all that he breaks the bread and pours the wine and uses these mysterious words to explain it.

While it bewilders me that I managed to get a couple of postgraduate theological degrees under my belt without understanding much about atonement, it perhaps amazes me more that after 15 years as an Anglican priest giving out Communion each week, I faced these questions for the first time and realized I didn't know how to answer them. My experience since then of asking numerous unfortunate people over cups of tea the same questions is that many of us – even those who have done some theo-logical study, or those who hear these words on a regular basis – are a bit muddled about it all.[1] We realize Jesus was forming a new covenant, an agreement, a treaty – but with whom? Was it the Divine Christ making a covenant with humanity, or the Human Jesus making a covenant with God? And why – what did it do? How did making a covenant bring about atonement, if it did? This appears to be a fragment that has been lurking under the carpet for long enough to gather a fairly heavy coating of dust.

As soon as you start thinking about it, all sorts of strange things become apparent. Blood 'poured out for many for the forgiveness of sins' sounds as if it hearkens back to sacrificial atonement, but the sacrifices brought forward for atonement did not form new covenants. Nor did anyone drink blood (God forbid!) to form a covenant. Does the linking of the broken bread with the cup of wine mean that the bread, too, is connected somehow to this new covenant? And why, in our Christian history of *theosis*, and Christus Victor and the theories of sacrificial atonement, moral influence atonement and penal substitutionary atonement battling for supremacy in the atonement stakes, is Jesus' own choice of story so frequently ignored or made one element of a different story?

That's not to say that no one studies covenantal theology. One could probably fill an average-sized cathedral with books written about the biblical covenants. But 'covenantal atonement' does not have the familiar ring that many of the other atonement theories do for the average pew-dweller or sermon-preacher, and that fascinates me.

So, what did Jesus mean by 'this is my blood of the new covenant'? And what does this have to do with atonement? Before diving into the world of biblical covenants to unpack the questions at the beginning of this chapter, I have an important caveat. Our explorations of sacrificial and victorious atonement have been rather like film trailers: they give you a general idea of what's going on and let you see in advance a few of the most memorable moments including, frequently, giving away the plot completely. But they are not the films. The films themselves may be far more complex, far longer, and potentially worthy of intense study. That is even more the case for what we are about to cover of covenantal atonement. You may feel that what follows is overly complex, but in reality there are so many ways of understanding the biblical covenants that what we will cover here is even less representative of the richness of the story than a film trailer would be. Perhaps it comes closer to a YouTube clip of scenes from the film, cobbled together by someone who's seen enough of the film to fall for the leading actor. The angle presented is not false, but is highly selective. I hope, however, that it may do what trailers are meant to do, and encourage you to seek out a fuller version.

The Charter and the covenant

We are all familiar with some form of covenant. Treaties, such as the Treaty of Versailles, the Treaty of Waitangi, or even the Magna Carta, are essentially covenants, and some of us may still use the slightly archaic phrase 'the covenant of marriage'. In its simplest form a covenant is an agreement between two or more parties outlining the shape of their relationship going forward.

When one party is God, things become a little complex, and when the stories the covenants are embedded in are the rich and ancient foundational stories of our faith, we will swiftly find ourselves back in the realm of mysterious and supernatural ideas we have engaged with for much of this book. Even with something as legal-seeming as a covenant, we need to bring our imaginations with us if we are to understand it. So let's once again prime our minds to be receptive to this strange world by approaching it through the story of a world that makes no claim to be anything but fantasy. This is a world created by the Australian author Garth Nix: the world of the 'Old Kingdom'.[2]

The Old Kingdom is a land in which everything is held together by a powerful Charter, formed at the time of Creation. The people of that Kingdom (unlike our own), know their mythic history well, because the repercussions of the events surrounding Creation can be felt through to the present day.

Before the Old Kingdom, everything was filled with Free Magic and inhabited by Free Magic creatures called the 'Nine Bright Shiners'. Free Magic was wild, limitless and untamed, of immense, perhaps inexhaustible, power. One Bright Shiner succumbed to the lure of that power and became the Destroyer, Orannis, sweeping through the universe, devouring burgeoning worlds as It went.[3] As It approached what would be the Old Kingdom, however, seven of the other Bright Shiners were ready for It. Together they had created a Charter which bound Free Magic within defined limits, pushing it back to allow life to exist, filtering it into the manageable and useful forms of what became known as Charter Magic. By pouring many of their own lives into the Charter's formation they made it strong enough to bind Orannis Itself and bury It deep underground.

The Charter, then, underpinned and connected all of life in the Old Kingdom by holding the power of Free Magic in strict control. People of the Old Kingdom were baptized by having a Charter Mark placed on their forehead, and this Mark connected them to one another and to their world through the countless interlocking threads of the Charter.

However, Free Magic still existed beyond the Charter and the lure of power continued to tempt the Old Kingdom people. Occasionally someone would discover how to reverse a part of the order of creation – how to bring a dead creature back into life by feeding it the life-blood of the living, for example.[4] Each time this happened, it caused a crack to form in the Charter, allowing Free Magic to seep through, and giving the Charter-breaker access to its destructive powers. Free Magic and life cannot coexist for long, however, and wherever the Charter was broken, the land became contaminated, plants died, rocks broke. Even the one foolish enough to think he could tap into the power unscathed would discover he was being slowly destroyed himself.

The heroes of this series are the Abhorsen, people whose mission is to rebuild the Charter to cover any cracks, to right imbalances and turn reversed orders back to where they should be. It is their work that enables life to continue.

Creation and covenant

It always fascinates me when profound and complex biblical ideas are communicated vividly by writers who make no claim to the Christian faith. The 'creation story' of this fantasy world has uncanny parallels with both our own creation story and with an understanding of biblical covenant which is central to covenantal atonement. Covenant and Creation are tightly connected for the people of the Old Kingdom, as are the Charter and Creation. Both creation stories paint pictures of wild forces kept at bay by divine power. The 'baptized' people of the Old Kingdom, countless years after Creation, are still alert to their responsibility to keep the Charter, and are still well aware that breaking the Charter has physical repercussions (pollution, death and destruction seeping in, chaos monsters rising) and relational ones (the bond connecting them to the Charter, each other and the world is snapped). Those of us who have long since lost any true sense of connection to our foundational stories have also largely lost any awareness of similar repercussions in our world.

Our creation stories in Genesis and Job are as mysterious and beautiful as any told before or since. They are stories of a limitless, formless darkness and deep – 'free magic' – being pushed into controlled channels so that life can exist. Wild darkness becomes part of a rhythmic pattern of day and night. Swirling waters are pushed apart by the firmament to make water above and water below, with space in between for life. The waters below are divided and limited by the creation of land: space for land-creatures to live. Creatures themselves are divided and limited by the distinctiveness of their species. Stars, moon and sun are placed within a careful pattern to give regularity to seasons. The whole creation, in fact, is held together in a complex relationship of powerful limits and patterns, very similar to Garth Nix's Charter, created in our case by one God, and held in place by God's faithfulness.[5] We are all familiar with the story as told in Genesis 1, but we hear something very similar as God thunders his challenge to poor Job towards the end of his story:

> Where were you when I laid the foundation of the earth?
>   Tell me, if you have understanding.
> Who determined its measurements – surely you know!
>   Or who stretched the line upon it?
> On what were its bases sunk,
>   or who laid its cornerstone
> when the morning stars sang together
>   and all the heavenly beings shouted for joy?
> Who shut in the sea with doors
>   when it burst out from the womb? –
> when I made the clouds its garment,
>   and thick darkness its swaddling band,
> and prescribed bounds for it,
>   and set bars and doors,
> and said, 'Thus far shall you come, and no farther,
>   and here shall your proud waves be stopped'? (Job 38.4–11)

Out of darkness and the swirling void, God has carved and controlled the elements within strict limits to create a lush place of life and harmony which God said was good.

Then God makes humans. They, too, are deemed 'good' and they too are given a limit or boundary to ensure that they stay within the harmonious and beautiful order of creation. So far, so good. But uniquely among all created things, humans have the ability to choose to break through their limit.[6] The sea, the darkness, the stars, plants and animals – all are held in harmony with each other through God's faithfulness. Humanity is different. We are made in God's image, and that means we ourselves are capable of faithfulness. Our place in the intricate pattern of relationships that is creation was established by God, but we can choose to uphold it, to maintain it, to be faithful to it – or not.

It is a daunting picture. A space is carved out of lifeless chaos for all the carefully crafted beauty and peace of Eden, and two small, weak, soft-skinned and dreadfully gullible creatures are given the power to live in it peaceably or break it.

Breaking the limits

Whatever Eve was thinking in this story as she reached out to pluck the forbidden fruit, it was certainly not that she was about to launch the whole muddled history of humankind down a path of unfaithfulness. Yet unfaithfulness was at the heart of it: a breakdown in trust and trustworthiness in the relationship between God and humanity. The beautiful little *Jesus Storybook Bible* traces Eve's and Adam's actions to the insidious suspicion that God didn't really love them and could not be trusted. In this, as in so much in that little book, Sally Lloyd-Jones is making a profound theological observation.[7] Maybe Eve and Adam were hungry for power or knowledge, but at the base of it all was the fracturing of their relationship with God.

The snake in this story was no fool. It realized that for the human to disobey God she had first to doubt him, to distrust him. So the snake told her that God had lied to her. The only reason God didn't want her to eat the fruit was that it would make her as knowledgeable as God, he said. There was power available to her, just beyond the limits that were set on her, if only she reached out for it. God was selfish, power-hungry, insecure and was deliberately stopping the woman from being all she could be, whereas he, the snake, wanted the best for her. So Eve and Adam had on one side the God who had made them from dust and bone and created the wonder of peace and goodness around them, and on the other side a snake who was, well, a snake. They chose to believe the snake. Lies and slander tend to have that sort of power.

A striking thing about this story is that this act of unfaithfulness towards God impacts on far more than that one relationship. As with Nix's 'Charter' in *Abhorsen*, the repercussions of breaking that which holds the order and balance of creation in place are both relational and physical. The humans no longer have intimate access to God, and are exiled from their Eden. But it is also as if by breaking their limit, by succumbing to the lure of the wild power beyond their reach, they have caused a crack to form in the structure holding chaos at bay. Chaos seeps through, sucking life from the land, bringing fear, mistrust, exile and death to humanity. The two – a breakdown in relationships, and a suffering creation – are inextricably connected in our own creation story.

As the generations unfold, relationships between God and humans, and humans with one another, continue to degenerate and the cracks in creation widen. Cain kills Abel and Cain's exile is deepened, while his descendants grow progressively more brutal. Eventually the crack is so wide that creation begins to undo itself, and God decides to take control before everything is lost. He starts with one small act of new creation through separation: he 'chooses' and separates Noah and his family to create the seed of a new humanity. Then God takes away the remaining limits on the water, and it gushes up from below and down from above and once again covers the earth, covering also the humanity who had so dismally failed to preserve all God had given them.[8] For 40 days the controlled chaos of the flood reigns until God pushes it back again and releases Noah and his family to try once more.

Before God lets Noah loose completely, however, he explains what is going on. He tells Noah that he is making a *covenant* with him and all living creatures on earth.[9] You may have been wondering when we were going to get to the point of all this, and here we are at last: the first mention of 'covenant' in the Hebrew scriptures.

On one level, God's covenant with Noah does what we expect covenants to do: it establishes a particular relationship between God and humanity with, in this case, instructions on the proper relationship between humanity and the rest of creation built in. It is a chance for God to remind humanity of his own faithfulness, and give people another opportunity to be faithful in return. But it is more. It also marks a starting-again, a new creation. When God puts this covenant in place, the crack that humanity had caused in the order and balance of creation is covered over or healed; the firmament is re-sealed above and the waters below forced back to their proper place; the relationship between God and humanity is re-established, and order, balance and life are restored. The covenant returns us to a state of harmony which is not Eden repeated, but a new way of being at peace.[10] We could say, then, that covenant is a work of atonement.

Was bringing 'atonement' in there a bit of a jump? It isn't really. We haven't yet made much of the familiar idea of breaking the word 'atonement' down into its component parts ('at-one-ment'), but now that we're looking at covenantal atonement it becomes of central importance.

At-one-ment and covenant

If we picture the world of Noah as one where, as in Garth Nix's Old King-dom, chaos and destruction is held at bay purely through the network of limits and boundaries created and (in our world) held in place by God's faithfulness, then the 'bad news' of Noah's day was the damage humanity kept inflicting on this complex harmony. Imagine a bunch of decidedly dim people punching holes in a dam upstream from a village, wanting to access the power of the water for themselves. Punch enough holes and the dam will burst and wipe out the whole village.[11] Or imagine the girders of a building being twisted, one after another. At some point – quite quickly – the building will collapse. This cracking or twisting of something good is one of the many ways 'sin' is understood in the Hebrew scriptures. When we looked at sacrificial atonement we saw how it focused on deal-ing with the bad news of sin *polluting* the world. Covenantal atonement deals with the bad news of cracks and twists forming in the order and balance of creation, and humanity's seeming inability to stop adding to them.

But there's a beautiful little picture at the start of the Noah story that gives hope. God instructs Noah on how to build the ark and 'cover it inside and out with pitch'.[12] Make sure, in other words, that all the cracks are covered and the waters raging outside will not be able to enter. What is intriguing about this is that the Hebrew word used for 'cover' is one of the many variations of the word we translate 'atone'. 'Atonement' in this sense means to cover over a crack or gap, to seal it. Understood figura-tively, the same root word could then come to mean making up for any sort of lack, or even paying a debt ('I'll cover that bill', for example). We are used to associating that figurative sense of 'payment' with our atone-ment stories, but what if the picture this word is meant to give us is of God's covenants 'atoning' by 'covering' the breaches made by human sin, sealing them with pitch so that chaos can no longer seep in, preserving the 'ark' of our world in peace, and thus restoring order and at-one-ment to creation?

Each biblical covenant, for all their differences, shows something being done to 'cover over' the breach between God and humanity, heal that relationship, and launch a new creation. Covenants are good news of atonement.

It would be pleasant to stop there, but while that is, perhaps, the most important idea to keep in mind from this chapter, there are a few more complexities to deal with before we can move on. For while the presence of covenants and the atonement they bring about is exceptionally good news, we have to face the daunting fact that throughout the Hebrew scriptures God has to keep making new ones. Whenever God creates a covenant with humanity, there is a tacit acceptance built in that humans are going to mess it all up again.[13] It is not long after the story of Noah that we read of humanity deciding to breach the limit between humanity and God in a thoroughly concrete way, and up goes the Tower of Babel. Shortly afterwards, down it comes again along with the 'chaos' of a multiplicity of languages which effectively divide humans from one another.

God decides to start again – again – which brings us to an unassuming old man called Abram.

Notes

1 This is also an effective way to narrow down your friendship group to the truly patient and loyal among them.

2 Garth Nix, 2003, *Abhorsen*, Old Kingdom Trilogy, Crows Nest, Sydney: Allen and Unwin. This precis of the world is drawn from across all three books of the trilogy.

3 Orannis is referred to by the capitalized pronoun 'It' throughout the series.

4 This is another good example of the motif of 'blood is life' reappearing in fantasy works.

5 Jeremiah also celebrates the idea that it is God's faithfulness that holds creation together: Jeremiah 31.35–36; Jeremiah 33.19–21.

6 We could understand this today in terms of the laws of nature (such as gravity) that all beings 'follow' because they do not involve choice, and the 'moral law' that we are all conscious of but can, and do, choose to break. See the first chapter of C. S. Lewis's *Mere Christianity* (Glasgow: Collins, 1952) for the classic discussion of that topic.

7 Sally Lloyd-Jones, 2007, *The Jesus Storybook Bible* (Grand Rapids, MI: Zonderkids), p. 30.

8 I may be getting ahead of myself here, but does that raise any uncomfortable echoes in your mind of the present day?

9 Genesis 9.8–11.

10 Remember that in this new world, Noah is allowed to eat meat, under certain restrictions. That's one small sign that it's not Eden repeated, but a new peace in a new situation.

11 It is not hard to apply this analogy to much of our Western consumerist society.

12 Genesis 6.14.

13 See, for example, Deuteronomy 31.16.

12

The Backstory (2): A Covenant People

Without wanting to discourage you, I must admit that we are now at the point where many discussions and learned books on biblical covenant *begin*. God's covenant with Noah does not fit as neatly into patterns of ancient Near Eastern covenants as later biblical covenants do, so scholars have often chosen to focus on the covenants with Abraham, Israel and David. The Abraham story is where things begin to be grounded in something resembling history rather than myth, so I can sympathize. On the other hand, I find that it is in our scriptures' wonderfully rich and mythic prehistory tales that many theological threads find their beginnings, so I am unapologetic for having taken you on a rapid tour through them.

The Noahic covenant was a kind of re-creation of all creation. In later covenants the accompanying act of new creation is on a different scale: that of a person or a people who will, God hopes, realize the importance of the covenant and be faithful to it (do their bit to hold it together), for the sake of all humanity. For the remainder of this 'backstory' journey we will explore how Abraham, the people of Israel at Sinai and David are chosen, separated out, like light from darkness or land from sea, to be the new covenant-bearers: the faithful who will maintain the vision of peace and harmony (at-one-ment) which is God's design for creation. Somehow, we are told, the faithfulness of these few will bring blessing to the many. That is God's promise to Abraham when a covenant is 'cut' between them, and that is the promise repeated to Abraham's son.[1] They are chosen not for themselves, but to be upholders of the covenant for all people.

Later, the people of Israel, a nation chosen and created by being set apart from Egypt to be the new covenant-bearers, are given a huge and complex law to guide them as they try to understand what faithfulness and obedience mean in everyday life. It is a lot to live by, but Israel was created and called specifically for this, and if it ceases to be a covenant people, it ceases to be a 'people' at all.[2]

As we know, they had mixed success and the consequences were dire, which is where many of us decide we'll stick to reading the New Testament. For if we look seriously at God's words attached to the covenant at Sinai, we find a list of blood-curdling, brutal and horrifying curses that will fall on Israel if it fails.[3] We don't like to think of curses. We particularly don't like to think of curses that apparently come from God. But they are there, clear and uncompromising, in the Hebrew scriptures. They are also a key part of understanding Jesus' words at the Last Supper, so we have to attempt to understand them however distasteful they are. Let's try.

The covenant curse

From what we can tell by looking at covenants in other ancient Near East cultures, human-to-human covenants were regularly accompanied by a list of blessings that would ensue if the covenant was kept, and a list of curses that would fall on the weaker party should they break it. We find the same in the human–divine covenant at Sinai, with the horrors of Leviticus 26 and Deuteronomy 58 being graphic descriptions of what was promised should Israel prove unfaithful. These passages provide what are possibly the most disturbing passages in all scripture. Here's an example:

> But if, despite this, you disobey me, and continue hostile to me, I will continue hostile to you in fury; I in turn will punish you myself seven-fold for your sins. You shall eat the flesh of your sons, and you shall eat the flesh of your daughters. I will destroy your high places and cut down your incense-altars; I will heap your carcasses on the carcasses of your idols. I will abhor you. I will lay your cities waste, will make your sanctuaries desolate, and I will not smell your pleasing odours. I will devastate the land, so that your enemies who come to settle in it shall be appalled at it. And you I will scatter among the nations, and I will unsheathe the sword against you; your land shall be a desolation, and your cities a waste. (Leviticus 26.27–33)

How do we read such passages and not have the suspicion flit through our minds that we're nicer than our Creator? We wouldn't wish such things on anyone, so how can God do so? There are at least two things to keep in mind here. The first is that, as Rabbi Jonathan Sacks says:

> The reason the curses are so dramatic is not because God seeks to punish, but the exact opposite. The Talmud tells us that God weeps

when He allows disaster to strike His people: 'Woe to Me, that due to their sins I destroyed My house, burned My Temple and exiled them [My children] among the nations of the world' (Brachot 3a). The curses were meant as a warning. They were intended to put off, scare, discourage. They are like a parent warning a young child not to play with electricity because it is dangerous. The parent may deliberately intend to scare the child, but they do so out of love, not severity.[4]

He goes on to clarify the difference between a prediction and a prophecy:

If a prediction comes true, it has succeeded. If a prophecy comes true, it has failed. The Prophet tells the people what will happen if they fail to change. A prophecy is not a prediction but a warning. It describes a fearful future in order to persuade the people to avert it.[5]

God does not 'wish' the curses on anyone. God does not manipulate events to ensure evil falls on the wicked. What God does do is warn us of what will happen as an inevitable result of ignoring God's warnings.

The second thing to keep in mind is that we may conceive covenants differently to the way ancient peoples conceived them. Perhaps we have difficulty understanding these curses because we don't think of covenants, agreements and treaties as having any power in themselves. Symbolic (or perhaps legal) power, yes, but that is all. The Hebrew people, in contrast, did believe that covenants held innate power, and that belief brought consequences with it. We know to handle powerful things carefully. The same power that enables fire to warm us and cook for us when used rightly can also cause widespread destruction if used wrongly. Take away fire's power for destruction and you render it useless for good. If a covenant with God was going to be powerful enough to actively bring blessings, then breaking it had to have powerful repercussions: the knowledge that the curse would hit them if they disobeyed was, in a way, a guarantee of the blessing reaching them if they obeyed.

A daunting corollary to this is that it seems that any covenantal curse *has* to run its course before God can make a new covenant. There is no avoiding it (perhaps the prodigal son had to go through all he did before he could come home and right his relationship with his father). God weeps over the mess his children are making of things throughout the Hebrew scriptures, but it is only once the curse has been 'exhausted' that God can step in with a new covenant. It may seem tough, but it also makes sense. Actions have consequences. It is a variation on the theme we have been playing all through this chapter: break the covenant, and chaos and death and bad stuff come in and things fall apart. They just do. We don't have to think of bad stuff as something decreed by a vindictive God (which is how we tend to think of curses), any more than we should blame an appliance manufacturer for our burns if we decide it would be a good idea to iron our clothes while wearing them.[6] We have been given instructions, we have been given brains to think with, and experience to learn from, so really we have no right to complain.

Having said all that, look again at the foundational covenant with Abraham in Genesis 15. When God's covenant with Abraham is 'cut', Abraham is instructed literally to *cut* a series of animals in half, and lay them out in a row with a gap between the cut parts. This in itself is not strange for a covenant ceremony, and in any normal covenant between a greater and lesser power, the scene would now be set for the lesser power – Abraham – to move between the cut carcasses, rehearsing his own fate should he break the covenant. But here's the amazing thing: it is a *light from God* that passes through the pieces.[7] It is almost as if God were saying he would take the brunt, the curse of any breaking of this covenant, on himself. This is very strange.

Many years later when the family have become a people grumbling in the desert, God cuts another major covenant with them at Sinai. This time the covenant doesn't involve cutting beasts and birds in half, but rather the even messier ritual of throwing blood on the people – and on the altar. The symbolism is clear again with regard to the people: things will get messy and bloody if you break the covenant. But note that again God is involved in this. The altar, too, has blood thrown on it.[8] The inevitable outworking of the covenantal curse is more complex than it seems at first.

The seeds of promise

As the history of God's people continues, a familiar pattern forms. God makes a covenant with them, they rebel, chaos breaks out, and suffering overcomes them. You could pick any few chapters of Isaiah and you will see the same pattern repeated. At the end of each cycle, God, in his infinite mercy, *atones* by repairing their relationship, 'covering over the cracks' that had allowed such suffering in, and renewing or reforming his covenant to enable them to start again. Try Isaiah 24—27, or 50—54, or 58—59. Read the first few harrowing chapters of Hosea, where the covenant is portrayed as a marriage (which is indeed a covenant relationship), and Israel as an unfaithful wife who breaks her husband's heart and unleashes his anger, but who is promised forgiveness and love if she would only return.

The sheer repetitiveness of it all could easily give rise to hopelessness. Yes, God does always fix things eventually, but is there any point when we just break covenants again and unleash curses and chaos on the world? What does God hope to achieve? The Hebrew scriptures insist there is a point, and that there are glimmers of hope that something fundamental might change at some time in the future. This hope hangs primarily on the two covenants we are still to look at (briefly, I promise!).

The first is when God makes a covenant with his chosen king, David, promising him that David's line would be kings for ever. Within a few generations it became evident that that would not literally be the case, but the prophetic writers did not let the promise drop. Instead, they maintained the hope that one day a new 'David' might appear who would reign for ever (hence the Messiah being 'of David's line').[9]

Now, an important thing to know about the kings of Israel is that they were spoken about and thought about as representing their whole kingdom. King and people were 'bound together in such a way that what is true of the one is true in principle of the other'.[10] When David is blessed, it's the equivalent of the whole of Israel being blessed; to say 'We have no portion in David' is a way of saying we have no portion in David's kingdom.[11] Perhaps, then, this future 'David' could embody all that the original David, and therefore Israel, were *meant* to be, to make up for the disappointing reality of their failures.[12] Perhaps this David would finally keep the covenant faithfully *on behalf* of those chosen to do so, and peace would come.

Or take it a stage further. Was it conceivable that this man could somehow save Israel by letting the inevitable curse of the broken covenants fall on him instead of on the people he represented? Isaiah's vision of the 'suffering servant' suggests that possibility:

Surely he has borne our infirmities
and carried our diseases;
yet we accounted him stricken,
struck down by God, and afflicted.
But he was wounded for our transgressions,
crushed for our iniquities;
upon him was the punishment that made us whole,
and by his bruises we are healed. (Isaiah 53.4–5)

If so – if that curse could finally be completely exhausted – then, just as God swore never to flood the earth again, so he swears that he will never 'rebuke' Israel again, but will hold her fast in his love and covenant of peace:[13]

> For the mountains may depart
> And the hills be removed,
> But my steadfast love shall not depart from you,
> And my covenant of peace shall not be removed,
> Says the LORD who has compassion on you. (Isaiah 54.10)

The covenant of peace

Here, with the 'covenant of peace', we reach the goal, aim and purpose of all the covenants. 'Peace' in this context is something deeper than the non-violence we considered under our discussion of victorious atonement. 'Peace', or *shalom*, in the Hebrew scriptures means a state in which everything and everyone is in right relationship with everything and everyone else, as it was at creation.[14] In other words, it is the very thing that 'at-one-ment' brings about. A covenant of peace would mean that humanity's distrust of God, which began with Eve and Adam, is healed.[15] A covenant of peace would mean that the scattering of humanity at Babel is reversed, warfare is over, and humanity is one.[16] A covenant of peace would mean that the broken bonds that lead to the unravelling of creation, seen at the time of Noah, are healed and a new creation formed in which everything and everyone will be in right relationship with everything and everyone else.[17] This would not be a return to Eden, as God is a creator God who never needs to repeat himself. But it would be a new creation, a new state of peace.

Imagine a world where a lamb could cuddle up safely to a wolf, or where a snake would watch benignly as a toddler plays on its nest.[18] Fantasy, we think, of course. So imagine instead another of Isaiah's visions of peace:

> No more shall there be in it
> an infant that lives but a few days,
> or an old person who does not live out a lifetime;
> for one who dies at a hundred years will be considered a youth,
> and one who falls short of a hundred will be considered accursed.
> They shall build houses and inhabit them;

they shall plant vineyards and eat their fruit.
They shall not build and another inhabit;
they shall not plant and another eat;
for like the days of a tree shall the days of my people be,
and my chosen shall long enjoy the work of their hands.
(Isaiah 65.20–22)

Is even that so impossible? Apparently so. The people of Israel never managed it. No one has. The inevitable breaking of one covenant after another suggests we are incapable of reaching the peace that is the heart of the purpose of them all. Yet God kept healing the breaches, rebuilding the covenants, *atoning* for his people as if there was hope. And as we reach the end of the Old Testament, the promise of a future covenant of peace is still there, rising to tantalize us.[19] It is the original cliff-hanger. Will the promise be fulfilled in the next instalment? How?

Fortunately for us, we don't have to wait several hundred years for the sequel.

Notes

1 Genesis 12.2; 22.18; 26.4. 'Cuts' is the term used to form a covenant in the Hebrew scriptures. You'll see why soon.

2 Bernard Och, 'Creation and Redemption: Towards a Theology of Creation', *Judaism* 44.2 (1995), p. 234. See also Hosea 1.9 and Hosea 2.23.

3 Deuteronomy 58; Leviticus 26.

4 Jonathan Sacks, 'The Core Idea', *Covenant and Conversation*, 2, https://rabbi sacks.org/wp-content/uploads/2020/05/CandC-Family-Behar-Bechukotai-5780. pdf (accessed 03.10.2022).

5 Sacks, 'The Core Idea'.

6 I have seen warnings not to do this, both on a piece of clothing and in the instruction manual for an iron. That it needs to be said beggars belief.

7 Genesis 15.

8 Exodus 24.8.

9 For example, Jeremiah 23.5.

10 N. T. Wright, 1993, *The Climax of the Covenant*, Minneapolis, MN: Fortress Press, p. 46.

11 Isaiah 55; 2 Samuel 20.1.

12 Isaiah 11.1–10, where the 'root of Jesse' will embody all David was meant to be, and therefore all Israel was meant to be.

13 Isaiah 54.9–10; Ezekiel 34.25; Ezekiel 37.26.

14 For more on this, see the excellent short video on *shalom* created by the Bible Project, https://bibleproject.com/explore/video/shalom-peace/ (accessed 30.10.2023).

15 Jeremiah 31.31–34.

16 Isaiah 2.2–4.

17 For example, Ezekiel 34.25–27.

18 Isaiah 11.6–8.

19 The Hebrew Bible has the books in a different order to the Christian Old Testament, but in the Old Testament it is the prophets who have the last word, scattering these words of promise through their writings.

13

The New Covenant

One of the satisfactions in reading a well-crafted book or series is finding how tiny allusions or incidents you encounter early in the story suddenly gain significance or make sense towards the end. Think, if you are a Harry Potter reader, of the threads that draw together in the final chapters of the seventh book, and make little sense until then. Or, for you Narnia readers, think of the pleasure of finding Reepicheep meeting us at the gates of Aslan's country. Or, if murder mysteries are your genre of choice, the chances are that a significant factor in your enjoyment of them is finding all the incidental elements coming together to make sense of the solution.

Perhaps that is one reason why the story of Jesus is so fascinating: it is crammed full of these little light-bulb moments. There is much that is strange and inexplicable in the Old Testament's portrayal of covenant, including the valiant triumph of optimism over experience shown by the prophets who, despite all past evidence, persisted in believing in a coming eternal covenant. Yet we, having read the 'sequel', realize they were right. These threads of audacious hope from a 1,000-year-old narrative draw together in Jesus. Or, to use the analogy we started the book with, all sorts of apparently random scuff-marks scattered through the stories of covenant in the Old Testament reveal themselves to be a track of footprints leading straight to the Last Supper, Gethsemane and beyond.

In this chapter we are going to retrace our steps, following that track of footprints *back* through time, viewing what we have already read in light of what happened next – rather in the manner of someone who, having finished a carefully crafted mystery novel, wants to appreciate how many clues there were along the way pointing to 'whodunnit'.

The first major covenant we re-encounter walking backwards through time is God's covenant with David. There, you will remember, God promised that David's line would be kings for ever.[1] Given the hiatus when there were no kings of David's line, that made little sense as we reached the end of the Old Testament, but we now discover David's descendant being called 'King of kings' by his followers and being king over a kingdom that will never end.[2] ('Oh! *That's* what those Old Testament passages meant', we think).[3] There's also the delightful double irony of Pilate putting a sign above the crucified Jesus, saying he was 'King of the Jews'.[4] Pilate likely meant it to be ironic, yet it was, unbeknown to him, true.

That is all quite fun, but there is a deeper significance to Jesus being of 'David's line'.[5] Remember that it is the king, not a prophet or priest or any other person of importance, who can represent, in himself, Israel. Jesus inherits in his human heritage the kingly line of David, and so is able to embody the role of Isaiah's 'suffering servant' who 'bears the iniquities' of the world.[6] What Jesus the King did was done on behalf of all; what happened to him happened to all. That's the first, vital insight that the Old Testament covenants can give us into the nature of Jesus' atoning acts.

We walk on back through scripture over multiple hillocks of small covenants until we reach the two major covenants at Sinai and with Abraham. Now that we know about the Last Supper, we find that these covenants are linked in a new way. At Sinai, picture how the blood was thrown on both people and altar, as if God were offering to share the inevitable consequences of that covenant being broken. Then think of Jesus taking the wine and saying it is his own blood, poured out so that past sins could be atoned for and a new covenant formed. Remember how the light from God passed between those broken carcasses laid out by Abraham, as if God were foreshadowing a time when he would, himself, be broken. Then picture Jesus taking his 'flesh' and breaking it in half, telling his followers that this was being done on their behalf.

There, in graphic and stark terms, Jesus shows us why he is going to die, and gives us an answer to the questions that this whole section began with. What did Jesus mean by linking his actions at the Last Supper to covenant, and how are they linked to atonement? Jesus is showing that he is willingly taking on the consequences, the curses, of these two ancient foundational covenants, as humanity's representative, so that the cracks and distortions caused by our unfaithfulness can be covered over, atoned for, once for all. His blood will be shed and his body torn, and the curses will be exhausted.

That, I believe, is at the heart of Jesus' words and actions at the Last Supper. Jesus' followers were about to enter a time of confusion and disillusionment and grief as the man they loved, and had begun to learn to venerate, allowed himself to be slandered, tortured and killed. Jesus could have tried to explain, but words can be hard to take in, particularly in times of grief or stress. Instead, he acts out his purpose, simply, directly and memorably. He gives them something material that they take into themselves: bread and wine, hoping that eventually, when their grief has receded, they will understand.

They eventually did. They understood both what Jesus had done and why. They also understood the significance to them of atonement coming through a new covenant: something that, in God's work, is inseparable from the birth of a new creation. They realized that they, a bunch of confused, fearful people, with Christ's body and blood within them, were to take on the mantle of the patriarchs and Israel itself, to become a new creation, to become the new covenant people: bearers of the covenant of peace for the sake of the world.

Peace with God and one another

Although I will be looking at this in more detail in a few chapters, it is worth stopping here to think a little about what this means. What did the covenant of peace promise? It promised, first, the restoration of relationships between God and humanity. Previous attempts to get this right had not gone well, but this time, at the covenant meal of the Last Supper, it is different. This time it is Jesus the Human who makes this covenant with God the Father on behalf of humanity, and the unity of the relationship between the Father and Son is eternal and unbreakable. That is a covenant bond which now will never be broken or warped. There, amid all the change, doubt, instability and fear of our world, is something firm and sure: God's 'steadfast love shall not depart' from us.[7]

That is something we can cling to as the foundation of everything else. But the covenant of peace envisages even more. Jesus is not just Jesus the Human, he is Christ the Lord, and the covenant is also between him and his followers. A little like the war we discussed in the previous section which is won and yet ongoing, covenantal atonement still gives us a part to play: not in our 'eternal salvation' but in the bringing of God's kingdom on earth. Secure in the knowledge that nothing in life or death can now separate us from the love of God, we are to seek peace with one another for the sake of the peace and wholeness of creation.[8] As bearers of the new covenant, we are to be one, as Jesus and the Father are one.[9]

Surrounded as we are by factions and denominations within our own faith, and the division and suspicion and racism of our world, it looks as if we haven't done too well. But there are two clear signs of hope in the New Testament world. The first is the 'undoing of Babel' on the day of Pentecost, where instead of everyone being divided by different languages, everyone heard the numerous disciples speaking in their own language, whatever sounds they were uttering. Where God's Spirit is at work, there can be understanding that reaches out across seemingly irreconcilable differences.

The second sign is the remarkable movement of Christianity beyond the Jews into the world of the Gentiles:

> Christ redeemed us from the curse of the law by becoming a curse for us – for it is written, 'Cursed is everyone who hangs on a tree' in order that in Christ Jesus the blessing of Abraham might come to the Gentiles so that we might receive the promise of the Spirit through faith. (Galatians 3.13–14)

We are so used to Christianity being a worldwide religion that our natural response to all that Paul and others write about the Gentiles being welcomed in could well be a subconscious 'of course'. But there was no 'of course' about it. The mysterious God with an unpronounceable name, YHWH, was the God of the Jews. The Greeks and Romans had their own gods, as had the Canaanites and any other tribe. I imagine that you would be fairly annoyed if complete strangers started claiming your mother as their mother too, or your famous ancestor as theirs as well. That annoyance would be exacerbated if these strangers were people you'd rather not be associated with because of their political, social or moral positions. That scenario is possibly as close as we're likely to get to imagining how strange it was for the early Jewish followers of Jesus to comprehend Gentile Christianity. It wasn't just that Gentiles weren't Jews, it was that they behaved strangely and had no respect for the Law given to the Jewish people by YHWH himself. It wasn't just that they committed the occasional sin; it was that their whole lifestyle was drenched in sin. To let them start claiming Abraham as their ancestor and God as their Father could shake the foundations of the Jewish faith and identity, uproot all that was vital in their religion.[10]

And yet, despite this deep and real fear, or these profound and justifiable reasons for keeping Christianity within Judaism, the early Church spread at an amazing speed across cities and countries far beyond Judea. The peace that Jesus brought was not the accepted peace of the world, but his own peace.[11] This was a peace that drew back together the humanity that had been separated, breaking down the walls that divide. Paul puts it far better than I could:

But now in Christ Jesus you who once were far off have been brought near by the blood of Christ. For he is our peace; in his flesh he has made both groups into one and has broken down the dividing wall, that is, the hostility between us. He has abolished the law with its commandments and ordinances, so that he might create in himself one new humanity in place of the two, thus making peace, and might reconcile both groups to God in one body through the cross, thus putting to death that hostility through it. So he came and proclaimed peace to you who were far off and peace to those who were near; for through him both of us have access in one Spirit to the Father. So then you are no longer strangers and aliens, but you are citizens with the saints and also members of the household of God. (Ephesians 2.13–19)

I'm not sure we always recognize the grace involved on the part of the early Jewish Christians for them to welcome us into the family of God, or how powerful their experience of Christ must have been for it to have been possible. Something fundamental changed between the Last Supper and Pentecost. Christ's atonement healed not only the breach between humanity and God, but between peoples, creating 'one new humanity in place of the two': a people joined across race, gender and place in society, invited into the peace of God, invited to be the people of the new covenant.

One last covenant

We may be content to stop there in our journey of footstep-following back through time. If you feel you have read more than enough about covenants for now, skip these few paragraphs and jump straight to the summing-up at the end, because already the covenantal curses have been exhausted, the cracks in our relationships with God and one another have been covered over and the new act of creation launched. Atonement has been made. But if you are keen to dig deeper still, there is the covenant with Noah ahead of us. Is there any connection here with Jesus' atonement?

As we take some exploratory steps into the 'prehistory' section of the Old Testament, we also enter a realm of imaginative speculation. That is almost unavoidable. God's covenants with Abraham, Israel and David, while vast in scale, are primarily about the relationship between God and his people and the very practical ways that should be worked out. With the Noahic covenant we are working on the cosmic level of creation itself, and risk 'occupying ourselves with matters too great for us, or with marvels that are beyond us'.[12] But they are matters and marvels that are pressing on us today.

The covenant God makes with Noah is that he would never again release the boundaries formed at creation to allow chaos to destroy the world. As the Arctic and Antarctic melt and the waters around us continue to rise, the certainty of this promise is looking more problematic every year. Climate change is one of the most overwhelming 'bad news' issues we are facing, and one feels that this story of Noah must have something to say about it. That is a question for our 'good news' chapters, and we will return to it there.

For now, there is this more foundational question of whether the covenant with Noah has anything to do with Jesus and the covenantal theory of atonement. What connection is there between the bonds holding creation together and Jesus? There is, perhaps, a rather mysterious connection, hinted at in at least two places in the New Testament, and pointing us to something we have not yet mentioned in this chapter: the resurrection.

The first place is a strange verse in Romans 3, where we read that we sinners are '... justified by his grace as a gift, through the redemption that is in Christ Jesus, whom God put forward as a sacrifice of atonement by his blood, effective through faith'.[13] What does *not* come through in this translation is that 'sacrifice of atonement' is the translator's interpretation of the word *hilasterion*. The *hilasterion* was literally the elaborate cover of the Ark of the Covenant: the gold box that held the stone tablets God gave to Moses. Literally, then, Jesus is put forward by God as *the one who holds the covenant within him* as the Ark of the Covenant did. That reads a little differently, doesn't it? Now take that idea with you as you read this beautiful passage from Colossians:

> [Jesus] is the image of the invisible God, the firstborn of all creation; for in him all things in heaven and on earth were created, things visible and invisible, whether thrones or dominions or rulers or powers – all things have been created through him and for him. He himself is before all things, and in him all things hold together. He is the head of the body, the church; he is the beginning, the firstborn from the dead, so that he might come to have first place in everything. For in him all the fullness of God was pleased to dwell, and through him God was pleased to reconcile to himself all things, whether on earth or in heaven, by making peace through the blood of his cross. (Colossians 1.15–20)

Christ, here, is both the one through whom heaven and earth were created, and the one who continues to hold all things together. It sounds, again, as if in some sense *Jesus contains the covenant itself in himself*: that power which kept the chaos of the flood at bay, that power which holds creation in harmony and peace.

Perhaps it will help if you think back to the story of the Old Kingdom Charter in Garth Nix's book *Abhorsen* with which we began. In order to give that Charter the power it needed to control Free Magic, some of the Bright Shiners put their very lives into it. The Charter contained both the power to hold creation together *and* divine life: both the action of God and, in a sense, God Godself. Or, as John puts it, Jesus is both God's creative, active Word *and* God.[14]

I did warn you that covenant was complex! And this part of the discussion is, as I said, imaginative speculation. But the beauty of approaching the Last Supper along this path is that it broadens and enlarges the view we get of it. Jesus referred to the bread and wine as both his body and blood *and*, in some sense, the 'new covenant'. If we bring the bright, magical stories of Noah, creation or even Nix's Charter into our understanding of Jesus' words, it becomes easier to see his atoning action as something of immense power, working on a cosmic scale. It is the covenant, embodied in Christ, that holds creation together, and at the crucifixion we see that body broken, its life-blood shed.[15] But that is not the end. At the resurrection we see that body made new and that life become eternal. So, too, is the new covenant, held in Christ, an eternal covenant: steadfast, cosmic in scale and God's means of everlasting peace.

Summing it up

That was a long and complex journey, so I hope you are still with me. I do believe it is a worthwhile atonement journey, as it can shape our understanding of Christ's work in ways we might not glean from other stories.

When we think of Jesus' atonement in terms of covenant we see the depth of Jesus' love, taking upon himself the curse of all humanity's unfaithfulness, on behalf of us all. We have the deep security of seeing how an eternal covenant was created that was not dependent on wayward humanity for its survival. The relationship between God and the people of the new covenant is unbreakable: God's steadfast love will not depart from us. We can, of course, ignore or reject it. If we were to accept it, we would find it comes with some challenges to the ways we sometimes think about our faith. Suddenly, atonement is about more than my personal relationship with God, my personal decisions and my personal salvation: rather, it is tied to the whole of creation. At the same time, it makes my personal relationship with God, my personal decisions, and my personal salvation more important. We are not here as autonomous and isolated individuals scrambling to ensure our place in heaven. We are called to be part of a new creation, a new covenant people, as were Noah and Abraham and the people of Israel. In that sense, my relationship with God and my personal decisions become my contribution to the upholding of that new covenant: my role within a people entrusted to uphold this covenant of peace for the sake of all people – indeed, perhaps, all creation.

Notes

1 2 Samuel 7.

2 1 Timothy 6.15; Revelation 17.14; 19.16; Luke 1.33. See also Peter's speech at Pentecost in Acts 2.

3 There is a school of thought that objects to reinterpreting Old Testament passages as pointers to Jesus, but Jesus doing so himself seems to validate it. 'Then beginning with Moses and all the prophets, he interpreted to them the things about himself in all the scriptures' (Luke 24.27; incidentally, this has to be one of the most tantalizing verses in Scripture. Couldn't Luke have given us a couple of extra chapters unpacking this statement?)

4 Mark 15.26.

5 Luke 1.32–33.

6 Isaiah 53.1–12.

7 Isaiah 54.10.

8 Romans 8.35–39.

9 John 17.11.

10 This, of course, should make us question whether there are groups of people today whose lifestyles we believe are too 'drenched in sin' for us to allow them full participation in the Church. If there are, we may have to think again.

11 John 14.27.

12 Psalm 131.2, adapted.

13 Romans 3.24–25.

14 John 1.1–2.

15 Note that at the point of Jesus' death, darkness covers the land. The very first thing that is controlled by God at creation breaks through its allotted boundaries as Jesus, the one holding it all together, dies.

14

Covenantal Good News (1):
Restoring Relationships

When I was seven years old, I devoured as many of the Jungle Doctor books by Paul White as I could find, usually many times over. There was one story, however, that I found so disturbing that I never read it a second time – and yet it has stuck in my memory for almost 50 years. As I remember it, it goes like this: a conceited monkey, while showing off one of his extravagant jumps between trees, falls to the ground and finds himself sinking in quicksand. A friendly giraffe stretches his neck out over the quicksand and offers to help him out, but the monkey cries, 'I can pull myself out by my fine whiskers!' Similarly, an elephant, and a troop of monkeys dangling in a chain from the tree, all offer to help, and each time he responds, 'I can pull myself out by my fine whiskers!' Many hours later, all that can be seen are two little monkey paws sticking out of the quicksand, clutching two little bunches of torn-off whiskers.

I did not give that book to my own sons, and I do not enjoy the story now any more than I did when I was seven. But it is a pitifully clear representation of the secular 'good news' pervading our Western world: the alluring conviction that we can tackle any quicksand that life dumps us in by strengthening our whiskers, arms and self-confidence.

This conviction, and the radical individualism it is part of, has – weed-like – spread itself so widely across our Western worldview that it is difficult to find where the tap-root lies, or all the places it is likely to sprout again. I suspect, however, that if we are to live out covenantal atonement's 'good news' of peace, we will have to find ways to dig it out of our own lives. While we are going to range over a variety of topics in the next few chapters, they will all be exploring how covenantal atonement challenges this worldview and offers good news of a different sort altogether.

The story of God's covenants is based on the belief that there is a pattern to how the world should be: a network of limits and connections that, when they are maintained, lead to *shalom*. We are as much a part of that pattern as a slug or sunrise, with the one difference that we can choose to try to step out of it, thus breaking the *shalom* of the universe. Over thousands of years of history, humanity has repeatedly warped and broken those limits and connections, and God has patiently repaired them through each new covenant.

This covenant story offers one set of assumptions about ourselves and our relationships: that interconnectedness is at the heart of how the world should be, and that we are part of a larger pattern; that we were never meant to 'go it alone'; that broken relationships are behind the wrong in the world; that our relationship with God is of prime importance. For Jews and Christians, being covenant people means, first, faithfulness to God and, as a result of that, faithfulness to one another and creation. Mess up or abandon the first, and the other two begin to unravel as well.

The monkey in the Jungle Doctor book lived from a different set of assumptions. He was sufficient in himself; his success was up to him and him alone; he could find the strength in himself to tackle anything that came along. He was not part of any network or pattern, but a proud individual. He ignored the help of his own kind and others alike – even those with demonstrably greater strength. To admit the need of others would be to demean himself.

Although this mentality is rife today, it is not new. Rabbi Sacks gives us a telling insight into a man thousands of years ago whose life was centred on himself, cut off from the pattern of the universe: the writer of Ecclesiastes. It is worth quoting quite a long section of his comments here:

Here is the ultimate success, the man who has it all – the houses, the cars, the clothes, the adoring women, the envy of all men – who has pursued everything this world can offer from pleasure to possessions to power to wisdom, and yet who, surveying the totality of his life, can only say, 'Meaningless, meaningless, everything is meaningless.' Kohelet's failure to find meaning is directly related to his obsession with the 'I' and the 'Me': 'I built for myself. I gathered for myself. I acquired for myself.' The more he pursues his desires, the emptier his life becomes. There is no more powerful critique of the consumer society, whose idol is the self, whose icon is the 'selfie' and whose moral code is 'Whatever works for you.' This is reflected in today's society that achieved unprecedented affluence, giving people more choices than they had ever known, and yet at the same time saw an unprecedented rise in alcohol and drug abuse, eating disorders, stress-related syndromes, depression, attempted suicide and actual suicide. A society of tourists, not pilgrims, is not one that will yield the sense of a life worth living. Of all things people have chosen to worship, the self is the least fulfilling. A culture of narcissism quickly gives way to loneliness and despair.[1]

I find seeds of this despair whenever I ask young people to tell me what the 'bad news' and 'good news' is for them today. As I mentioned in Chapter 5, there are two almost universal responses to that question. One is the fear that the weight of expectations they carry, often without a recognizable source, may prove too much for them. That sounds very much as if they are living with the belief that their only choice is to pull themselves up by their own whiskers. The other most commonly voiced concern is, naturally, climate change. Soberingly, it has not so far spontaneously occurred to any of the young people I speak with that Christianity might have anything helpful to say in response to either concern.

These two issues, one personal and one cosmic, may be different in scale, but on a daily basis the amorphous pressure of unfulfillable expectations has a similar effect on an individual as the possible extinction of human life. In response to the first, a bright, enthusiastic young student chilled me to the core by saying matter-of-factly that she wasn't at all sure she'd make it to 40, given how many people killed themselves before then. On the other hand, climate change looms so menacingly that young people must either cling to a hope that scientists will find a way to deal with it (blocking from their minds the dire possibility that they won't find a way), or else allow themselves to be overwhelmed by the hopelessness of it all. The bottom line is that both issues, personal and cosmic, raise the question of whether there is any point in planning for the future.

Does the death of a man on a cross 2,000 years ago have anything to offer as a meaningful response to either of these crushing issues? Or is Christianity no more than – as Karl Marx claimed – the 'opium of the people' after all, helping us through by dulling our sense of pain and urgency?[2]

I am writing as an 'armchair theologian', not a psychologist, sociologist or scientist. I cannot begin to claim that I understand what causes the horrific youth suicide rate across the UK, New Zealand, Australia and other Western countries. Nor is this the place to discuss the science of climate change or the very practical societal changes we must seriously contemplate if we are to care for the creation entrusted to us. My aim in these chapters is a more theoretical one: to consider what, if anything, our understanding of covenantal atonement might say to the bad news of our time. Admittedly, when the situation is as urgent as this one is, it might seem a waste of time to start theorizing about it all, but I believe it is important. Whether or not we stop to consider it, we all act out of whatever theoretical basis we have constructed, so it is helpful occasionally to stop and check what that basis is. When we drive anywhere the goal is important, but so is the functionality of the vehicle.

In the rest of this section, then, we will explore what covenantal atonement might offer us and our pressured young people as we try to keep our 'vehicle' functioning even when the road is rough. You will find more chapters in this section than in the previous ones, for good reason. In the same way as the covenantal theory of atonement infiltrates the whole biblical story, it also infiltrates our lives, and the scope for exploration is bewilderingly wide. There is a unifying theme, however, in the areas I have chosen to ponder. At the back of them all will be the hope of *shalom*, the goal of the covenants, seen in right relationships with God, one another and creation.

We will look first at the age-old issue underlying our relationship with God: forgiveness. How does the forgiveness found through covenantal atonement restore the network of relationships necessary for *shalom*? What does that, in turn, teach us about restoring relationships with one another? In the next chapter, we will tackle covenant and creation, consider honestly our bleak prospects, and wonder, tentatively, what Christ's covenantal atonement might say to us in terms of hope even now. Finally, after a brief detour through a consideration of *shalom* and truth, we will return to the covenant of peace and explore how this might be good news even for those who do not realize it.

Peace with God and one another: the covenantal theory of atonement and forgiveness

When Jesus held up the wine at the Last Supper, he said, 'This is my blood of the new covenant which is poured out for many for the forgiveness of sins.'[3] The one unarguable thing about covenantal atonement, then, is that it involves forgiveness. Forgiveness is the key ingredient in righting our relationship with God, covering over the breach caused by our unfaithfulness, and bringing peace. We have looked at forgiveness already under the sacrificial theory of atonement, but just as each atonement story gives us a different way of viewing God's work through Christ, so does each illuminate different angles on forgiveness – not all of them completely comfortable.

For example, one of the striking aspects of forgiveness seen through the story of covenantal atonement is that it does not stop our actions and choices from having consequences. All that we have discussed about chaos and curses underlines this truth, but the covenant with Noah brings it home most graphically. After generations of bloodshed between people, God made a covenant with Noah and started again, which was wonderful – but the flood had still happened and the people and animals who died were not miraculously returned to life.[4] Forgiveness does not return the past.

You could be excused for thinking that this is a rather depressing thought to base a chapter on 'good news' around, but it is only when we start with this level of stark honesty that we can find where the good news is lurking.

Forgiveness and relationship

As covenantal atonement makes clear, forgiveness is not a 'get out of jail free' card which lifts from us all responsibility for our actions. We can reach out our hands to receive God's grace at Communion, but the plastic bag we carelessly drop in the church car park may still find its way to the sea and potentially bring death there. Forgiveness does not excuse us from chasing the bag down before it gets away, or from trying our best to cut our plastic use in the future. Nor does forgiving another mean no harm has been done, nor that no action is needed on their part, nor that we are expected to somehow believe it never happened. Our choices do impact the world, and forgiveness does not pretend otherwise.

What forgiveness does do is make it possible for a *relationship to be restored* in a re-created form, and that is the basis of healing. Covenantal atonement does not wipe the past clean; what it offers is to take all the broken pieces of our past and build something new from them. With the biblical covenants, that 'something new' always starts by bringing us back to God: welcoming us into, or back to, the steadfast love that is eternally present. In the same way, the forgiveness we are then asked to offer one another is primarily relational: it seeks to heal and rebuild our relationships with each other. It creates peace.

One of the saddest developments in recent popular teachings on forgiveness has been the idea that we do not forgive someone for their sake, nor for the sake of our relationship, but for our own sake. Forgiveness has become one ingredient in our well-being recipe. We know it is bad for our well-being to hold a grudge, so we set ourselves free by deciding to forgive. On one level it amounts to a similar thing: if I am tied to you by resentment and choose to undo the knot, I am setting you free as well as myself. But why I find this approach so sad is that it is one more example of how, in a society rife with loneliness and filled with people longing for connection, we continually encourage one another to conceive of ourselves in isolation. Today, this rich chance for peace and connection is sacrificed at the altar of personal well-being. We need to reclaim the good news of forgiveness: that it enables relationships to be restored, rebuilt, maybe formed for the first time or in a completely new way.

Forgiveness and grace

So, covenantal atonement does not change the past, but rebuilds the future. The next – and related – lesson covenantal atonement can teach us is that forgiveness is radically different to making excuses for someone. This way of misunderstanding forgiveness sneaks in easily because it sounds so virtuous. Surely 'to know all is to forgive all'? Surely if we can excuse someone, find or invent a reason that almost justifies their actions, then 'forgiving' is not so difficult? It is true that a vital aspect of loving our neighbour is to do our best to understand their actions rather than gleefully condemn them – but only to the extent that honesty allows. Making excuses for someone is not forgiving them; it is removing the need to forgive. Sometimes we can understand someone's actions perfectly well and realize there *was* no excuse, and that is where we discover just how confronting the forgiveness offered by God, and expected of his covenant people, is.

The forgiveness offered us through covenantal atonement is pure grace. It looks squarely and honestly at things that are inexcusable and, without softening them at all, forgives. God, 'knowing all', takes us no further than his sure knowledge of our weakness and inexcusable unfaithfulness to every covenant he makes. God, 'forgiving all', means Jesus taking on the full brunt of the resulting curses, neither downplaying their severity nor excusing us, but dying for us anyway, 'while we were yet sinners'.[5] *That* is the extent of God's love for us: not that he understood us and so excused us, but that he understood us, found no excuse, and loved us anyway.

There is an honesty in this understanding of forgiveness that we need to hear today. Too often forgiveness is spoken of as if it meant pretending what the other did was either not as bad as it was, or excusable. That is both dishonest and an insult to our experience. It also causes problems when we are the one seeking forgiveness, leading us to go to any length to justify our actions to God and one another. That is not only unwise and dishonest, but exhausting.

The irrational grace-filled forgiveness offered through covenantal atonement offers us the chance to come to God with complete honesty about our weaknesses and faults, about those things both petty and great that we hope no one ever discovers. We do not need excuses, we do not need to justify anything, we do not need to pretend to be more than we are. We can let go of all that. It allows our lives to still be a mess as the result of what we have done or not done, and yet for us to be forgiven. It allows us to be incomplete and insufficient, and yet forgiven. And that is good news. That is vital news for people today.

Forgiveness and the weight of expectations

Our young people know that social media plays a large role in burdening them with expectations of who and what they should be and, for many, their parents add considerably to the weight. But even when they are well aware of the social media perils and have parents who carefully do not attempt to shape them according to their own expectations, the pressure to be perfect is still there. Young people may laugh and shake their heads and say they have no idea why they feel it, but they admit they still do. It's part of the air they breathe.

It shouldn't surprise us. For decades we have propagated a worldview that assumes that the way to a fulfilled life is to believe we are good and lovable and have the strength within ourselves to be and do anything we dream of. For two reasons, this is a philosophy that is a logical outcome of a society without God.

First, if there is no divine, forgiving grace, if we do not believe we are loved despite our unlovable characteristics, then – since we all want to be loved – we have to persuade ourselves we *deserve* love and are worthy of it.

Second, if there is no creator God able to take the broken fragments of our lives and build something previously undreamed-of from them, then we have to find the strength within ourselves to patch them together, or to pin a smile on our faces as we walk over shattered glass. And so our world 'ties up heavy burdens' of expectations and lays them on our shoulders,[6] insisting we believe it is possible to be and do and cope with anything ourselves, if only we think positively and build up our personal resilience; if only we work hard enough on our mind and psyche and body. In other words, we ask monkeys stuck in quicksand to pull themselves out by their own whiskers.

None of us is good, lovable and strong all the time. Few of us are all those things even *some* of the time. Most of us have periods where we are *none* of those things for any of the time. And keeping up the pretence that we are, in order to survive among peers and on social media, sucks us dry.

Think of all the weights that this covenantal understanding of forgiveness can lift from us:

1 It lifts the weight of having to pretend a strength or virtue we do not have.[7] God's steadfast love will not depart from us no matter how unlovable we are. He will not be shocked by the reality of our weakness: he has always known it, and yet always loved us.

2 It lifts the weight of having to justify our actions to ourselves and others, and removes the lurking fear that they may not believe us – and that we may not believe ourselves. God's forgiveness does not rely on us having any excuse for what we've done. Grace is gloriously unreasonable.

3 When life cripples us, we do not need to feel guilty that we are not strong enough to pull ourselves to our feet. Sometimes our own whiskers are not enough to pull ourselves out of our private quicksand puddle, and that's OK. We were never designed to be able to cope with life in isolation; we were not designed to cope with life without God and one another.

4 When faced with the wreckage resulting from something we or another has done, we need neither deny it nor despair. If we were the cause of it we must face it honestly, repent, and do all we can to make it right, but we are not doing so alone. We are working with God who is a creator God and whose covenants always involve new creation.

And each new creation seeks to move us further along the path to peace. Each new creation begins with making a relationship right. When the bedraggled prodigal son finally crawled home he knew that despite the range of things he had done wrong, his prime concern was the way he had betrayed and broken his relationship with his father. The ring and cloak and fine feast were all, I am sure, delightful, but what mattered most was his father running to meet him; his father sweeping him up in all his grime and pain and failure, barely attending to his stumbled apologies in his joy at his son being returned to him.[8] Their relationship would never be what it had been – God never repeats himself – but what it would become, built on the pain and loss and love and forgiveness of the past, would be something new and strong and beautiful.

That is what God built for us through the new covenant in Christ, and what is echoed each time we bring the mess of our lives back to him to be gathered up in love and forgiveness. It is good news.

Notes

1 Jonathan Sacks, 'Succot for our Time', *Jonathan Sacks: The Rabbi Sacks Legacy*, https://www.rabbisacks.org/ceremony-celebration-family-edition/succot-family-edition/ (accessed 04.07.2021).

2 Karl Marx, 'A Contribution to the Critique of Hegel's Philosophy of Right', *Deutsch-Französische Jahrbücher*, 7 and 10 February (1844), https://www.marxists.org/archive/marx/works/1843/critique-hpr/intro.htm (accessed 22.09.2022).

3 Matthew 26.28.

4 Hence no unicorns, much to my grief as a young child when I first heard 'The Unicorn Song' by the Irish Rovers.

5 Romans 5.8.

6 Matthew 23.4.

7 '... A strength or virtue we don't have *yet*.' We are to keep trying!

8 Luke 15.11–24.

15

Covenantal Good News (2):
Climate Change and Hope

Jeremiah was a prophet at a time when it was a particularly tough role to volunteer for – or, in his case, to have thrust upon him by God. The people of Israel had been ignoring their role as the covenant people for a long, long time, and Jeremiah's generation had not only inherited the effects of their ancestors' faithlessness, but were busily making matters worse. Jeremiah was God's last-ditch offensive against their complacency: an attempt to shake the people out of their false reality and decadence by painting new and lurid pictures of the exile and death and suffering that would result from a shattered covenant. 'Wake up, people! Look what's coming! DO something!'

As was so often the case, Jeremiah failed. In fact, *most* of the prophets failed to make any impact on God's people, but that didn't stop God trying.[1]

If someone dared to ask Jeremiah today for some good news about the state of our world, they would risk being hit by a blast of his frustration. I can hear Jeremiah muttering about people who prefer to look at pictures of cats and baby elephants on social media than face an unpleasant reality.[2] He was scathing of false prophets who pretended there was 'Peace! Peace!' where there was no peace, false prophets who assured the people that their gaping wound was a mere scratch.[3] You would have to be foolhardy or very brave to confront him with such a request.

Foolhardy, brave – or desperate. And that would make a difference. If the request came from a desperate shivering soul who believed Jeremiah's prophecies of doom all too well, they may have been given a different message. Yes, things were going to be tough – but there was always hope on the other side of tragedy:

For surely I know the plans I have for you, says the LORD, plans for your welfare and not for harm, to give you a future with hope. Then when you call upon me and come and pray to me, I will hear you. When you search for me, you will find me; if you seek me with all your heart, I will let you find me, says the LORD, and I will restore your fortunes and gather you from all the nations and all the places where I have driven you, says the LORD, and I will bring you back to the place from which I sent you into exile. (Jeremiah 29.11–14)

Or:

The days are surely coming, says the LORD, when I will make a new covenant with the house of Israel and the house of Judah. It will not be like the covenant that I made with their ancestors when I took them by the hand to bring them out of the land of Egypt – a covenant that they broke, though I was their husband, says the LORD. But this is the covenant that I will make with the house of Israel after those days, says the LORD: I will put my law within them, and I will write it on their hearts; and I will be their God, and they shall be my people. (Jeremiah 31.31–33)

The message of biblical covenants is both tragic (breaking them *will* have repercussions) and hopeful (God is a God who never seems to give up). We need always to keep both realities in mind if we are to look at an issue such as climate change clearly.

Having said that, in this chapter I have committed to focusing on hope (the good news). This is not because it is more important than the repercussion side of the story (the bad news) – far from it. We need, and have needed for a long time, voices that would cry out, 'Wake up, people! Look what's coming! DO something!' The Church is beginning to do so, but it is running to catch up with the secular prophets who, in this case, have shown us the way. We still have much more to proclaim in this area. Our urgent message must be the need to *act*, to change, to repent; to bring our theology to bear on how we have ignored or warped our responsibility to be stewards of the earth and faithful covenant-bearers; to spread the news that if our apathy, denial and faithlessness to our covenantal responsibility continues, we may be exiled from the earth, not just from our home.

We must do all this with confidence that here, as in every part of life, God must be at the centre of our thinking and living. Increasingly, even secular experts are starting to talk about climate change as a spiritual issue (although not necessarily a Christian one), and there is much, much more to be unpacked over how fundamentally our faithfulness to God is linked to the health of our world.[4] It is not hard to find bad news and challenges in our present and future situations, and we must all – Jeremiah-like – plead for a deep change of heart before it is too late.

The problems of proclaiming good news in the face of climate change

Those of us who have chosen to be part of God's covenant people should be at the forefront of any movement or action that recognizes and heals the fractured relationships between humanity and creation. This is not an optional extra or 'add-on' to our faith: it is bound up with the heart of our calling. As we saw earlier, when God chose Abraham, the people of Israel at Sinai, and David, they were chosen, separated out, like light from darkness or land from sea, to be the new covenant-bearers: the faithful who would maintain the vision of peace and harmony (at-one-ment) that is God's design for creation. And they did so on behalf of the world. If we claim to be people of the new covenant, that is now our vision and calling.

Given the urgency of the situation and the importance of that calling, this is a time when proclaiming the bad news would be much easier than proclaiming the good news. In fact, the prospect of writing a 'good news' chapter on climate change has been so daunting that I have been putting it off for months. It would be too easy to offer facile answers. I feel the same sort of reluctance that you might feel if obliged to speak of good news to someone who has just been diagnosed with a terminal illness. God's faithfulness means there always *is* good news, somewhere, but blurting out our version of it risks trivializing the devastating reality that they are dealing with.

My reluctance is compounded by those both within and without the Church who have declared a form of good news that is based on decidedly shaky foundations: classic examples of proclaiming '"peace, peace" where there is no peace'. It can be dangerous to embrace good news without a clear recognition of the reality of the bad news. Any good news in this chapter is not, for example, aimed at a speaker I heard at a Pacific gathering who assured everyone that rising sea levels would never be a major problem because God promised Noah never again to flood the earth. Before that speaker can safely hear good news, he needs to realize that although God is faithful, humanity is perfectly capable of flooding the earth without God's help. Our choices impact the whole of creation. The biblical covenants make that clear.

Nor is this suitable good news for those who blithely assure us that the world was going to end anyway and that's fine because God will make a new one. Since their belief is based largely on the book of Revelation, they probably need to ponder the verse that says:

The nations raged,
but your wrath has come,
and the time for judging the dead,
for rewarding your servants, the prophets
and saints and all who fear your name,
both small and great,
and for *destroying those who destroy the earth*.
(Revelation 11.18, italics mine)

I, also, believe in the promise of new creation, and I believe it is a promise that we can – and should – hold on to as a sure and steadfast hope even when things look unutterably bleak. But is the fact that you could buy a new present for a friend a reason for the friend to break the first one through carelessness or greed? Is the fact that we will all die an excuse for hastening the death of another? Does the resurrection excuse murder? Each life is unique, precious, irreplaceable and belongs to God. God does not take our carelessness with one another's lives lightly, no matter how able God is to form another foetus in another womb. I do not believe God takes our carelessness with the world lightly either, and that is some bad news we need to face up to before we're ready to consider good news.

So I am writing this for those who are like Jeremiah's terrified questioner, who already believe all too strongly in the bad news, the prophecies of doom, and who are already doing all they can. I am writing it to explore a glimmer of good news for a generation who are seriously wondering whether they should bring children into this world. I dare do little more than point out where one glimmer might be found and (to revert to an earlier atonement picture) suggest that even the smallest spark of light, if it is the light of Christ, can defeat the darkness.

One glimmer of hope: the possibility of change

Our hope comes from the fact that we follow the God of the Hebrews, not the gods of Greece or Rome. If you are familiar with Greek myths, you will know they do not have many 'HEA' endings.[5] Almost without exception they have the cold inevitability about them that you find in

Tess of the d'Urbervilles where you as a reader, and the characters themselves, are helpless to do anything to stop the protagonist's fate pacing inexorably towards them. One of the most famous figures of Greek tragedy, Oedipus, has a dire fate hanging over his life, and everything he does to try to avoid it leads him steadily closer to its fulfilment. The gods or the 'Fates' decide a future and there is nothing mere humans can do about it.

At first glance this worldview may seem foreign to us, but our Western mindset is a strange mixture of Greek and Hebrew in this respect. At times, both science and Western philosophy have followed this Greek assumption that life is predetermined and that we are helpless victims of fate, although, most recently, scientific determinism replaced gods with genes as the determining factor in what we foolishly call our 'choices'. (Scientific determinists also replace the captivating *stories* of the Greeks with far less appealing *theories*. Genes aren't nearly as much fun as capricious gods and goddesses.) Nor is it just the scientists and philosophers. Some branches of Christianity have a tendency to fall into the same mindset, ascribing everything to God's 'providence', which, if carried to its logical extreme, paints a picture of humanity as helpless pawns living in hope that God won't sacrifice us for the sake of winning the game.

Battling against this attitude is the secular, positive understanding of humanity's power, whose latest incarnation is the positive thinking movement in which we can achieve the frankly impossible simply by thinking the right way. We have encountered this already in earlier chapters. This attitude generally feels more familiar to us than Greek fatalism, but there are times when it deserts us. I am interested here in the moment most of us have experienced at some time when it seems our fate – or, in this case, the fate of the world – is beyond anyone's control or influence; the moment when positive thinking and self-confidence smacks up against the reality of our limitations or the reality of death. It is the moment when we are overwhelmed with hopelessness and impotence: when our life is rolling over us and trundling heavily on, unheeding of anything we try to do to change its direction. It is the moment when it seems impossible that our puny individual choices could make any impact on the inexorable forces at work around us. These are moments we are going to be increasingly prone to as we deepen our awareness of the climate crisis and as reality chips away at our ability to deny or minimize it.

Covenant gives us two key elements we need for hope in this sort of crisis. A covenantal understanding of how the world is holds God and humanity in partnership, with both having roles to play. This means, first, that it defies any determinist mindset with the knowledge that God has given us the freedom and power to be agents of change ourselves. Blaise Pascal gave us that famous phrase, 'the dignity of causality', when describing what God has granted us through prayer, but this causality is not through prayer alone.[6] What we do can change things. We are not chess pieces being moved around a giant board by a game-playing god, nor is our destiny predetermined by our genetic make-up.

That is one side of the covenantal story. The other side assures us that while we are not passive chess pieces, neither are we left to fumble our way through to the end of the game alone. Covenants are between two parties. A covenantal understanding of the way the world is gives us what no positive thinking programme can give us: knowledge that the earthly forces which are beyond the control of our mind games are infinitely smaller than the God who is faithful to the covenant of creation. God is *so* faithful to that covenant that he was willing to take the impact of the covenant curse on himself in Jesus. God is *so* faithful to the new covenant, so *invested* in it, that the biblical language talks of Jesus *as* the covenant itself, the covenant that holds creation together, the covenant that is the seat of atonement.[7] That is how deeply God is involved.

As Christians we have no grounds to feel hopeless, no matter how bleak things may seem, because there is truly God. We have no grounds to feel impotent, because there is truly freedom.

There is one question here we do need to address before moving on. Christian theology since the Reformation has got itself tied in knots over the need for us to acknowledge our helplessness when it comes to earning salvation. Protestant and Catholic alike realize that we are saved by grace, although they still debate whether it is 'grace' or 'grace alone'. We did nothing to deserve existence in the first place. We deserve nothing of the life God gives us. We did nothing to deserve the love and self-giving of God in Jesus. But that does not mean we can do nothing of meaning to shape the future. Debates over words like 'predestined' have resulted in us losing something of the Hebrew celebration of freedom and hope, so perhaps a fresh look at one verse that has tied us to belief in God's 'providence' will be helpful here.

Working together with God

N. T. Wright is the kind of biblical scholar who seems to be able to recite anything from the Bible at will. He has so steeped himself in the words and teachings of scripture that when he gives a talk he pulls verses out of his head effortlessly in an unending stream. Yet he was brought up short in recent years when a student of his challenged the traditional under-standing of Romans 8.28: 'We know that all things work together for good for those who love God, who are called according to his purpose.' Being a scholar, Wright allowed his preconceptions to be challenged, examined the proposal in depth himself, and came to the conclusion his student was right. Now he asserts that we have mistranslated the signifi-cance of this sentence, which is not that God pieces together the world's story neatly, regardless of human activity, but that God works *together with* those who love God. The verse should better be translated: 'We know that God works all things for good together with those who love God …' Or, as he says in a later interview, 'God is taking those who love God as his partners in doing what he wants to do.'[8] In other words, God and God's people are in a covenantal relationship where they work *together* for the good of the world.

Perhaps you may be thinking it would have been better news to find that the present, past and future, and every emotion we experience, are all engineered entirely by God. If so, I sympathize. In some ways it would be nice to sit back, 'eat, drink and be merry', and let God take care of it all. But the people of the Bible seemed to believe that freedom was so pre-cious that it was worth the responsibility that came with it. For myself, I would rather live in Jeremiah's world than Oedipus' world.

I believe the image of God and humanity working together in a coven-antal relationship is vital for hope in the face of the climate crisis. Fear can be paralysing. As we are bombarded by the increasing woes of our climate and our ecosystem through every form of media, the situation can begin to feel too big. It seems to be unfolding inexorably, driven by forces beyond our control (scientific, commercial and political). Our story risks taking on the feel of tragedy.

Against this we need to bring the powerful voice and conviction of biblical hope. Our story is not driven by fate, but by choices – our own and God's. The future is yet unwritten and therefore there is always hope that it can surprise us. When our choices break the covenant, the eternal way-the-world-should-be with faithfulness to God at the centre, then, yes, our impact on the future is bad. We know that. We have a faith that chooses the gloom of the biblical prophets over the blind and delusional self-confidence of an Oedipus. But when we return to that covenant, we find that God has been faithful, and that Christ's new covenant is ever-lasting. We find that while we have our part to play in writing the future, we do so as 'co-authors' with the God of all creation:

We face an open future, because we are free. We, with God, are co-authors of the script, which has not been written in advance ... There is no evil decree that cannot be averted. That is the difference between Aeschylus and Isaiah, or between Sophocles and Jeremiah. It is the difference between Greek tragedy and Jewish hope.[9]

This glimmer of hope is the foundation for all hope, since it is the reason we *can* hope. The future can be changed, and the one changing it with us is the God of all creation. If our faith told us to be determinists, we would not have hope: we would wait for our fate to unfold. Apathy would be the sensible response. If our faith told us that everything was up to us alone, the enormity of the problems facing us could easily swamp and overwhelm us. But God's choice of a covenantal relationship with humanity tells us that God works *together with us* to write a future as yet unwritten. Yes, God has a clear idea of what the 'HEA' will be, but in the meantime we have a calling as covenant people to be both faithful and hopeful, and thus be part of the healing of the world.

Notes

1 Ironically, the one who *did* succeed was Jonah and he was (a) dead against prophesying, (b) preaching to non-Israelites, and (c) fed up at succeeding. Go figure.

2 To which I must plead guilty. Not so much cats, but I do love baby elephants.

3 Jeremiah 6.14.

4 Try googling 'climate change spiritual' and you'll get an idea of how much is being written and discussed in that area.

5 HEA is, apparently, recognized shorthand for 'Happy Ever After'!

6 Blaise Pascal, 1966, *Pensées*, A. J. Krailsheimer (trans.), London: Penguin Classics, number 513.

7 Romans 3.25; Colossians 1.15–20.

8 You can hear N. T. Wright talking about this on a YouTube interview, starting at around 4 min 30 sec. 100huntly, 'NT WRIGHT: Coronavirus Part of End Times Prophecy? God's Grief & Shock', YouTube, https://www.youtube.com/watch?v=-J384Gx9nbkw (accessed 30.10.2023).

9 Jonathan Sacks, 2017, *Numbers: The Wilderness Years (Covenant & Conversation)*, Jerusalem: Maggid, p. 112. This quote shows that I am indebted to Rabbi Sacks for the initial direction of this chapter.

16

An Aside

The nonviolent resister is not fighting simply for 'his' truth or for 'his' pure conscience, or for the right that is on 'his side'. On the contrary, both his strength and his weakness come from the fact that he is fighting for the truth, common to him and to the adversary, the right that is objective and universal ... For this very reason, as Gandhi saw, the fully consistent practice of nonviolence demands a solid metaphysical and religious basis both in being and in God.[1]

Shalom and truth

In this chapter I am pausing for a moment to prepare the ground a little. Each of the 'good news' chapters in this section deals in some way with *shalom*, peace, since that is a key aim and purpose of God's covenants with us, but there is, I believe, something we need to face up to before we can go any further down that path. What covenantal atonement teaches us about peace is that it is essentially relational. What happens to peace, then, in a society that is fiercely individualistic? Does the peace of covenantal atonement provide us with good news to speak into that society? I believe it does, but in order to get there we need to start with some foundational questions about ultimate reality. If that sounds daunting to you as a reader, imagine what it is like setting out to write about them! So I will start with something I am familiar with, music, and we will build from there. However, since this is more of a preparatory chapter than one that deals directly with covenant, you are also welcome to skip the chapter completely if it is not helpful.

I am a pianist, which means that, unlike other musicians, I can come to my instrument and sit and play without spending a few minutes ensuring I have the tuning right. However, when I accompany someone who is on another instrument, I need to play the 'A' on the keyboard repeatedly until they have twisted or extended or warmed up their instrument to the point that their 'A' can play in unison with mine – without us both flinching or the dog howling. In an orchestra, multiple instruments seek to match their 'A' with the purest 'A' available, played on an oboe. Once that note is in tune, then hopefully their other notes will also blend in harmony.

Some people are better at tuning than others. Some are born with what we call 'perfect pitch' where they can pull an 'A' out of the air. Most of us ordinary mortals, however, have to do our best to approximate it. Either way, harmony depends on a mutual agreement that 'A' has a certain frequency and that everyone is going to try their best to get as close to that frequency as possible (be patient – you will hopefully see the relevance of all this soon).

What would make harmony next to impossible would be if everyone decided to invent their own 'A's. Imagine an orchestra where everyone was taught that the concept of an ideal 'A' was outdated, and each player was to find the true 'A' within themselves, in their lived experience. At the same time, they were to be tolerant of whatever 'A' another created, since that too was the truth according to that person's lived experience. Admittedly, some twentieth-century classical music sounds as if it was based on that premise, but in general the music thus produced would not be conducive to peace or beauty.

I realize that this is not a subtle analogy, and that by using it as an introduction to what I am about to say I will be oversimplifying a complex situation. But sometimes beneath complex situations there is a simple, central thesis which needs to be brought out from obscurity: in this case, the thesis that once a society has rejected or lost belief in a reality outside themselves (a true 'A'), *shalom*, or harmony, is very difficult to reach. I believe, therefore, that if we are to be co-workers with God in the quest for the *shalom* that is the aim of the covenant, then the single most important piece of good news we have is the existence of God.

Did you expect that, or were you expecting something more subtle or obscure, perhaps? After all, isn't it obvious to those within the Church that we have to start with God's existence? It should be, but it is not, and once the existence of God (or even 'god' or 'gods') slips into obscurity, so does the existence of any reality beyond ourselves: any true 'A'.

I have spoken with countless teachers, students and parents at Church of England or Anglican schools, and God is rarely mentioned. Values, yes – they come up in almost every conversation. The chapel as a place for reflection, yes. Spirituality, yes. God, no. Those things that are 'personal' or individual and contribute to our well-being are acceptable. The idea of a potentially demanding divine being causes instant discomfort. Nor is this tendency limited to schools. When speaking publicly, Christian leaders of mainstream churches are often more likely to seek common ground – along those same three comfortable paths of values, reflection and spirituality – than to talk of the one thing we have to offer that the secular world cannot approximate: God. We seem to forget that 'good news' doesn't consist of telling people what they already know, but is rather the bringing in of the unexpected, the different, the longed-for-yet-not-yet-found – and in our world, that is God.

Belief in the reality of God is, obviously, not tied specifically to coven-antal atonement, but we have got to the point in the West where in order to give any credence to the focus of the next chapter (which will, eventually, be about peace, covenants and relationship with one another) we have to start here. The Church in the West is taking a while to realize how fundamentally things have changed in recent decades. Once, a long time ago, the existence of some sort of god or gods was taken as given. For centuries now that has been a matter of debate. But what is happening today is that it is not just God's existence that is doubted, but the existence of a transcendent *anything*.

Ultimate truth

Think of 'truth' itself. Once we took it for granted that there were truths beyond ourselves, 'ultimate truths' that we may not yet fully understand, but towards which we strive (a common 'A').[2] This premise is every bit as important for science as for religion. Every experiment, every theory, presumes that there is some truth that the experiment is testing, or the theory may bring us closer to. We don't yet fully understand the world, but scientists work on the premise that there are realities to be understood. Yet this fundamental assumption is gradually being wiped from the general consciousness in the Western world. We and our young people are slowly being conditioned to believe that personal experience is a stronger and even more virtuous basis for truth than reason or facts. Experts are discovering that their expertise is disregarded: that an increasing number of people are convinced that the pitch my search engine or friend or gut feeling tells me is 'A' *is* 'A' regardless of science or musicianship. Once there is doubt about the veracity of ultimate truths, then reason and facts, which try to point to these truths, are suddenly not nearly so persuasive.

As a result, society often claims that 'my truth' has just as much authority as yours. Tune your instrument however you like, play away regardless of anyone else, and find the path to peace through tolerance of whatever truth another follows. This is even assumed to be a virtue: it is argued that with the removal of abstract truth, we are all free to construct our own truth and the wars over religion and other ideologies will be things of the past. *You* are to tolerate my chosen pitch, and *I* am to tolerate yours. We may picture tolerance as multiple parallel lines, each running its own path and never intersecting.

If this way of living were possible, it is true that conflict may be avoided – there is no conflict between parallel lines – but what a picture of loneliness and isolation it creates. Knowing no better, the secular world calls that absence of conflict 'peace', but it could hardly be further from the interwoven network of relationships that is biblical peace.[3]

In reality, however, the lines of our lives rarely stay parallel. What do we do when they intersect, or find themselves clustered together? What do we do when we are forced, through proximity alone, to decide *together* how to live and what goals our society should be seeking? If there is no Truth beyond ourselves nor even the possibility of one we're yet to find, then on what basis is your 'A' more 'A-like' than mine? How do we decide whose lived-experience-truth we follow? Rabbi Sacks talks of Jewish 'arguments for the sake of heaven' where two people argue not to win, but to come closer to the Truth. But if there is no ultimate Truth that we are both seeking, then we cannot come closer to it through listening to each other. The only option we have left is to try to 'win', to conquer another's truth with our own.

And that's what we do, often with great passion. There is another dimension to this understanding of truth, you see. If your truth is interfering with my truth, and both our truths are constructed from our lived experiences, then I will naturally take any threat to my truth personally. It *is* personal. If you challenge what I am saying, you are not engaging with an idea or issue or truth 'out there' but attacking my identity, my lived experience. When we realize this, it makes sense of how the same people who passionately promote tolerance of one group of people who are 'different', can respond with vitriolic *intolerance* to those who question them. For them, to question or think differently is to criticize my truth, and since my truth is my lived experience, you are criticizing me. That is not a recipe for peace.

Tolerance, the sad little diluted version of peace that society encourages us to aim for, can only survive as long as another person's truth exists alongside mine without challenging it. It creates a world of individual melodies that, at best, allows us to share a room with those whose melodies have enough in common with ours for us to overlook the notes that clash. But it is a world away from the harmony of the St Matthew

Passion or a Beethoven symphony. It is a world away from the harmony of people, animals and God as pictured in Eden or in Isaiah's vision of the world to come. It is a world away from the peace for which Christ gave his blood of the new covenant.

Peace with others

It is perhaps ironic that religion, which has been at the root of so many wars over the centuries, is also our only hope for peace. When our 'ultimate truths' were found through science and reason, we ended up with Charles Darwin and Friedrich Nietzsche: a merciless world where the fittest and strongest survive. As we recoiled from that in slow motion, we relocated truth to our individual being and experience. We planted a hopeful seed of tolerance, and are bewildered to discover deep loneliness, insecurity, and desperate, defensive conflict sprouting from it. Where do we go next?

We need God. For all the problems religion has caused in the world, we still need it. We need belief in ultimate somethings. We need a cosmic 'A' to tune to. Ideally, if we are to build true peace, we need to rediscover harmony rather than promote a world of soloists. In turn, that might mean we need to believe that there is such a thing as a musical score, and that it will go much better for everyone if we find out what part we should be playing and play it.

So here's some good news: God is. Here's some more: there is an ultimate score God wants us to follow, a cosmic symphony. Or perhaps a better analogy would be jazz, where we have been given the key and modulations; we have been given the players in our generation's band; and have been given the freedom to improvise within those parameters and in harmony with those around us.

The peace of covenantal atonement is not the temporary peace of tolerance, but the peace that reaches out to difference and welcomes it as another element in our increasingly complex harmony. It is not only something God has designed for us but also one of our deepest longings. That will be the subject of the next chapter.

Notes

1 Thomas Merton, 1967, 'Blessed are the Meek: The Roots of Christian Non-violence', *Catholic Peace Fellowship*, http://www.catholicpeacefellowship.org/wp/wordpress/1960s-cpf-pamphlet-blessed-are-the-meek-the-roots-of-christian-non violence-by-thomas-merton/ (accessed 02.03.2021).

2 This is the basis of religion, science and even most philosophy. Think of Plato and his 'eternal forms' and the lasting influence his thought has had in the West.

3 Try listening to someone practising the alto line in a series of hymns, and then contrast that to the beauty and interest of hearing a full choir. I am an alto myself and can testify that alto lines in most hymns are dreadfully dull in themselves.

17

Covenantal Good News (3):
The Covenant of Peace

My husband is not the most organized of human beings. Searching for keys, wallet or phone are part of our daily routine, and on any one day the chances are slim that his phone diary and paper diary will show the same appointments. But there are some elements of disorder that drive him to distraction, and one of them is a picture hung crookedly. Now, given that we live in an old house where the floor and ceiling are rarely parallel, this does cause difficulties: the picture hanging over our piano can align with the ceiling or the piano, but not both. My husband averts his eyes as he walks past.

A few years ago our younger son discovered this quirk in not only his father but *also* in (joy of joys!) his elder brother. For months afterwards we would come into a room and find each picture had been gently and subtly nudged in one corner ... *just* out of alignment. Then one morning my husband turned on his computer to find the screensaver had been changed to one of those fingernails-on-a-blackboard pictures where a painted line on a road had included a manhole, and the manhole had been replaced out of alignment.

There is something in us that reacts at a visceral level to pictures like that. For many, like me, the discomfort is slight, but it still elicits a slightly hysterical laugh. For some it is almost painful. But then there are other pictures that give you an instant sense of rightness, of peace. These are pictures in which everything is in right relationship to everything else: the state the Bible calls *shalom*. I have given talks on the biblical concept of *shalom* in a number of schools, and it's a time when PowerPoint slides are very useful. Show a series of those uncomfortable scenes where things are *almost* right but not quite, and then bring up a picture where things are aligned perfectly, and there is frequently an audible sigh of relief. My favourite 'peace' picture is of a bunch of scruffy white-toed gym shoes arranged in a circle, toe-inwards, so that the white toes all align. You don't notice the scruffiness of the rest of each shoe. Your eyes are drawn immediately to the lovely rightness of the perfectly aligned toes forming a slightly off-white circle.[1]

For me, it's one of the best visual images of biblical *shalom* I have come across. We are a scruffy bunch, God's people, but when our relationships with one another are 'right' it can be beautiful. It can exude a sense of peace.

In this chapter I want to look more at this understanding of the *shalom* underlying the 'covenant of peace' and why I believe it is such good news. At a time when many in the Church have niggling doubts over how good our good news is for the average person they meet, *shalom* is something that goes straight to the core of human longing. At a time when individualism is fast becoming the ultimate loneliness of self-worship, the covenant of peace guides us back to relationship as the foundation of well-being. As people of the covenant of peace, we are given a story to be part of, a heroic goal to strive towards, and unquenchable hope. That sounds pretty good to me.

Longing for *shalom* with one another

The presentations on biblical peace that I mentioned above were professional development sessions for the staff and boards of various Anglican schools. The audience was always a mixed group. One or two would be Christians. Most would know or care little about Christianity, but were happy to go along with 'promoting Christian values'. A few were definitely on the defensive. What fascinated me was that when I talked about *shalom* at the deep level of our longing for right relationships with one another, creation and God, people would suddenly begin to listen and focus. Even those who have no connection to the Church 'get' this.

Those of us who believe that there is such a thing as truth, that there is some 'ultimate reality out there', shouldn't be surprised by this reaction. The point of the 'covenant of peace' is that there *is* a right way for life to be, and if there is, it makes sense that we should have a deep, if often misunderstood, longing for it.

We find it easiest to recognize the truth of this in our longing for right relationships with one another. We do have that longing, even though we don't always seek its fulfilment wisely and often destroy the very thing we seek. But the reality of the longing itself comes through in the countless novels, films and plays based around the dream that somewhere there is someone (child, parent, mentor, friend, lover) who will fully understand me as well as love me, and be fully understood, as well as loved, by me.

Countless other storytellers write poignant or cynical tales in which this dream is unfulfilled or shattered. Both take the longing, the dream itself, for granted. Where they disagree is over whether or not it is a realistic dream.

Christianity, as usual, takes some paradoxical approaches to the situation, being both realistic and idealistic about it. It is thoroughly realistic: given who we are as entirely fallible humans, it is next to impossible that we will learn to form perfect relationships this side of eternity. That knowledge should go some way towards protecting us from disillusionment. All our relationships with one another *will* require work, repeated repairs and forgiveness: it is not simply a question of finding the right partner or parent or child and everything will be perfect.

On the other hand, Christianity is ridiculously idealistic: given who we are as covenant-bearers, the impossibility of our relationships with one another ever being perfect shouldn't discourage us in the slightest from trying to make them so. If we believe that the desire for right relationships that we find in ourselves exists because that is what we are made for – that it is part of a reality beyond ourselves – then the goal is worth aiming for, even if at present our efforts are flawed. When a toddler draws his mother there is no reason he should be discouraged because his drawing has his mother's arms and legs sticking out of her enlarged head. The important thing is his desire to draw this thing he loves to the best of his ability, however imperfectly. There is hope: even Michelangelo or Renoir would have created similar images as children. *Shalom* between people is part of God's plan and promise, and in seeking, however imperfectly, to fulfil that longing we are responding to one of our deepest nudges from God.

Our second paradoxical approach to *shalom* with one another is that Christians believe the key to right relationships with each other is starting with our focus somewhere else. Not on the other, not on ourselves (despite all the encouragement our world gives us), but on God. *Shalom* with others, *shalom* with creation (and, as a result, *shalom* with ourselves) are grounded in *shalom* with God. Fortunately for us, we find that the longing for this *shalom* is every bit as strong as the other longings, even if we rarely recognize it.

Longing for *shalom* with God

Saint Augustine, who wrote thousands of profound sentences back in the early fifth century, is largely remembered for a mere half of one of them. It is found in the opening paragraph of his *Confessions* where he writes to God: '... you made us for yourself and our hearts find no peace until they rest in you'.[2] Augustine was someone who had sought the peace of fulfilment and completeness in a colourful range of relationships, philosophies and religions, and finally found it, rather to his surprise, in the place his mother had been recommending all his life. His writings on the Christian life and faith were so immensely influential for over 1,000 years that it was inevitable that he would fall out of fashion in some circles today. Yet his understanding of the deep longing we have for God was profound, and his portrayal of conversion as a process of falling in love with the beauty of God is something we could spend the rest of our lives unpacking.

But I am going to leave it to C. S. Lewis to go to the heart of this Augustinian longing, as I know of no one who has done it better. There is an experience that Lewis calls 'joy', and it is closely tied to the longing I am describing: the longing for some 'rightness' where all is fulfilled, completed, at peace. Lewis suggests that joy is a taste, a glimpse, of what there is beyond. It is a 'strangeness' that unaccountably moves us, a beauty that 'stabs us', wonder 'laying a fingertip on our heart'.[3] Far from being a kind of cheerful happiness, joy is an ache: the ache of being woken, momentarily, to the reality of our deepest desires. It's a homesickness, it's the shy desire for beauty and love beyond our imaginings. I remember it first when I was home alone as a teenager and had a record of Rachmaninov's second piano concerto playing. The yearning that poured out through the music swamped me, and I remember wondering in bewilderment how I could feel so *homesick* when I was sitting safely in the home I loved. I believe that was a glimpse of our yearning for God – what Lewis describes as the 'desire for our own far-off country'. It is hard to better his description of it in his essay 'The Weight of Glory'. There he uncovers the ways we hide our shyness over this vulnerable longing by attributing it to nostalgia, memory, a book or music – and with that comes a story:

> The books or the music in which we thought the beauty was located will betray us if we trust to them; it was not in them, it only came through them, and what came through them was longing. These things – the beauty, the memory of our own past – are good images of what we really desire; but if they are mistaken for the thing itself they turn into

dumb idols, breaking the hearts of their worshippers. For they are not the thing itself; they are only the scent of a flower we have not found, the echo of a tune we have not heard, news from a country we have never yet visited.[4]

Could there be a more wonderful word-painting of the inexpressible experience of our longing for God? Did any of you who read that for the first time feel a sense of wonder to discover that you are not alone in that experience? We may quench our awareness of such moments with busyness or cynicism, or we may use these glimpses we are granted to infuse poetry or music or art, but these experiences are more universal than many of us realize.

We were made for God, and our restless, peace-seeking hearts vibrate to every touch of God's 'unutterable beauty'.[5] Yet, mysterious and wonderful as that is, the final longing I want to look at is infinitely more so. Somehow, for no conceivable reason, God too appears to long for us.

God's longing for *shalom* with us

When I started theological college, there were two subjects I was nervous about. One was philosophy. The philosophy students I'd met as an undergraduate tended to 'see through' the world, and if they deigned to discuss anything, it was with a raised eyebrow, knowing look, and deep condescension for our childish illusions. I dreaded being surrounded by them or, worse, becoming one. The other nerve-wracking prospect was studying the Old Testament. It was scary, strange, full of violence and other things that threatened my carefully constructed faith.

I am sure God chuckled. In any case, I ended up with a Masters in Old Testament with a minor in Philosophy.

It was in my first year there that I first studied the book of Hosea, first fell in love with the Old Testament, and for the first time cried while reading the Bible. There are few parts of the Bible as full of God's pain and longing as in the book Hosea. It's easily obscured behind our horror at the language used of Hosea's wife, but it is there – deep and almost wild grief.

This is a depiction of God that could only come through story, never through the impersonal, clinical philosophical debates of the ancient Greek world. Hosea reminds us that when we discuss 'covenantal atonement' as an interesting theory, we are miles away from the covenants God has with his people. The biblical covenants are essentially the living, vibrant, difficult story of being loved beyond our imagining, not in the style of a sentimental, pink-covered romance, but in a style closer to a Shakespearian tragedy with all its gut-wrenching bewilderment and complexity. I am not even thinking of us as the Juliet to whom Romeo pours out words of love and who responds with equal infatuation. In the first chapters of Hosea we are King Lear. You don't have to know all the story, but King Lear was a man who was offered deep and true devotion from one daughter but was disturbed by the honesty of it, and turns instead to the false and easy words of the others, who betray him. The result is sheer, appalling tragedy. Death.

In the first few chapters of Hosea, the prophet is told to take a wife (in the covenant of marriage) who will turn from his faithfulness to the false and easy promises of her lovers. Everyone will see it, will see the pain and betrayal the prophet goes through, and maybe – just maybe – they will understand something of the situation between God and Israel.

For the story of God's relationship with Israel is not that of a dispassionate God being annoyed that his plans have been disobeyed. This is God's heart breaking. Here is the core of it. God's wife, Israel, says,

> I will go after my lovers;
> they give me my bread and my water,
> my wool and my flax, my oil and my drink.
> (Hosea 2.5)

And then come some of the most poignant words in all scripture from God:

> She did not know
> that it was I who gave her
> the grain, the wine, and the oil,
> and who lavished upon her silver
> and gold that they used for Baal.
> (Hosea 2.8)

Here is God as a lover as well as a husband, lavishing Israel with gifts in the intensity of his love, and then watching her turn away without noticing where the gifts came from. Worse, she seeks out the same gifts soiled and second-hand through the baals, when God is holding them out to her, freshly created for her. Yes, the passages that follow are deeply disturbing as God then lashes out, blocking her way with thorns, humiliating her, doing anything he can to put her in a position where she finally has to realize the truth and turn back. But he does this with the desperation of a love that cannot bear to see her blindness lead her into the sort of tragedy that ends in nothing but death. I still find the passages disturbing, and we probably should. But the point is that this is no cool, calculating, distant and controlled God, but one so desperate in his love that he is willing to accept the humiliation of only being chosen because there was no other choice left; to have his 'wife' only turn back because all her other paths were blocked. How many of us would take back an unfaithful spouse on those grounds alone? Yet God accepts her. More, he blesses her, restores his covenant with her, essentially makes atonement with her, and starts all over again ... again.

We have seen how the pattern of covenant, fall, disaster and new covenant permeates the Bible. From the tale of Adam and Eve onwards it is invariably triggered by the same thing: Israel wandering blindly off, seeking in all the wrong places for what only God can give. We long for peace with God, but so often refuse to go where that longing can be met. The amazing thing the Bible shows us is that the longing is not one-sided: that the longing we feel for peace with God is an infinitesimal taste of the longing God has for peace with us, and that when we in our foolish blindness could not find the right path to God, God in his love came down the path to meet us. That alone may have been reason enough for the incarnation.

Jesus came to 'guide our feet into the way of peace'[6] when we ourselves could not recognize the way. He also came to do what we could not do: bring about peace with God, fulfil the covenant on our behalf, establish something that could survive the worst we do. And Jesus came to wave his hand in front of our distracted faces and say, 'Look! Here I am. There's no point in wasting your time searching down all these blind alleys when what you're looking for is here. Come to me. Come to the source of Life directly and don't be fooled by the cheap, brightly coloured imitations the world holds out to us. I am the way, the truth and the life.'

This is why we needed the previous chapter on truth before coming to this point. If there is no truth, there is no 'imitation' of truth; there are simply passing fashions of thought with no foundation or root. If, however, there is Truth and that Truth is, as Jesus claimed, found in God, then it is possible to build something of eternal strength on it.

It is also possible for there to be an endless and potentially tragic stream of imitations.

Shalom substitutes

Human beings are complicated creatures. We are animals with 'eternity in our hearts' and our longing for God, whether or not we recognize it as such, is deep and real.[7] That is encouraging for those of us who want as many comrades as possible on the quest for *shalom*. We sometimes need to be reminded that the good news did not seem good to us only because of some unusual inner quirk or our private choice or our upbringing, but because it is good news for the world. If human beings are searching blindly for something, it can only be good news to learn that that Something has come to find us.

How can we be sure people are still searching, still seeking an answer to that inner longing? Because the 'Baals' continue to run fine marketing campaigns and humans continue to fall for them. That is both tragic (how can we not notice the depth of love being held out to us by the one eternally faithful source?) and, ironically, encouraging. People may be looking in the wrong places, but at least they're still looking.

One place this can be seen is in the interesting changes of emphasis within our education system in recent years. It seems that as that system has been progressively and systematically purged of Christian faith and influence, a number of rather uncomfortable holes have been revealed which need plugging. To admit that perhaps this suggests we need religious faith after all would be unthinkable, so schools have found secular imitations of religious practices and beliefs and enforced them on students in a way that we would never dare enforce our own faith.

In New Zealand, schools have been encouraged for a number of years now to introduce mindfulness practices: to help students not just still themselves, but connect with ... well, they're not sure what, so probably connect with themselves. They're promoting the practices because they find that something approximating prayer and meditation surprisingly helps student well-being in all sorts of ways. This is presented as a new discovery. Hmm.

Well-being itself is a second major focus. I must be careful not to disappear down this rabbit hole, as well-being, 'positive psychology' and the like are huge and complex issues. Our well-being programmes are based on psychology, which, having the reputation it does as a science, is seen as a valid basis for encouraging all students to take on its practices and beliefs. And it *does* help! Imitations are only imitations because they are in some way like the original, and they will therefore have some of the same effects as the original. But imagine eating only banana flavouring and never a banana. Consume nothing but imitations for too long and things start to sicken.

The 'sickness' that underlies countless self-help strategies is the creeping decline of individualism into self-worship. The effects of our Western 'individualistic society' have been obvious for decades, not only in rising levels of loneliness and isolation, but also in a growing need for artificial forms of affirmation and connection. Tragically, we have sought to heal the wound caused by self-centredness by slicing deeper, to the point where we are close to amputation. Where Christian meditation was always relational, a way of opening ourselves up to God in order to be strengthened to be *shalom*-bringers to others, mindfulness is an individual exercise for our own well-being. Programmes for well-being focus on making us autonomous individuals, discovering all the strength we need contained within our own skins. Even actions that a few generations ago would have been unquestionably relational are now turned in on ourselves. As mentioned earlier, I am encouraged to forgive others because it is good for me, not because of any impact it might have on a relationship. We take on an 'attitude of gratitude' not because there's anyone to be grateful to, but because it's good for us to have those warm feelings inside.

We are being encouraged to pour our love into ourselves, and self-love has to be one of the loneliest states imaginable. We are encouraged to see ourselves as the centre of the universe, and then wonder at the rise in narcissistic personality disorders. Maybe we do 'find peace' best when we are by ourselves, but that only shows that we have not worked out how to have peace with one another. Nor is the form of peace we find alone truly *shalom*. Peace in isolation is blowing a whistle that plays one note. *Shalom* is a symphony orchestra. Both, arguably, produce music, but they are not the same.

If we are to be people of the covenant of peace, we need to break out of our culture's suffocating obsession with the self, and instead to seek 'well-being' where the 'real thing' is to be found: through right relationships with God, one another and creation. And we need to help others do so also. We are like flies, stuck in a bottle and faithfully bashing ourselves against the glass sides, convinced that because the sides, like air, are transparent, they are what we seek. Maybe if some of us decide to look upwards we may see, find and lead others to the freedom and freshness of the real air outside.

Notes

1 See, for example, https://www.gettyimages.co.nz/photos/shoes-circle (accessed 30.10.2023).

2 St Augustine, 1961, *Confessions*, R. S. Pine-Coffin (trans.), London: Penguin, p. 21.

3 C. S. Lewis, 'Against Too Many Writers of Science Fiction', *My Poetic Side*, https://mypoeticside.com/show-classic-poem-16799 (accessed 08.08.2022).

4 C. S. Lewis, 'The Weight of Glory' in Walter Hooper (ed.), 2013, *The Weight of Glory: A Collection of Lewis' Most Moving Addresses*, London: William Collins, pp. 29–31. (Sermon first published 1941.)

5 G. A. Studdart Kennedy, 1927, *The Unutterable Beauty: Collected Poems*, London: Hodder and Stoughton, p. 96.

6 Luke 1.79.

7 Ecclesiastes 3.11 (NIV).

PART 5

A Whole New Kind of Rabbit

The Story of Theosis

18

Preparing the Ground

Dear Jesus, help me to spread Thy fragrance everywhere I go. Flood my soul with Thy spirit and love. Penetrate and possess my whole being so utterly that all my life may only be a radiance of Thine.[1]

There was a time in my twenties when I made a serious effort to read a number of the 'classics'. Most I am glad, in retrospect, to have ploughed my way through, but Kafka's novella *The Metamorphosis* was a mistake. The story begins with a man waking up one morning to find he is a giant cockroach, and goes downhill from there. It was disturbing, as it was meant to be. It was also decidedly creepy.

I had a similar reaction when, as a young child, I accidentally saw snippets of the old black-and-white film *The Fly*. I was, admittedly, easily spooked at that age, but those few, accidentally glimpsed scenes haunted me for years. In that story, a man voluntarily enters a machine which was designed (in Harry Potter terms) to 'disapparate' him from one place to another. He doesn't realize that there is a fly in the machine with him, and when he is put back together his human head is attached, in tiny form, to a fly body, while the fly's head appears enlarged on a human body. One particularly horrific scene was when the fly, complete with human head, gets caught in a web and calls out desperately for help as the spider approaches. Although I strongly suspect the special effects would make it all embarrassingly comic today, at the time it was indeed disturbing.

Film-makers, writers for television and authors of horror stories know the visceral discomfort we feel when humans are reduced to something bestial. They also know they can evoke a similar reaction from us by reducing a human to something robotic. Think of a *Dr Who* episode where a man's face is peeled off to reveal cogs and gears, or – perhaps most powerfully – the ghastly concept of the Stepford Wives in the film of the same name. Somehow the idea of a human being being transformed, metamorphized, in this way is the stuff of nightmares.

And yet, think of Beatrix Potter's Mrs Tiggy-Winkle, a hedgehog in an apron, busily ironing Peter Rabbit's little blue jacket and serving hot, strong cups of tea to her visitors. There is nothing creepy there, despite her being a very human-like animal. Children who read countless stories of animals and toys that talk and act like human beings are not given nightmares, whether it is the animal-like Winnie-the-Pooh or the mechanical Thomas the Tank Engine. If anything, such stories are a comfort and delight. C. S. Lewis's Narnia is a whole, beloved world of talking beasts and living trees and it feels right and good. We feel, deep down, that our dogs *should* be able to talk with us; that trees *should* have living spirits within them.

It seems, then, that when we imagine something as being *more* human than it would otherwise be, rather than less, it turns from horror to delight, from creepy to a sense of rightness.

What, then, would it look like for humans to metamorphize into something *more human*? It is not a simple question. Would we want to increase our rational powers? Would embedding computer chips in our brains make us more human or less? It might be fun to have super-hero strength but, again, would it make us more *human*? Perhaps.

Possibly the word 'humane' can help here. If you met someone who was strikingly more humane (compassionate, considerate, wise, gentle, outward-looking) than most humans, would they be creepy? Or would they garner your respect? Was Mother Teresa creepy or did we vaguely feel that she was someone whose life was beautiful in a way that our own wasn't? When we see footage of the Dalai Lama and Archbishop Desmond Tutu – two people who knew all too well what it is to suffer the indignities, pain and tragedies of division and prejudice – laughing uproariously together, or deep in a discussion of joy, we are drawn to it because there is something there we know is right and rare. It is a glimpse of humanity as it could be; of humanity growing into something more.

It seems, then, that as long as we are moving deeper into what we, deep down, believe we should be, it is not creepy. It is beautiful.

As long as these essential *humane* qualities are growing, less 'spiritual' qualities can be imagined to grow as well. If you have read the final chapters of C. S. Lewis's *The Last Battle*, remember how glorious it felt to imagine swimming up a waterfall and racing over hillsides without being tired. Being changed into a being who could do that is as much 'fantasy' as being turned into a cockroach is, but it is a change filled with anticipation and joy, not horror.

As Christians, we are allowed to believe there is a reality that those glimpses of joy are pointing towards. We are allowed – even encouraged – to believe that the reason we are drawn to people of unusual compassion or heroism is that they give us faint insights into the 'something more' that is the goal of our lives. Fantasy stories that give us glimpses of that state are like chords which, when played, set up a sympathetic resonance within us. Deep down we recognize that that is what we are designed for.

We have an ancient story of Christ's atonement which tells us that the whole point of everything is for us to become ever more fully human, and thus, mysteriously, *like God*. 'Like God' not just as a vague and passing resemblance, but in the sense that we will become 'gods'. It is a story that is central to the Eastern Orthodox Church, and although it was often sidelined in the West, it never disappeared completely. Traces can be found even in Martin Luther's and John Calvin's writings, and it is the atonement story clearly most beloved of C. S. Lewis.[2] It is what is called *theosis* – or, sometimes, *divinization*.

This is yet another solidly biblical atonement story that we rarely discuss in our churches. Why? We may be too squeamish to find sacrificial atonement appealing, and too wary of abuse to explore victorious atonement deeply, but what is our problem with *theosis*? Possibly it is because the concept of becoming 'gods' sounds embarrassingly presumptuous. Yet why does it sound presumptuous to us in the West and not to the Eastern Church?

At least part of the reason is that the roots of the Eastern Church are firmly in the writings of the first few centuries AD, whereas our atonement thinking is strongly shaped by the medieval theologian Anselm and, later, the Reformation.[3] It is difficult to understand *theosis* without understanding the significance of this difference.

Paying the debt?

In the West we are used to thinking of atonement mostly in terms of Jesus' death on the cross paying the debt for our sins, either because God's honour or God's justice demanded it.[4] In contrast, the Eastern Orthodox Church starts with the question, 'For what was humanity created?'[5] They answer, 'For full communion with God.' They set their eyes on the goal first, and the problem (the universal 'bad news') then becomes apparent. It is the question of what is stopping all humanity, in all time, reaching the goal and purpose of their existence:

> [A] properly theological grasp of sin requires that we begin, not with how it allegedly affects God [e.g. by offending his honour] but how it truly affects [humankind]. What is the deprivation caused by sin? It is the loss of the divine life, the true human destiny.[6]

Atonement is then understood as the *process of restoring the divine life in humanity*, and bringing that communion, that destiny, about. It is a huge picture, involving all creation and all time. For the Orthodox, God's purpose was always atonement, beginning at creation, working through the incarnation, life, death, resurrection and ascension of Jesus, and on through the lived experience of the Church.

As a result, they can be a little bemused by the West putting so much weight on the cross alone, as if all that mattered was that sin was 'paid for'. They do believe that Christ's death defeated sin, death and the devil, but are wary of pinning down the 'means' to one theory. They seem especially wary of viewing Jesus' death as a payment to satisfy God. After all, although sin is real and the idea of a 'debt' is very biblical, so is God's grace and forgiveness.

Here is their point: how can it be 'forgiveness' to demand that someone – anyone – pays a debt? You would be unimpressed if I absolved you of a debt you had already paid, so where is the grace in God 'forgiving' us of a debt that had been paid in full? When Jesus tells us stories of debtors it is precisely in order to illustrate that God forgives *without* the debt being paid. Re-read Matthew 18.23–35: not only does the 'master' forgive an unpaid debt, but he gets angry at another for demanding their debt be paid. Or Luke 7.36–46, where a creditor cancels two debts not because they are paid, but because the ones owing them could not afford to pay. That's grace; that's true forgiveness.[7]

So without ever downplaying the depth of sacrifice on Jesus' part and the weight of sin that he lifted from us, let's focus for a few chapters on that bigger story. We have a goal to press on towards, the greatest goal imaginable: perfect communion with God, participation *in* God – in other words, *theosis*:

[God said] that we were 'gods' and He is going to make good His words. If we let Him – for we can prevent Him, if we choose – He will make the feeblest and filthiest of us into a god or goddess, a dazzling, radiant, immortal creature, pulsating all through with such energy and joy and wisdom and love as we cannot now imagine, a bright stainless mirror which reflects back to God perfectly (though, of course, on a smaller scale) His own boundless power and delight and goodness. The process will be long and in parts very painful; but that is what we are in for. Nothing less. He meant what He said.[8]

Our journey

This section will be a little different to the previous three explorations of atonement stories. Up until now we've started with the Old Testament and used its themes, stories and images to help us make sense of the New Testament stories. While *theosis* is also firmly grounded in the Old Testament, the Orthodox start with Jesus, seeing him as the lens through which all time, BC and AD, is viewed. We will be talking about the creation story, for example, but as something that can only be seen clearly once Jesus has lived and died and risen and ascended. With this atonement story, the emphasis is on the story of Christ making sense of the Old Testament stories rather than the other way around.

As a result, we will be moving between Testaments, often overlaying one with the other. We will also be dealing more with theological concepts that arose in the first few centuries *after* Christ than in the centuries before. The Church Fathers are of paramount importance to the Orthodox Church, and you cannot spend time with the Church Fathers without finding yourself tangled up in amazingly complex theological debates. I will try to navigate them as painlessly as possible, but do not feel bad if they make your brain spin. You are not alone.

Since we are not using our usual pattern of starting in the Old Testament and moving to the New, it will be helpful to have an alternative framework to guide us through this complex story. Here Maximus the Confessor (c. 580–662) points the way. Maximus was deeply influential concerning the direction of the Orthodox Church, and it is from him that we get the idea of there being three ways in which humanity needed salvation in order for atonement to be complete:

A in its *being*
B in its *well-being*, and
C in its *eternal being*.[9]

This will provide a structure for the following chapters. You may find that those three headings do not mean exactly what you are used to them meaning, but that will become clear as we move through them.

As you read on, remember that what I am trying to encapsulate here is 2,000 years of complex theology, largely in a tradition that is not my own. If any Orthodox Christian reads this, I apologize in advance for the inevitable inadequacy of what will follow. I hope, though, to spark enough interest in Western readers for them to dig deeper into the riches of this tradition.

Notes

1 Daily prayer of St Teresa of Calcutta, https://www.worldprayers.org/archive/prayers/invocations/dear_jesus_help_us_to.html (accessed 18.12.23).

2 Try reading the final section of Lewis's *Mere Christianity*, or his essays, 'The Weight of Glory' and 'Transposition'.

3 Anselm (AD 1033–1109) was a brilliant theologian and an apologist (someone who defends the faith, generally through logical arguments). In order to reach his people with the good news, he sought to explain atonement in terms of the language, worldview and 'bad news' of his day. He started with humanity as it was, then and there, which people of his time knew and understood. That's fine and good and is, after all, what this book is largely about. But there is a danger in approaching theology this way: the danger of attempting to fit the eternal truths of God and humanity into the passing circumstances of one small period of time. So when Anselm asked himself what atonement needed to 'put right', he started with the problems of the day and transposed them on to the divine–human relationship. In a culture ruled by honour and shame, sin came to be understood as an affront to God's honour; and atonement was therefore something that satisfied that honour and in doing so restored right relationships, thus returning 'right order' to the universe. The crucial part of Christ's mission (almost the only necessary part) was the cross, which was where our debt was paid and God's honour satisfied.

4 Note the link between 'crucial' and 'cross': 'crucial' originally meant 'cross-shaped', 'cruciform'. Just one of the numerous subtle ways our worldview is reflected in our language.

5 Patrick Henry Reardon, 2015, *Reclaiming the Atonement: An Orthodox Theology of Redemption: Volume 1: The Incarnate Word*, Ancient Faith Publishing, Kindle edition, location 836.

6 Reardon, *Reclaiming the Atonement*, location 954.

7 Reardon, *Reclaiming the Atonement*, location 789–819.

8 C. S. Lewis, 1952, *Mere Christianity*, Glasgow: Collins, p. 172.

9 Reardon, *Reclaiming the Atonement*, location 961–1003.

19

Transforming our Being

The Velveteen Rabbit is a dearly loved children's book about a toy rabbit who is told by a wise old Skin Horse that it is possible to become 'real' through the love of a child. The process takes time, and along the way you are likely to become rather tattered and torn, but if a child loves you long enough and hard enough, you become real in the child's eyes:

> 'Real isn't how you are made,' said the Skin Horse. 'It's a thing that happens to you. When a child loves you for a long, long time, not just to play with, but REALLY loves you, then you become Real.' 'Does it hurt?' asked the Rabbit. 'Sometimes,' said the Skin Horse, for he was always truthful. 'When you are Real you don't mind being hurt … Generally, by the time you are Real, most of your hair has been loved off, and your eyes drop out and you get loose in the joints and very shabby. But these things don't matter at all, because once you are Real you can't be ugly, except to people who don't understand.'[1]

When the Rabbit is chosen to be the boy's special toy, day and night, he learns what that means, and as his fur is rubbed off and his nose gets shiny from being kissed, he believes that he has indeed become real. But one day he sees two creatures moving of their own accord through the forest – creatures that look a little like him, but have movable hind legs, and can bounce without being thrown.

They must have been very well made, for their seams didn't show at all, and they changed shape in a queer way when they moved; one minute they were long and thin and the next minute fat and bunchy, instead of always staying the same like he did. Their feet padded softly on the ground, and they crept quite close to him, twitching their noses, while the Rabbit stared hard to see which side the clockwork stuck out, for he knew that people who jump generally have something to wind them up. But he couldn't see it. This was a whole, new, unheard-of way of being 'real'. They were evidently a new kind of rabbit altogether.[2]

Shortly afterwards, the boy catches scarlet fever, and once he recovers everything he had had contact with is sent out to be burned to prevent contagion – including the Rabbit. But at the point where the Rabbit is convinced it is the end, something happens:

> Of what use was it to be loved and lose one's beauty and become Real if it all ended like this? And a tear, a real tear, trickled down his little shabby velvet nose and fell to the ground. And then a strange thing happened. For where the tear had fallen a flower grew out of the ground, a mysterious flower, not at all like any that grew in the garden.[3]

From the flower comes a fairy: a fairy with the power to transform the Rabbit completely, and make him *Real*. 'Wasn't I real before?' the Rabbit asks. 'You were real to the boy … because he loved you. Now you shall be real to everyone,' is the reply. The Rabbit finds himself in a glade with the strange creatures he had met before, but now he discovers he has hind legs to scratch his nose with. He is still himself, but he can leap and bound and twist. All he had only done in his imagination he could now do with his own body; the life he had imitated was now Life in reality.

That is the story of *theosis*.

If at any stage in the next few chapters you feel weighed down by theological concepts or convoluted analogies, I recommend putting this book down, finding *The Velveteen Rabbit* in your nearest library, and reading it – or re-reading it. It is the simplest and most delightful way of understanding (as opposed to analysing) *theosis* that I have encountered. Anything I write now will be by way of a rather long footnote to this story of the Rabbit, the boy and the fairy.

Still, some people enjoy footnotes, so let's have a go at finding sources and connections and expansions of the story that might enrich our understanding a little.

In each of the atonement stories we have explored there has been an interweaving of what theologians call the 'already and not-yet': that which has been done by Christ, and the unfolding story of which we are a part. Remember that when we talked about Christ being victorious over Satan, we noted that the worldview that put Satan in place was still very much a part of our world. There are things we could not do to save ourselves, but there are also things we are given to do as part of bringing in the kingdom. We cannot make the sun rise, but we can be sure it will, and in the meantime we are to be candle-bearers. The same idea can be found in this story.

Think about the three areas in the last chapter that Maximus the Confessor identified as needing transformation: our being, our well-being, and our eternal being. Nothing the boy or Rabbit could do would change the essential nature, the 'being' of the Velveteen Rabbit. However hard they both imagined he was Real, he was actually made of velvet and stuffing. Nor could either of them avoid disease or the inevitable destruction of the toy (his 'eternal being'). The gift of 'life', of true reality, came from a power beyond them. Yet it was the love they gave and received that kindled the Rabbit's dreams of being Real and kept those dreams burning; it was that mutual love and giving that meant the Rabbit could weep a 'real tear'. So we will find that the transformation of our being and eternal being are pure gift, pure grace, as there was nothing we could do to bring them about. It is in the transformation of our well-being that God invites us to be active participants in our own story and the story of creation.

Of course, nothing is as clear-cut as that, and these three transformational needs cannot truly be separated out into three neat categories. But when we are trying to get our heads around mysteries like this, we have little choice but to simplify them. We must just keep in mind, always, that Reality is beyond anything we can presently imagine. Our goal is to become a whole new kind of Rabbit, and at present the stuffing in our heads makes comprehending that impossible.

Our created being

So, what does it mean to have our 'being' atoned for, saved, transformed? Our own story starts, as each of our atonement stories do, in the Garden of Eden, where we read the tale of the creation of the human being. The writer of Genesis tells of God creating humankind in God's 'image and likeness, male and female he created them'.[4] Here we face the first difficulty. I am sure the writer knew what he (or she!) meant by 'image and likeness', but it is by no means clear to us. What *is* that 'image' and how are we a 'likeness' of God? Is it because we have free will, or reason, or consciousness, or creativity? Is it because we love and can be faithful? Or is it something else?

I wrote earlier that, for the Orthodox, everything is viewed through the lens of Christ, so we need to start by remembering that Christ was there at creation.[5] It was through Christ, the Word of God and perfect image of God, that all things were made, and all things have their being in him.[6] The Church Fathers, Irenaeus (c. AD 130–202) and Clement (c. AD 150–215), suggested that we bear God's image because we have a spark or measure of Christ within us. Later, Athanasius (c. 296–373) wrote of us having 'the impress of His own image, a share in the reasonable being of the very Word Himself'.[7] So in this understanding it is not that we share certain qualities with God, but that, in some mysterious way, all that God is has been pressed into us in miniature.

Fractals are an ideal way of thinking about this. Fractals are patterns where every part of the pattern is a smaller version of the complete pattern. More than that, no matter how far you magnify the pattern, you will always find smaller and smaller versions of the original pattern reproduced within it. They're fascinating, and worth looking up on the internet.[8] Perhaps, then, we can think of ourselves as having impressed on our nature an infinitely small version of the pattern that is God.

Alternatively, think of copying and pasting a complex line-drawing into a Word document. Stop and try it, if you have a computer handy. If you shrink that image down and down, for a long time you can still see the general shapes although the finer lines start to blend together. Keep reducing it and there is less and less room for complexity, until eventually it looks like little more than a blob of grey or black. Take it down to the point where all the 'handles' you've been using to move it overlap, and it is unrecognizable. Yet you could still grab the handles and expand it. The *potential* for it to look like the original drawing is there.

Christ is like the full-coloured, 3D original of which the line drawing was an image. In the creation of humanity, God impressed a tiny, *tiny* version of that image into us, with its 'handles' ready for it to be expanded. Or, to take a more ancient analogy, Irenaeus believed that it was as if Adam and Eve were infants with the potential to grow the image of God within them so that as humanity matured, so did the image and likeness of God. They were 'morally, spiritually and intellectually a child' with all a child's potential and hope – and contrariness.[9]

We know what happened. It wasn't that the image was deleted (although there is some debate about that), but it stayed so small as to be almost unrecognizable, while Adam and Eve chose to paste a picture of themselves on top and expand that. That was the 'being' their children and children's children inherited: one that, while it retained the spark of God's image within us, had so obscured and smothered it with the image of humanity that any hope of growing into the likeness of God was obliterated.

Until, that is, one instance of a 'human being' appeared in which the Reality itself lived, not just a nearly obliterated image of it. That changed everything.

The Being of Christ and the problem with mysteries

It doesn't do to stretch analogies too far, so hold lightly to the whole idea of fractals, Word documents and line drawings. But also keep in mind that the Church has always stretched the meanings of words and used analogies and metaphors when talking about God. We have to.

So as we move now to consider a doctrine central to the whole idea of *theosis*, and go back to far more ancient concepts than computer cut-and-pasting, don't let the antiquity of the pictures and words give you the impression that the people who used them thought they were scientific, exact descriptions of God. Most of our foundational doctrines, like those found in the creeds, are not so much precise descriptions as fences marking boundaries beyond which we are stepping into dangerous territory. There are landmines out there, and all we know is that if we are to approach the Mystery that is God safely, we should walk along the inside of that fence.

Those landmines are called 'heresies' and the Church Fathers built the fences of 'doctrine' almost solely in order to avoid them. The debates that led to the formation of our creeds may seem ridiculously pedantic to some of us in the West 1,500 years later, but our faith would look very different without them. The Orthodox Church has never forgotten how important the work of the Church Fathers was, and in order for us to go further with their teaching we ourselves need to pause and have another look at some of that work.

One thing I found fascinating when studying Patristics (a word meaning the study of the first 500 years of the Church) was that it is difficult to think of a heresy that had not already been tried out by AD 500. All we have done since then is suggest variations on those ancient themes. That makes the work of the Church Fathers (and some 'Church Mothers') even more remarkable, as they had to tackle these heresies for the first time in all their unexpected and appealing brightness. And they *were* appealing. Heresies were the brainchildren of numerous intelligent and devout people, each of whom had a strong case for moving the fence in one direction or another. It took the combined insights of heads of churches from all over the known world, gathered together in councils, to discern the pitfalls ahead if certain paths were taken.

Remember, the role of these doctrinal fences wasn't to explain God (as if that were possible), but to mark out the points beyond which we could not safely go. So perhaps a better picture than a single fence is two fences running parallel, quite a long way apart. We know not to go too far to the right nor too far to the left, and *somewhere* in the vast area in between is the Truth.

So take, for example, the doctrine of the Trinity. It makes no logical sense at all, and of course that is inevitable. The ocean cannot be contained within a few neat containers and the Being of God certainly cannot be contained within a few neat human concepts. What the doctrine tells us, however, is that we cannot step over the fence in one direction to claim that we believe in three gods. Nor can we climb over in the other direction of deciding that Father, Son and Holy Spirit are one God in three different sets of clothes. God is Three and God is One, and that's the misty path we walk.

Or take the doctrine on which the Orthodox understanding of atonement – *theosis* – stands or falls, which relies again on the placement of two of these fences. They are the fences that guide our understanding of the Being of Jesus:

(a) Jesus is completely, perfectly divine, properly described by all the characteristics of divinity.
(b) That same Jesus is also fully, perfectly human, properly described by all the characteristics of humanity.[10]

Jesus, fully human and fully divine. The path marked out by these two boundaries is not one we understand, nor can we see clearly as we walk it, but we know it is the path of safety and truth.

Why is this so central to *theosis*? Peter Bouteneff, the Orthodox theologian whose words I quoted for these two 'fences', goes on to say that although Jesus does not sin, that does not mean he is no less human, since sin is not foundational to the human nature. In fact, by not being sinful, Jesus was *more* human than the rest of humanity.

Here things begin to fall into place. The amazing thing about Jesus, who was fully God and fully human, was that *as a result* of being both, he was the most *fully human* human being there has been. He was what humanity was always meant to be, and even more. In Jesus, the likeness of God and the goal of humanity were both complete and, in Jesus, human and divine were in perfect communion. The divine did not swallow up or destroy the human, but brought it to perfection. Jesus (if I can say this without offending anyone) was always the Living, Real Rabbit, showing us what we in our cloth-and-stuffing being could one day be, reminding us of what we were made in the image of, instilling in our hearts the desire to be Real ourselves.

But Jesus was even more than that. It was as if the world was full of velveteen rabbits, and Jesus was the first Real one to exist. *By existing, he made the existence of Real rabbits possible.*

Pause and think about that, as it leads us to the most mysterious part of this whole story.

The transformation of being

In trying to communicate how Jesus metamorphized the being of humanity and, in doing so, made that transformation possible for us, once again we are in the realm of mystery and I can only offer you a series of analogies.

The first is the one already suggested: Jesus as the first Real Rabbit. Jesus was the first perfect human to exist, the first human in whom the goal of perfect communion between divine and human natures was real. The fact of the incarnation itself made the existence of perfect humanity *possible*, made it a reality. If that picture is enough to spark your imaginative understanding, you may not need the rest of this little section. Otherwise, read on.

A Church Father who did much to shape our understanding of this mystery was St Athanasius. He was one of the most courageous and outspoken of the Church Fathers, and as a result probably holds the record for the number of banishments handed out to one person. (He was exiled five times by four different Roman emperors. Impressive.) Not one to be silenced by such treatment, he turned to the written word, penning, among other things, a little – surprisingly readable – treatise on the incarnation. In it he suggests that when Adam and Eve disobeyed God, the being of humanity became touched with a corruption that grew from one generation to the next.[11] But God and corruption cannot coexist, so when Jesus became a human being, the corruption was simply driven out. Think of turning on a light in a dark room. Jesus filled the dark, corrupted being of humanity with the light of holiness.

Here is another of Athanasius' ideas. If we start with the teaching that the image of God was 'imprinted' on the human being, how could that image be repaired if it is blurred or overlaid or destroyed? Humans could no more imprint themselves than a piece of paper could reproduce on itself a date stamp. Nor could angels help, 'for they are not the images of God'. Our only hope was that the Original would once more imprint Himself on us. So 'the Word of God came in His own person, because it was He alone, the image of the Father, who could recreate man made after the image'.[12]

Or, finally, think of human nature as a river stemming from a source that has become polluted. The head of that river is Adam. Now imagine that a new, fresh source, infinitely more powerful, springs out of the rockface and swamps the original source, taking all the pollution down and away. Now it is the living water of Christ, our Source and Head, flowing between the banks of human nature. We still can, and do, pollute our own little puddles, but that pure water is now there for us should we allow it to flow through us.

Whatever picture you like, the essential teaching is that the incarnation was a vital part of God's unfolding plan for atonement. In Christ, who was fully human and fully divine, divine and human in perfect communion, a 'Real rabbit' became a real thing. The being of humanity was transformed. Part one completed.

But that was not our only problem. The actions and choices that we make in our lives can work against that 'one-ness' with God that atonement seeks. We can blur the image of God in our act of living, just as humans have throughout their history. And even if that is somehow made right, we still face death. 'Of what use was it to be loved and lose one's beauty and become Real if it all ended like this?'

Sin itself needed to be 'undone' for our well-being, and death itself needed to be 'undone' for our eternal being. That is what we will explore in the following chapters.

Notes

1 Margery Williams, 2015, *The Velveteen Rabbit*, Toronto: HarperCollins, Kindle edition, location 5–6.

2 Williams, *The Velveteen Rabbit*, location 10–11.

3 Williams, *The Velveteen Rabbit*, location 18.

4 Genesis 1.27.

5 Even more mysteriously, it was the *crucified* Christ who was there at creation (Revelation 13.8).

6 John 1.3 and Colossians 1.16–20.

7 Athanasius, 1944, *St. Athanasius on the Incarnation*, translated and edited by a religious of CSMV, London: Mowbray, p. 28.

8 See this website for an animated example: 'What are fractals?', *The Fractal Foundation*, https://fractalfoundation.org/resources/what-are-fractals/ (accessed 31.10.2023).

9 Quoted in J. N. D. Kelly, 1960, *Early Christian Doctrines*, San Francisco, CA: Harper and Row, p. 171.

10 Notes taken from a series of lectures by Peter Bouteneff, 'The Orthodox Christian Church: History, Beliefs and Practices'. Written and narrated by Peter Bouteneff, Learn25Audio, released 13 August 2008, 9 hrs 39 mins.

11 Athanasius, *On the Incarnation*, pp. 29–30.

12 Athanasius, *On the Incarnation*, p. 41.

20

Transforming our Well-being (1): Recapitulation

I am an incompetent knitter and an inconsistent crocheter, so on the occasions that I get the urge to crochet a shawl or scarf (the limits of my ability) I become sadly familiar with the deep frustration of discovering, 40 or so rows too late, a very obvious flaw. Even more depressingly, frequently the flaw runs right through all I have done, as a result of my haphazard approach to reading the pattern. My options are to give up on the whole thing until inspiration hits again, or unravel it all (dealing with the numerous knots that form in the process), and try again, paying deeper attention to the instructions.

There is a theory tied up with this story of atonement that Irenaeus called 'recapitulation'. In essence, it means that Jesus, through his life and death, patiently unravelled the history of humankind and knitted it together once more in the pattern it was meant to have. Our problem, you see, is not just that our very being had become misshapen and corrupted (think of the 'wool' being badly spun and prone to snapping), but that over our individual lives and the whole history of humanity we have ignored or mis-read the pattern. We have lost sight of the goal, the pattern for which we were designed: perfect communion (at-one-ment) with God and therefore creation. We call losing sight of this goal 'sin'.

The Greek word we translate 'sin', *hamartia*, can also famously be understood as 'missing the mark'. The picture that immediately comes to mind is of earnest archers facing the target and every arrow landing wide of the bullseye. Our true problem, however, is not one bad shot or even a series of bad shots, but the fact that frequently we ignore the target completely and shoot randomly into the darkness. It is unsurprising that the result is painful for everyone involved.

In the holistic way the Eastern Orthodox approach atonement, it is not only our 'being' but also our whole history and tendency to wander further and further from God's pattern that needs to be made right, brought back to at-one-ness. This process of bringing us back into the pattern, of getting the bullseye back into our line of sight and slowly, slowly improving our aim, is the process of *theosis* we are involved with every moment. It is something as individual as every human life, and yet tied up with the whole of human history. It is also, they believe, the path to true well-being.[1]

How do we follow the pattern, improve our aim? How do we become more *like* God, more *one with* God? The answer is: we become more like Jesus. Jesus was the perfect human being because he was fully divine and fully human; within himself he held full communion between God and humanity. Having that full communion, he lived a life perfectly in accord with God's pattern and purpose, a life of perfect obedience, leaving us an example to follow and God's own presence in the Spirit to guide and shape us.

Stop there and take a breath. Did you find that paragraph frustrating? The words are, I believe, true, but if you are like me they will have left you with the helpless sense that you still do not know what to *do*. What does it mean in practice? As any of us who have tried to 'follow Jesus' for any time know, there is no simple set of tick-boxes along the way. There is one clear directive: 'love the Lord your God with all your heart, soul, mind and strength, and your neighbour as yourself', but, while clear in principle, that command is still anything but simple in practice. People are complex. We are complex. Life is complex.

As a result, the ways in which Christians have helped one another understand the journey to God-likeness are also complex and varied. They need to be. Fortunately, today we are blessed with access to more than 2,000 years of wisdom from fellow journeyers. We also have treasures from cultures not our own which may, through their very strangeness, help us see in a new way. That is my hope, as we delve deeper into the riches of the Eastern Orthodox story of atonement.

You may have seen already that we are in slightly different territory here to any we have traversed so far. The good news we have is all about what God has done; atonement is essentially about Jesus; the transformation of our being and eternal being are pure gifts from God. So far, then, we have focused on appreciating the wonder of all God has done and is doing. But the transformation of our well-being turns part of our focus back on ourselves and our own choices and actions. It is about our current lives, about God working *with* us to slowly instil divine life and being into the mortal, fleshly creatures we are. We could not do it alone, by sheer force of will, but neither are we passive in the journey. There are things we can do, disciplines we can undertake, that do not in themselves 'save' us but that are our way, the Orthodox believe, of working together with God on the '*theosis* project'.

Recapitulation is one key path to transformation for the Orthodox: both the recapitulation of history and recapitulation within our own lives. A second deeply important way of understanding this *theosis* journey involves the work of God's 'energies' in our lives: showing clearly how our own disciplines and decisions become inseparable from God's work in us. These will be our focus for the next two chapters.

Recapitulation

In the linear, one-directional way we think, it is easy to assume that Jesus was incarnate in human history for the sake of everyone who lived after him. The fate of those who lived in Old Testament times is something separate which we hope God can take care of. But when you conceive of humanity as an interconnected whole, interconnected not only across space but also time, then we cannot separate history so neatly into two. Deciding to follow the pattern halfway through the shawl is not enough: the whole thing needs re-doing.

When we were looking at the ways in which the 'victory' of Christ were thought of in the first few centuries AD, we touched briefly on recapitulation. There we saw how the early Church Fathers found numerous ways in which the Old Testament held 'types' or 'imprints' that the 'stamp' of Jesus fulfilled. Recapitulation meant Jesus taking these shadowy, incomplete, or plain wrong incidents in Israel's history, and fulfilling or making them right.

I gave some examples of recapitulation during that earlier discussion. Here is another: in the story of the Garden of Eden there was a virgin who did not heed the voice of God, a man who disobeyed God in order to please humans, a tempter who succeeded, and a tree that brought death. In the story of Jesus there was a virgin who obeyed the voice of God, a man who perfectly lived out the will of God, a tempter who was resisted, and a 'tree' that brought Life.[2] It is as if, as we have said, Jesus went back to the beginning of human history and, as a surge of pure water, swept the pollution out and away, leaving the river as it was meant to be.

If we accept that there might be some truth to the idea of the 'solidarity of humankind', then it does, for some mysterious reason, make a difference to us whether or not the rows that were crocheted at the beginning of the pattern of which we are a part were right. But this whole process of recapitulation is not solely a thing of the past. To 'recapitulate' something means to 're-cap' it, to bring it under a new head, a new *source*, as with the analogy of a new, fresh spring of water at the source of the river of history. As I commented earlier, we can choose to make our own little muddy puddles on the side of that river, or we can allow it to flush out our own lives as well.

This is where repentance comes in. Repentance, reorientation, deliberately allowing God to invade our lives and deal with the mess there (past and present) is a vital element in our journey towards God-likeness. A common practice among Orthodox Christians is to pray the 'Jesus Prayer' repeatedly for long periods, timing it with their breathing: 'Lord Jesus Christ, Son of the Living God, have mercy on me a sinner'. We are sinners, and Christianity goes right against the grain of our culture by insisting that the path to well-being – the way for our lives to be things of beauty and life – is to face that honestly and often, rather than pretending otherwise. It is that acknowledgement, with repentance, that opens the way for God to rework the tangles and flaws of our lives into the pattern for which we were designed.

The problems with repentance

Recapitulation is a helpful way of thinking about repentance, as it puts the emphasis where it needs to be: on God transforming our lives so that we grow closer to God's design for us. Jesus' recapitulation of the history of Israel was done out of love, not anger, but it did not come cheaply. The same can be said of repentance, of allowing Jesus to unravel and re-knit our own lives.

Whenever Christian teaching over the millennia has lost sight of either the love or the cost involved, it has tended to give rise to one of two problematic understandings of repentance. It has either implied that repentance is necessary to avoid God's punishment, or, more recently, that God is too nice to make a fuss about it all. Understanding repentance under this wider atonement umbrella of recapitulation steers us between those theological pitfalls.

Take first the idea that Jesus came to save us from punishment for our sins. The danger of this is that it is so close to the truth that it is easy to mistake it *for* the truth, but *theosis* pulls us back from the brink. Jesus came to save us not from punishment for sin, but from our *sins*.[3] It is our sins themselves that are the problem. It is sin that directs us away from the well-being, the *shalom*, that comes with God's purpose and design for us. It is sin, death and the devil that are defeated through Jesus' atonement, not God's anger. We must not confuse the two.

It is amazing how often we have got that confused, and set up God as our adversary, or as a cosmic and much less jolly Santa Claus who spends his time spying on us to check whether we've been naughty or nice so as to calculate the size of present we're to get at the end. Remember: God is on our side. It is Satan who is the accuser, not God.

But because God is on our side, God is determined to save us from sin, death and the devil, and we are not always keen to co-operate with what can be a difficult or painful process. I believe the story of a god who needed to punish someone, anyone, for disobedience, and was satisfied by punishing his completely innocent Son, is deeply disturbing. However, it is equally problematic to think that God takes sin lightly. To do so requires that we ignore large swathes of scripture and our own deep sense of justice. This is the second pitfall that recapitulation can help us avoid.

If we consider the president of Russia causing untold pain and death and destruction in Ukraine, or Royal Commissions around the world exposing the abuse and betrayal of children by those they trusted, everything in us should rebel at the idea that God would pat Putin or an abusive priest on the head and say it did not matter. God takes sin infinitely seriously because God loves us infinitely. God knows the true impact not only of huge atrocities but of the small things we allow to distort and darken us, and will not allow them to remain for ever. The tighter we hold on to them – the more we avoid giving them to God to deal with – the more painful it will be for us when God eventually separates us from them.

This is what we mean when we talk of God's judgement. Just because we believe in a God of love does not mean we can disregard all talk of judgement in the Bible. In fact, it is *because* we believe in a God of love that we must believe in judgement. Judgement is unavoidable, not as punishment but because things that are wrong have to be set right if we are to become more God-like. God does not destroy the crocheted shawl, but God does want it to be beautiful.

Judgement in the Bible is inextricably connected with peace (in the sense in which we thought of peace, *shalom*, in the previous section) because judgement is the process by which peace, rightness, is re-created. It is not an easy peace, but it is real. The mountains will be brought low and the valleys raised so that there is a level path, and if you have paid a fortune to have a mountain view, you might not like that.[4] The hungry will be fed and the over-fed rich be sent away empty: again, something the over-fed might object to.[5] In each of our lives the knotted, confused, ugly mess of knitting we produce will be restored to its pattern. Anything that is warping us, misdirecting us, misshaping us, anything that is not God's pattern for us, *will* be unravelled and re-knitted. While that is happening to us it is not comfortable, but surely we can trust the great Knitter.

God loves us too much to leave us as poor, warped, shrivelled versions of what God designed us to be. As Jesus calmly told his disciples, God designed us to be perfect.[6] This is, deep down, what we long for. This is what *theosis* is about.[7]

Let us draw near to Him with burning desire and ... let us take hold of the divine coal ... so that the fire of our longing, fed by the flame of the coal, may purge away our sins and enlighten our hearts. Let us be enkindled by touching this great divine fire, and so come forth as gods.[8]

Notes

1 At this point you will notice that what I am calling 'well-being' does not bear any immediate resemblance to the current 'well-being movement'. Sorry if this disappoints anyone.

2 The association of the cross with a tree is a very ancient one; hence the verse 'cursed is he who hangs on a tree' being associated with Jesus (Deuteronomy 21.22–23).

3 Matthew 1.21.

4 Isaiah 40.4.

5 Luke 1.46–56.

6 Matthew 5.48.

7 George MacDonald has written a remarkable 'Unspoken Sermon' on God as a consuming fire, and although it does not make easy reading for us today, who are used to a different style of writing, it is worth tackling. Here is a Protestant, Scottish preacher who understands *theosis* and the unavoidable importance of repentance and judgement:

For, when we say that God is Love, do we teach men that their fear of him is groundless? No. As much as they fear will come upon them, possibly far more. But there is something beyond their fear, a divine fate which they cannot withstand, because it works along with the human individuality which the divine individuality has created in them. The wrath will consume what they call themselves; so that the selves God made shall appear, coming out with tenfold consciousness of being, and bringing with them all that made the blessedness of the life the men tried to lead without God. They will know that now first are they fully themselves. The avaricious, weary, selfish, suspicious old man shall have passed away. The young, ever young self, will remain. That which they thought themselves shall have vanished: that which they felt themselves, though they misjudged their own feelings, shall remain – remain glorified in repentant hope. For that which cannot be shaken shall remain. That which is immortal in God shall remain in man. The death that is in them shall be consumed. (George MacDonald, 2012, *Unspoken Sermons*, Summit, NJ: Start, Kindle ebook, 11–12)

8 John of Damascus: *The Orthodox Faith*, 4.13, quoted in Patrick Henry Reardon, *Reclaiming the Atonement: An Orthodox Theology of Redemption: Volume 1: The Incarnate Word*, Ancient Faith Publishing. Kindle edition, location 708.

21

Transforming our Well-being (2): The Light of Christ

A bit of trivia for you. The common Hebrew word for 'grace', *hen*, does not appear at all in the book of Isaiah. This seemed odd to me when I first learned it, as Isaiah is full of stories of God's grace and forgiveness, of hope for the exile, of God patiently remaking covenants after the people have, once again, messed things up. As a Masters student at theological college, the puzzle intrigued me so much that I based my thesis around it. In it, I explored the way in which, rather than use the word 'grace', the writers of Isaiah used the image of light. Wherever the Light of God appeared, there was God's grace.

As I dug deeper, I realized there was a flip-side to this. In pre-electric times, light essentially meant fire, and whenever fire appears in Isaiah it was an image of the dangerous and awesome holiness of God. It seemed that grace and holiness were inextricably connected – that we cannot have what we think of as the gentle glow of grace without the daunting fire of holiness. On the other hand, it suggests that what can be terrifying images of a fiery God come to us as part of the story of grace, of free gift, of love.

These images of fire and light, of holiness and grace, are central to this next stage of *theosis*. It is not only our past God is interested in. *Theosis* is a process (that's what 'osis' means), and the point of it all – the point of our lives – is the process whereby we become steadily more filled with the fire and light of God, to the point where it spills out to give warmth and light to those around us.

The most famous image used to picture *theosis* is of metal in a forge, heated to red-hot. The fire fills the cold, lifeless lump of metal until it glows, until the fire and the metal are inseparable – and yet the metal remains itself. It is not destroyed, but it is transformed. So it will be with us as the fire of God infuses us ever more fully. Or imagine countless little coloured glass lanterns, unlit. Then picture what happens when candles are lit within them. Although it is the same light in each, it shines through each lantern with the lantern's own unique colour. Each of those colours is now brighter, more alive, than it was before – and is able to give light to others. In the same way, as we are filled with God's light we become *more* ourselves, more the unique being we were created to be – and we do so for the sake of others.[1]

There are two biblical stories particularly dear to the Orthodox Church when thinking about this mystery. The first is the story of the burning bush, where Moses saw God as fire and light. The bush was burning, but it was not being burned up: rather, it was transfigured. It became more than it had previously been, while what it had been remained. The second is Jesus' transfiguration, where the divine Light that had always been in Jesus was revealed to the three disciples, shining through and transfiguring his body and even his robes, while not consuming them.

While both these stories tell of the Uncreated Light shining through created 'stuff', they are also subtly different. In the first, God transfigures what had been an ordinary bush. In the second, while we call it 'the transfiguration', it was more of a revealing, a pulling-back of a veil, for that Light had always been within Jesus. Both stories have significance for us in our *theosis* journey towards 'one-ment' with God, and hence with God's creation.

The energies of God

Imagine you have been forced to stay within a dark room for days, weeks, months. Maybe it is an underground bunker in which many of you are sheltering while bombs fall outside. Phones provided light as long as their batteries lasted. Candles maintain some hope for a while longer, but they are almost gone and you ration their use, leaving you all for hours at a time in utter darkness.

A day comes when the trapdoor on the ceiling opens. There is a moment of terror, then overwhelming relief as you realize it is a friend, not an enemy. You are being welcomed out to the brightest, clearest, warmest day you can remember. As you all move your stiffened limbs towards the ladder, at first the light is too bright for your eyes, but you force them open as, in your turn, you climb out, move a little away to let others follow, and then simply stand still and marvel. How does it feel to be still and absorb the warmth and light of the sun after so long in darkness? To let it soak into you, to feel it renew your life? How does it feel to see through its light again as your tired eyes slowly adjust?

Then imagine if that same light and warmth and life and sight could reach into your innermost being. Imagine if a seed of it, a tiny spark or flame, began right in the deepest part of you and began slowly to grow, filling and warming the darkness, transforming you from the inside out.

This light, falling around us and growing within us is, in the story of *theosis*, the work of the Holy Spirit. This is also grace. This is also – to move to a term less familiar to us in the West – our experience of God's energies.

This is not a term we commonly use and it can be a little tricky to get our Western minds around it, so let's start with a voice that is more familiar to many of us. C. S. Lewis's essay 'A Slip of the Tongue' has many memorable sentences in it, but this is one that has stuck with me since my teens: '[God] has, in the last resort, nothing to give us but Himself; and He can give that only insofar as our self-affirming will retires and makes room for Him in our souls.'[2] It is the idea that God has 'nothing to give us but Himself' that is vital to start with here. Think about it for a moment. God, we believe, is the giver of *all* good things. How, then, can he be understood to be only giving Godself?

One response could be to think of God 'giving himself' through Jesus: giving his life for us. In this understanding, God's self-giving was completed in the incarnation, death and resurrection of Christ. No more was needed. In a sense that is true, but that is not quite what is being thought of here. God's self-giving is an ongoing reality.

Think of the sun. Our experience of the sun is not only that the sun was created billions of years ago, but that the rays of the sun reach us now, warm us now, bring us life now. Similarly, our experience of God is not only that God gave himself to us in Jesus 2,000 years ago, but that God continues to give himself to us, to pour out the warmth and life and light of God's real presence on us as surely as the sun warms and lightens and sustains life on the earth.

Here is the key thing. When we receive love, peace, justice, goodness, *grace*, we are, in some extraordinary way, *receiving God*, participating in God. God is qualitatively different to us, remember. It is not that God exhibits or 'has' love, peace, justice, goodness and holiness (the list could go on), but that God *is* love, peace, justice and so on. We experience or live those things: God is them. They are the light of God falling on earth; they are the fire of God within us, transforming us. They are God the Holy Spirit working, *energizing*, the world.

We can close our eyes, lock ourselves away, or seek the shadows where the flickering gift of our own small life seems to be all the light there is. Or we can walk into the sunlight, open ourselves to all the ways in which

God is giving Godself to the world and to us, and thus open ourselves to transformation.

For the Orthodox, these energies reach us in *three* key ways: through prayer, through the sacraments, and through opening our eyes. Regardless of whether or not you agree with their theology on these matters, it is worth at least beginning to understand them.

1 *Prayer*

In case you were wondering, the idea of God's energies was not something the Orthodox invented. Paul writes of *energeia* frequently, but we tend to lose it in translation.[3] If Paul had understood electricity, his use of the word would have been very close to the idea of us 'plugging in' to God so that God's *energeia* are able to fill us and strengthen us to do God's will. Look at Philippians 2.13, for example: 'It is God who is at work in you [think 'energizing you'], enabling you both to will and to work [think 'energize'] for his good pleasure.' The unique angle the Orthodox give us here is the idea that God 'working' in us is inseparable from God 'in' us. God does not send us some abstract force to change us: God gives Godself to change us – if we allow it.

God knows we cannot transform ourselves along the path to God-likeness through gritted teeth and determination, any more than our laptops can run without electricity. Prayer is a way of plugging into God so that God's power and energy and life can flow into us and transform us. Or, to suit a climate-conscious world, it is a way of turning our skin into solar panels and doing some divine sunbathing.

This is exactly what former Archbishop Rowan Williams suggests prayer is like:

> When you're lying on the beach something is happening, something that has nothing to do with how you feel or how hard you're trying. You're not going to get a better tan by screwing up your eyes and concentrating. You give the time, and that's it. All you have to do is turn up. And then things change, at their own pace. You simply have to be there where the light can get at you.[4]

I find this a fascinating angle on prayer. We are so used to using words in prayer. The Orthodox suggest that a key part of prayer is simply opening ourselves up for God to get to work on us; for God's energies – which are God with us and working in the world – to continue patiently the slow process of transforming us into God's image. In our achievement-centred world, the Orthodox risk 'wasting time' in silent openness to God.[5]

One thing to note, however. This is not simply a 'mindfulness' exercise for their own well-being (with a small 'w'). I remember learning even in school-level science that energy does not disappear, but is changed from one form to another. Similarly, the energies of God are understood to act in us and move beyond us, changing from one form to another. The burning bush was not transformed by God so it could feel good about itself. It had a bigger purpose, and so does God's work in each person. None of the atonement stories encourages us to think of ourselves in isolation: all face us outwards to at-one-ment with God and others. If the energies God fills us with are not flowing out to others through our own transformed lives, we need perhaps to check our connection.

2 The sacraments

Earlier, as we imagined together climbing out of that dark bunker, I invited you to think of that light and warmth and illumination starting inside you as well as falling around you, transforming the inner as well as the outer darkness. God gives Godself to the world as God gives the rain, to both 'just and unjust alike'.[6] But the process of *theosis* requires Light and Holiness to also transform us from the inside out. This is where sacraments come in. The Orthodox see sacraments as a door between the material world and the world of Mystery: the world of deeper truth and holiness and reality that is God. Through that open door we may glimpse the Mystery. And through that open door, the Mystery may enter us.

The Orthodox treat the Eucharist with deep awe, because they believe the sacrament opens the door to allow Christ to enter us through the bread and wine. Baptism is equally awesome, because as we sink below the physical water, the doorway is opened by the shared death of Christ, and as we rise again the Mystery enters us in Christ's shared resurrection. The Orthodox anoint the newly baptized with oil – sweet-smelling and sinking into their skin – as a sign and symbol of the Holy Spirit within them. They are given a candle as a reminder that they now carry a spark of the Light of Christ deep inside them, and with it the joy and responsibility of passing that Light to others.[7] Baptism, they believe, sets God loose inside the one baptized to transform them from the inside out.

This understanding of sacraments would not be universally accepted across the Christian Church, but it provides an interesting picture of God at work in us, and is one part of an even larger vision. For the Orthodox believe that what we recognize as 'sacraments' are a subset of the greater picture of God's energies at work in the world, if only our eyes were open to see it.

3 Opening our eyes

> When an attendant of the man of God rose early in the morning and went out, an army with horses and chariots was all around the city. His servant said, 'Alas, master! What shall we do?' He replied, 'Do not be afraid, for there are more with us than there are with them.' Then Elisha prayed: 'O LORD, please open his eyes that he may see.' So the LORD opened the eyes of the servant, and he saw; the mountain was full of horses and chariots of fire all around Elisha. (2 Kings 6.15–17)

Every now and then in the story of God's people, the veil is pulled back from someone's eyes and they glimpse something of the energies of God blazing forth in light and glory and burning holiness. We know about Moses with the burning bush and on Mount Sinai[8] and about the pillar of fire that led the Israelites on their journey. But there is also the experience of the priests who had to carry out the hazardous tasks required of them in the Temple. In the Temple the protective veil between the people and the burning holiness of God was very thin, and if things were not handled appropriately the consequences were dire.[9]

Or think of the light that blinded Saul and knocked him to the ground.[10] This is a wonderful example, because while the light surrounding and emanating from Jesus was so strong that Saul was blinded, it was also the first time he saw clearly. Jesus had a fair bit to say about people who could see what was physically in front of them but were blind to the Truth, and in Saul/Paul we see the reverse happen.[11] Then, of course, there is the transfiguration when Peter, James and John finally saw Jesus as he was behind the veil of flesh.[12] All these stories say to us that there is so much more to see, if only our eyes were opened.

Hamlet's famous line, 'There are more things in heaven and earth, Horatio, than are dreamt of in your philosophy' acknowledges this same mystery. So do numerous fantasy books. In Rick Riordan's delightful mash-up of ancient legends in present-day USA, there is a 'mist' that prevents ordinary humans from seeing all the gods, goddesses and monsters who are cavorting merrily or destructively around us. In the Harry Potter series, the Muggles would rather believe the most unlikely rational explanation of something than admit, even to themselves, that they have seen flying broomsticks or Dementors. In the opening book of Cassandra Clare's Mortal Instruments series, the heroine, Clary, goes from being an ordinary person (a 'mundane') to a Shadowhunter, able to see through the 'glamour' that magical beings cast to hide what is happening. At the end of the book, she is taking a ride on a flying motorbike:

> The wind tore into her hair as they rose up, up over the cathedral, up above the roofs of the nearby high-rises and apartment buildings. And there it was spread out before her like a carelessly opened jewelry box, this city more populous and more amazing than she had ever imagined: There was the emerald square of Central Park, where the faerie courts met on midsummer evenings; there were the lights of the clubs and bars downtown, where the vampires danced the nights away at Pandemonium; there were alleys of Chinatown down which the werewolves slunk at night, their coats reflecting the city's lights ...
>
> Jace turned to look over his shoulder ... 'What are you thinking?' he called back to her.
>
> 'Just how different everything down there is now, you know, now that I can *see*.'
>
> 'Everything down there is exactly the same,' he said ... 'You're the one that's different.'[13]

We have our own 'mist' blinding us to the mysteries in the mundane. When we begin to see the traces of God in the world, it is because *we* are changing, not the world. God was always there. In finally apprehending God around us we are seeing through a veil to how things truly are. Our eyes are opening.

And – this is key – there is something about focusing on the glory of Christ wherever it can be found, which is part of transforming our lives. What we gaze on, what we focus our vision on, shapes what we become.

> Now the Lord is the Spirit, and where the Spirit of the Lord is, there is freedom. And all of us, with unveiled faces, seeing the glory of the Lord as though reflected in a mirror, are being transformed into the same image from one degree of glory to another; for this comes from the Lord, the Spirit. (2 Corinthians 3.12–18)

It seems that when Paul recommended

> ... whatever is true, whatever is honourable, whatever is just, whatever is pure, whatever is pleasing, whatever is commendable, if there is any

excellence and if there is anything worthy of praise, think about these things ... (Philippians 4.8)

he was not simply giving a bit of positive thinking advice to make us happier. He was encouraging us to immerse ourselves in those things that are not only *of* God, but are God's own energies, because it is in opening our eyes and our hearts to these things that our vision becomes more like God's own vision.[14]

The closer we come to God-likeness, the more of the mystery we will see behind the veil of the mundane. But, equally, the more we seek to see that mystery, the more we are transformed.

Before we leave this section, one caveat. This understanding is very different to pantheism (the idea that nature is, in itself, divine). Nature is, in itself, a bunch of material atoms and is no more 'God' than a novel is its author. Apart from God, nothing has life or holiness in itself. But that is the mystery: God has chosen to 'charge' creation with glory, allowing it to bear mysterious traces of its creator, if we have hearts to see it:

If we immerse ourselves in the material world and make it the be-all and the end-all of our existence, then it becomes an idol, an obstruction standing between God and ourselves, and cutting us off from him. But the material world can become a way to God, joining us to him rather than cutting us off. It can become a door or channel of communication, through which he comes to us and we may go to him. If this is true, then even man's spiritual well-being demands that he should recognize and cherish the visible things of the world as things that are made by God and that provide access to God.[15]

Notes

1 This lovely analogy of the coloured lanterns came from a series of talks on Orthodoxy on YouTube, specifically this one by Frederica Matthews-Green, 2015, Theoria, 'Theosis Part 1: Glowing with the Light of Christ', YouTube video, 2:59, https://www.youtube.com/watch?v=Zr2avLzFSV4 (accessed 31.10.2023).

2 C. S. Lewis, 'A Slip of the Tongue' in Walter Hooper (ed.), 2013, *The Weight of Glory: A Collection of Lewis' Most Moving Addresses*, London: William Collins, p. 189. (Original publication date 1949.)

3 See, for example, Ephesians 1.19; 3.7; 4.16 or Colossians 1.29.

4 Archbishop Rowan Williams on *Pause for Thought*, Terry Wogan Radio 2, 18 October 2005, https://soulspark.online/sunbathing-with-god/ (accessed 14.03.2022).

5 Being honest with God does mean we will frequently pray with the reckless rush of words and emotions and desires and hurts that a child might pour out to a parent, but it is no accident that the Orthodox Church has maintained its centuries-old practice of meditation. Its whole theology of divine energies grew in clear expression after an ecumenical council was called in which the rationalist approach to prayer of someone called Barlaam of Calabria contested the deeply meditative prayer of Gregory Palamas and the monks of Mount Athos. The deep beauty, possibilities and holiness of Palamas' meditative practices, which he and the monks believed opened them to visions of the Divine Light, was recognized and affirmed by this ecumenical council.

6 Matthew 5.45.

7 Many non-Orthodox churches also use oil and a candle as part of baptism.

8 Exodus 3.2; 24.16.

9 Aaron's older two sons discovered this: Leviticus 10.

10 Acts 9.3–4.

11 For example, Matthew 15.14; 23.16, 24.

12 Matthew 17; Mark 9; Luke 9.

13 Cassandra Clare, 2007, *City of Bones*, London: Walker Books, p. 442.

14 While God is One, we perceive these energies only in part and so are able to give them different labels (grace, peace, hope, purity, justice ...). The greatest of them, of course, is love (1 Corinthians 13). The whole of John's first letter is drenched in this idea that by focusing on love, by opening our inner eyes to it and welcoming it in, we will grow to be more and more like God, because Love dwelling within us is God dwelling within us. 'God is love, and those who abide in love abide in God, and God abides in them' (4.16). 'Beloved, we are God's children now; what we will be has not yet been revealed. What we do know is this: when he is revealed, we will be like him, for we will see him as he is' (3.2).

15 John Macquarrie, 1997, *A Guide to the Sacraments*, London: SCM Press, p. 13.

22

Transforming our Eternal Being

Spoiler alert. If you have not yet read the final book in the Harry Potter series and plan to do so sometime, I do apologize for what follows, but the parallels with our current story are irresistible. If you have not read the series and do not plan to, you may want to start with note 1 at the end of this chapter.[1]

Tom Riddle was a wizard of exceptional powers and deep resentments who quickly developed the conviction that he was capable of defeating anyone and anything. With the possible exception of Dumbledore, nothing threatened this belief – except death. Death could not be defeated with a single spell or blackmailed into submission. Therefore, becoming Master of Death was a deep and complex challenge that soon became his obsession.[2] When he re-named himself, he chose the name Voldemort, with its French overtones of 'fleeing death'. When he gathered like-minded followers around him, he called them Deatheaters. And when he found a way of harnessing the death of others to preserve his own life, he seized it.

Murder is an act of such violence that it splits the soul of the one who commits it.[3] Rather than be horrified by this outcome, Voldemort manipulated it by murdering a series of people and storing the split portions of his soul in various objects which became 'horcruxes'. As long as any part of his soul survived, he was tied to life; no matter how many killing spells were directed at him, the scattered parts of his soul would render them powerless. The final book in the series, then, is the quest of Harry, Ron and Hermione to find and destroy every horcrux and thus remove Voldemort's self-created immortality. What they do not discover until the final few chapters is that Harry himself is one of Voldemort's horcruxes. Neither Harry nor Voldemort had realized it, but when Voldemort killed Harry's mother, his unstable soul split again and a sliver embedded itself in Harry.

The result? Voldemort cannot be killed while Harry is alive.

Thus, as the final chapters unfold and Hogwarts prepares itself for battle, Harry learns that he must put his wand away and give himself up to Voldemort to be killed if the world is to be freed from his evil presence. So, in perhaps the most moving chapter of the series, he quietly takes the lonely walk into the forest where he offers no resistance to the waiting Voldemort. And Voldemort kills him.

Or, at least, he tries to. The next scenes are deliberately surreal. Harry finds himself in an 'in-between' space which reminds him of a railway station (specifically King's Cross station, an observation that causes Dumbledore to chuckle). He discovers he still has a body, but this body no longer has a scar and no longer needs glasses. He meets with Dumbledore, who had died in the previous book, and learns that he himself could choose to 'go on' to whatever lies beyond death, *or 'go back'* to the ongoing battle at Hogwarts.[4] He also learns that the reason he has this choice is because of another mistake Voldemort had made when he – yet again – underestimated the power of love and life.[5]

Back in the fourth book, *The Goblet of Fire*, Voldemort had staged a dark inversion of resurrection in a graveyard, where the hideous 'thing', which was all that was left of him after his encounter with his own rebounding killing curse, is reclothed in a body built from flesh and blood seized from another. In his pride and vanity, Voldemort had decided he could not use just anyone's blood. It needed to be the blood of the one he most wanted to conquer: Harry. He did not consider that, by using Harry's blood, he was taking Harry's life within him, thus tying Harry to life as long as Voldemort lived.

We have, then, a Catch-22 situation. Voldemort cannot die while Harry lives, and Harry cannot die while Voldemort lives. But there is a resolution neither Harry nor Voldemort dreamed of. When Voldemort hurls the killing curse at Harry in the forest, it does kill something: it kills the fragment of his own soul that is lodged within Harry. All he is able to kill is his own darkness, his own evil, leaving Harry free from all traces of the taint he has been carrying since infancy.

That is not the end of Voldemort. He holds on to life on the strength of the one remaining piece of soul within him. But he has been disarmed: he no longer has any power over those Harry was willing to die for. When Harry returns and confronts him again, a furious Voldemort sends another killing curse towards him, which Harry meets, not with violence, but with his signature disarming spell. Voldemort's curse rebounds on to himself, and the final sliver of dark soul within him is destroyed. The one who would be master of death succumbs to it.

While Harry is not an allegorical representation of Christ, the whole series is drenched with Christian imagery and story, and these final scenes are particularly saturated: Harry's willing self-surrender out of love; his physical being in the 'next life'; the disempowerment of the evil one; Harry's return to finish things off; his refusal to use a killing curse but, rather, his victory through disarmament and protection – you could dig deeper and deeper into the parallels.[6] But for our purposes here, the key is that when the Orthodox write of Jesus saving our eternal being it is often in terms of Jesus taking darkness, sin and death into death with him, where death discovers that all it can destroy is itself.

Let's unpack this idea a little more. Remember that rather odd part of the story of Adam and Eve where God warns them that if they eat of the forbidden fruit, they will die? The reason it is an odd thing for God to say is that they don't die. They keep living to ripe old ages. What God presumably meant, then, was that by eating the fruit they made it inevitable that they *would* die; that by eating the fruit, they allowed death to enter them. Death embedded itself in humanity from humanity's 'infancy' as surely as Voldemort's dark soul was embedded in the infant Harry. There is, within each human being, the seed of the corruption of death.

When Christ took on human nature in its completeness, he also took on the death that was within it. Satan thought to exploit that vulnerability, to seize that bizarre, unthinkable opportunity to use death as a tool to defeat the immortal God. But just at the point when Satan was gloating over his victory, he discovered that all he had the power to kill was that taint of death itself.

By 'aiming a killing curse' at Christ, Satan killed and purged death from his human nature.[7] In the resurrection, Life rose again, uncorrupted and incorruptible, and we were given the mind-blowing promise that the same is offered to us: that this insuperable barrier between us and God-likeness has been defeated.

In one of John Donne's wonderful sonnets, his confidence in the reality of this promise leads him to defy and ridicule death. The poem begins:

> Death, be not proud, though some have called thee
> Mighty and dreadful, for thou art not so;
> For those whom thou think'st thou dost overthrow
> Die not, poor Death, nor yet canst thou kill me.

He closes with a satisfying verbal thumbing-of-the-nose towards the death that dared to think itself so powerful:

> One short sleep past, we wake eternally
> And death shall be no more; Death, thou shalt die.[8]

We are all invited to that same confidence.

Theosis and victorious atonement

The presence of Satan in this thread will naturally be reminding you of our discussion on victorious atonement. As you know, *theosis* is an understanding of atonement that incorporates God's actions from creation through Jesus' incarnation, life, death, resurrection and ascension – and on into the life of the Church. What we call 'victorious atonement' slips in as one element in that bigger story.[9]

Yet there are some differences in the way the Orthodox understand this story. They would disagree strongly with my argument about the 'ransom' being paid to Satan, for example. Not that they think it was paid to God. The Orthodox do not believe it was paid to anyone. They agree wholeheartedly that Jesus' sacrifice defeated sin, death and the devil, but not in the sense of any real 'payment'. It would, they argue, be unthinkable to suggest that God pays Satan anything. On the other hand, we have already dismissed the idea that God was demanding that his honour was satisfied, so God did not require payment either. In what sense, then, was Jesus' self-sacrifice a ransom or payment?

Think of the way we usually use the word 'sacrifice'. We sacrifice our peace to entertain our children. We sacrifice our financial dreams to follow a job or vocation that will provide deeper satisfaction. We sacrifice short-term pleasures for longer-term goals. The point is that none of these sacrifices are made *to* anyone. We are just making them. If anything, we are making them in order to reach a goal or overcome a particular condition or situation.[10] That is an Orthodox view. Christ's sacrifice achieved the goal of overcoming a particular condition in humanity that we were helpless to overcome ourselves: the condition of death and corruption.[11] While death ruled in our bodies we could never become God-like, so that seed of corruption which had been within humanity from the beginning had to be defeated for atonement to be complete.

Where, then, does the defeat of Satan himself fit in? Since Satan is the keeper and source of death, the resurrection was sign enough that he too was defeated. But maybe there is more happening here. Before we close this section, let's look at one more little gem the Orthodox can give us in this unfolding atonement story.

Between the death and resurrection

This element of the Orthodox story of atonement may easily be dismissed due to its tenuous biblical foundation, but I am including it because, frankly, I find it appealing, and you may too. It involves a period of time that we in the West do not generally know what to do with.

If you have ever been heavily involved in Catholic or Anglican Holy Week services, you will know that the whole week is a journey, a time when we enter liturgically into the story of the journey to Jerusalem, the Last Supper, the desertion of the disciples and the crucifixion. Then we pause. Between the darkness of Good Friday and the celebration of Easter Sunday is ... nothing. Holy Saturday is a strange, limbo time which has its own deep spirituality of emptiness. Jesus is dead, and the world waits.

For the Orthodox, Jesus is, in fact, very busy. He is busy storming the gates of hell and rescuing everyone who had been imprisoned there, starting with Adam and Eve. Jesus' victory is a thoroughly active and completely triumphant one, even before the resurrection.

If you are able to pause here and find a picture of an Orthodox icon of 'the harrowing of hell', do. It is also worth seeking a person or website that can help you 'read' it. If you are unable to do those things, picture a beautiful, stylized picture of Jesus standing on what turns out to be the broken pieces of the gates of Hades. In many of the icons it looks as if we have caught him in motion, robes swirling around him, in the very act of pulling Adam and Eve up from the depths, one hand grasping each. It is as if the gates have only just been smashed and Jesus has raced in in a whirl of activity to rescue those who are long-bound. On either side of Jesus are witnesses: on one side, typically, John the Baptist, David and Solomon (Jesus' 'forerunners'); on the other, various figures including Abel, the first martyr. All this is as it were in the foreground – that which stands out in bright, living colours. When you look closer, however, there is something in the darkness below the fragments of hell's gates. Locks and bolts galore are scattered around – all that had held these people in prison – and among them the shadowy, skeletal figure of Satan lies in the darkness, bound head to foot: no longer the proud 'prince' of this world.[12]

The biblical support for this story is admittedly thin. We do have the fascinating verses in 1 Peter though:

> For Christ also suffered for sins once for all, the righteous for the un-righteous, in order to bring you to God. He was put to death in the flesh, but made alive in the spirit, in which also he went and made a

proclamation to the spirits in prison, who in former times did not obey, when God waited patiently in the days of Noah, during the building of the ark, in which a few, that is, eight people, were saved through water. (1 Peter 3.18–20)

As a parent who has experienced reading a bright little Children's Bible to my son, only to find him completely traumatized by everyone being drowned in the story of Noah, I find these verses cheering. That wasn't the end of the story for them. But the scope of cheer still seems a little limited, referring as this does only to the people of Noah's time. However, in the next chapter (1 Peter 4.6), we read again that Jesus spent time preaching to the 'souls in prison' so that they, too, had the chance to repent, and this time it suggests a more general audience.

The casual certainty with which Peter talks about this event implies that it was part of a well-known belief, and that there was presumably more to the shared story than he mentions here. Even the meagre allusions he provides allow us to speculate a little. For one thing, if Jesus preached to the souls in Hades as Peter says, presumably he would have had to 'break down the gates' that Satan had set up to keep them imprisoned, and it would have been much simpler all round if he bound up Satan and got him out of the way while he did so. Immediately we have a picture that is very like the icon.

That is certainly how a mysterious writer in the fourth century understood the situation. This is where we get the real details for this story: from the 'apocryphal' Gospel of Nicodemus:

And while Satan and the prince of hell were discoursing thus to each other, on a sudden there was a voice as of thunder and the rushing of winds, saying, Lift up your gates, O ye princes; and be ye lift up, O everlasting gates, and the King of Glory shall come in.

And the prince said to his impious officers, Shut the brass gates of cruelty, and make them fast with iron bars, and fight courageously, lest we be taken captives.

And the divine prophet David, cried out saying, Did not I when on earth truly prophesy and say, O that men would praise the Lord for his goodness, and for his wonderful works to the children of men. For he hath broken the gates of brass, and cut the bars of iron in sunder. He hath taken them because of their iniquity, and because of their unrighteousness they are afflicted.

While David was saying this, the mighty Lord appeared in the form of a man, and enlightened those places which had ever before been in darkness, and broke asunder the fetters which before could not be broken; and with his invincible power visited those who sate in the deep darkness by iniquity, and the shadow of death by sin.

Then the King of Glory trampling upon death, seized the prince of hell, deprived him of all his power, and took our earthly father Adam with him to his glory.

(Gospel of Nicodemus 16)[13]

Regardless of the questionable nature of the provenance of this 'gospel', doesn't it seem to you that there is something apt about this? We regularly proclaim in our creeds that Jesus 'descended to the dead', so what do we think he was up to while there? He could not have dissolved into nothingness, so his 'being' must have been somewhere. If he was in the realm of the dead, the realm of Satan, do we picture him being literally or metaphorically bound for the duration of Holy Saturday, just managing to fight his way out in time to make it to the tomb by dawn on Sunday, with the clock ticking? That would make a great film script but makes little theological sense. Death was defeated through the cross. Jesus would have arrived as the victor. Imagining him sweeping into death and darkness as eternal Light and Life makes far more sense than either a last-minute escape or a more passive picture.

Take it a little further. Within the framework of Eastern Orthodoxy, if you are going to talk in terms of 'recapitulation', then Christ's salvation did have to 'work' backwards in time as well as forwards. If you believe that God 'desires everyone to be saved and to come to the knowledge of the truth',[14] why should that only be the case for those who lived after Christ? Is anything or anyone beyond the mercy of God? It is worth pondering on.

Wrapping it up

You may have found the flood of analogies overwhelming in these *theosis* chapters, but that is the difficulty when talking about the sorts of ideas we have been covering. We embodied beings tend to come closest to indescribable and incomprehensible mysteries when we use the concrete and symbolic as an aid. We simply have to remember to alter our depth of focus to look *through* the tools we use rather than *at* them.

Similarly, I may have raised some eyebrows in this and previous sections when I have built theological arguments out of the Garden of Eden as if it 'really happened' the way the author(s) of Genesis tell it. But surely what the story is for is to communicate theological truths, not historical ones. Those who depict icons know that the faces they create for Jesus and Mary or any of the biblical characters are not photographic depictions of the original: rather, as with symbols, they provide us with something to look *through* more than at. Just as the glory of God is burning behind the veil of the material world, so is it burning behind the veil of stories such as Eden, and so might it be glimpsed through the veil of the icon.

Most pertinently, that glory is also burning behind the veil of the outward lives of others who, like us, are called by God on the transformational journey of *theosis*.

If we approach our neighbours with this knowledge, if we look for the mystery nestled within them behind the material surface, we may find we can glimpse something of the divine Light and Life of Christ slowly metamorphizing them into the likeness of God. For this was God's plan for us all from the beginning. This is the ongoing story of bringing us back to one-ness with God: a oneness in which we bear the bright image of God, our being unobscured by corruption, our well-being unclouded by disobedience, our eternal being untainted and unrestricted by death. Or, to see it another way, our being transformed by the incarnation of God, our well-being transformed by the Life and energies of God, our eternal being transformed by the death and resurrection of God.

By this stage, you may have automatically begun to ponder some specific 'good news' we can draw from this story. I would love to hear your thoughts, which would be as varied and wide and glorious as our differences are. For now, though, I will explore a few ideas that have struck me most strongly as I read and wrote about this strange idea of *theosis*. As always, some of the following chapters will be more relevant to you than others. Some you may disagree with. That is fine. They are simply explorations, launching pads into the vast mysteries and unplumbed heights (can one plumb a height?) of all God has done, and is doing, for us.

Notes

1 If you are not a Harry Potter reader, all you need to know is that Harry, Ron and Hermione are the heroes of the series, and are young wizards/witches. Dumbledore was the beloved and wise head of the school they attended: Hogwarts School of Witchcraft and Wizardry. He is killed in the sixth book. Voldemort is the central evil character, who interpreted a prophecy to mean that he could only be destroyed by Harry, so naturally wants to destroy Harry first.

2 This is contrasted with Dumbledore's similar temptation, fall and ultimate resistance. J. K. Rowling, 2007, *Harry Potter and the Deathly Hallows*, London: Bloomsbury, p. 571.

3 J. K. Rowling, 2005, *Harry Potter and the Half-Blood Prince*, London: Bloomsbury, p. 465.

4 Rowling, *Deathly Hallows*, p. 566.

5 See, too, J. K. Rowling, 2000, *Harry Potter and the Goblet of Fire*, London: Bloomsbury, pp. 556, 70.

6 You can also admire how many different atonement stories Rowling uses.

7 I am holding myself back from indulging in too many explorations of the parallels Rowling creates in order not to overload you as the reader, but one little thing here. Remember how being hanged on a tree was a curse? Remember the talk about 'curses' when we discussed covenant? Satan really did fling a killing curse at Jesus.

8 John Donne, 'Death be not proud', available from *Poetry Foundation*, https://www.poetryfoundation.org/poems/44107/holy-sonnets-death-be-not-proud (accessed 21.10.2022).

9 The Orthodox are happy to use many of the stories I am writing about to understand the efficacy of Jesus' death and resurrection, but it does seem that victorious atonement is a favourite.

10 Notes taken from a series of lectures by Peter Bouteneff, 'The Orthodox Christian Church: History, Beliefs and Practices'. Written and narrated by Peter Bouteneff, Learn25Audio, released 13 August 2008, 9 hrs 39 mins.

11 1 Corinthians 15.

12 Think (again, for Harry Potter readers) of the hideous 'thing' under the bench in that between-worlds misty scene in Rowling's, *Deathly Hallows*, pp. 565–6.

13 Find this and further explorations on David, 'The Resurrection Icon and the World Without Charles Darwin', *Icons and their Interpretation*, https://russian icons.wordpress.com/tag/harrowing-of-hell/ (accessed 31.10.2023).

14 1 Timothy 2.4.

23

Good News of *Theosis* (1): A Society of Possible Gods and Goddesses

> It is a serious thing to live in a society of possible gods and goddesses, to remember that the dullest most uninteresting person you can talk to may one day be a creature which, if you saw it now, you would be strongly tempted to worship, or else a horror and a corruption such as you now meet, if at all, only in a nightmare. All day long we are, in some degree, helping each other to one or the other of these destinations ... There are no ordinary people. You have never talked to a mere mortal. Nations, cultures, arts, civilizations – these are mortal, and their life is to ours as the life of a gnat. But it is immortals whom we joke with, work with, marry, snub, and exploit – immortal horrors or everlasting splendours. (C. S. Lewis)[1]

The foundational, mind-blowing good news of *theosis* is that each human being is of more mystery and worth and potential than we could ever imagine. We each bear the image of God. We are all made to grow in that image in the way unique to each of us. None of us is a 'mere mortal'. God's love for each unique individual is so great that Christian teachers throughout the centuries have claimed that if there had been only one of us to save, Jesus still would have died for that person (think of Aslan and Edmund in *The Lion, the Witch and the Wardrobe*). We proclaim this conviction contrary to every sneaking belief that we have to justify our right to be loved or even exist; that our worth can be judged by the number of 'likes' we get on social media; that 'collateral damage' is unimportant. There are few pieces of good news more important for us to hear today.

And in case we are tempted to think that this is a sweet, sentimental idea suitable for bumper stickers, we need to remember it cost God his life. We need to remember that this conviction is the ground and purpose of our being. We were made to participate in God, for our nature to become ever closer to the divine nature, for that spark of God's image in us and others to be nurtured and strengthened and grown until we too become eternal beings.[2]

I would love to continue in this positive vein since this is, after all, meant to be a 'good news' chapter. But this foundational belief, which has quietly shaped much of the world for almost 2,000 years, is no longer providing the solid base it once did. If any of you have experienced wood-worm or termites (white ants) while renovating a house, you will know that they work away steadily in the middle of a plank or post. One day you lean unsuspectingly on what looks like a perfectly normal part of your house and find it caving in and disintegrating: nothing but empty air behind the surface. So it is with this essential teaching of the Church.

Tragically and bizarrely, the Church itself has often been as active a woodworm or termite as anyone else, happily joining the colony in hollowing out the very support it is sitting on. So, unfortunately, I need to start this good news chapter with some signposts of bad news.

Becoming gods ...

As we discussed *theosis*, some of you may have wondered how this idea of us becoming 'like God' could be a good thing, when it was precisely the offer to become 'like God' that was the temptation the snake held out to Adam and Eve. In that scenario, it was not a good thing. How can we now say it is?

The key difference is the path we take: we can try to be gods without God, or we can try to be like God through God. The fatal danger of the first path is that if you take God out of the equation in your quest to be a god, there is nothing between you and the illusion of absolute power. There is nothing to curb the darkness within you, and as your power grows the darkness grows.

Legend tells us that this was the path Satan took: seeking to be god apart from God. But we do not need to look into ancient tales for veri-fication of this danger. Human beings simply do not seem able to hold unlimited power without the hunger for more of it becoming insatiable. It is likely (well, at least possible) that Hitler and Stalin and Putin and numerous dictators across space and time started off with a genuine set of ideals and a genuine desire to better their country. But as they grew more 'god-like' in their power, their ruthlessness and carelessness with the lives of others also grew.

We are learning that anyone from doctors and lawyers to church leaders, if accorded god-like status by their patients, clients or congregations, can head down a path of darkness, not light. C. S. Lewis warns us in the quote that opened this chapter that there are two types of eternal being we can become. Those who, knowingly or not, are stumbling along the path of love and humility and faith, following what they understand of Light, have God at the end of their path, and are slowly becoming angelic. Those whose chief goal is themselves ... are not.

The image of God, revealed to us in Christ, is of a suffering, serving, life-giving, other-focused love. Unless that is the God-likeness we are praying to develop, it is the snake, not God, we are listening to, and it will be the snake, not God, into whose likeness we grow.[3]

The Great Myth[4]

The danger is not only for those in power. The danger is for all of us who have been swept up by the entrancing Great Myth of human progress: the myth that tells a story in which progress is inevitable, in which humanity is evolving towards bigger and better versions of itself.[5] It is a story in which we are becoming more god-like, but God is nowhere in the picture. God's place is taken by humanity working in co-operation with the blind and inexorable natural forces of the cosmos.

We cannot, in fairness, blame Charles Darwin for this. His research fell on ears that were already convinced of this Myth, and which seized his scientific discoveries with glee as a way of validating it. And so, by the beginning of the last century, the scientific discoveries of Darwin had been translated into 'social Darwinism': the conviction that humanity was progressing as inevitably as evolution did, with some races and groups of people further along the journey than others.

Can you see the immediate danger of that last point? Now that 'a more progressive humanity' was the image we were being changed into rather than God, it was inevitable that those in positions of power saw themselves as being further along the journey than others and, logically, *took themselves as models for that image*. Since those most enamoured of these theories were white, Western, heterosexual and intellectual men, then of course the 'higher', 'more developed', 'superior' race of beings that we were apparently destined to transform into were white and Western, heterosexual and unrestricted by anomalies such as intellectual or physical differences. Those who did not fit this model were lesser mortals who, by existing at all, were holding back humanity as a whole from its necessary progress, thwarting our very reason for being. For the greater good, they should be removed.[6]

By the beginning of the last century, many in society, including (to our shame) a number of mainstream church groups and denominations, had become so caught up in the mission to work alongside and assist this inevitable evolution of humanity towards a higher, more developed, superior race that this conclusion made sense to them. This brings us back to a topic already referred to when we were thinking of victorious atonement: eugenics.

As we saw earlier, the Englishman Francis Galton, a cousin of Charles Darwin, led the way by inventing the word 'eugenics'.

> Galton's gospel of eugenics found fertile soil in Britain, in the intellectual salons of Europe, and in the United States. Beginning in the early years of the twentieth century, eugenics scientists called for programs to manipulate human reproduction. They advocated for laws to segregate the so-called feebleminded into state colonies, to live out their lives in celibacy. They led the drive to restrict immigration from countries whose citizens might pollute the national gene pools. And they supported sterilization laws aimed at men and women whose 'germplasm' threatened the eugenic vitality of the nation.[7]

Within a decade, eugenics societies were established across the UK and the USA, and eugenics became a topic at their universities. By 1907, Indiana had passed a law for forced sterilization of those deemed 'defective'. In 1912, three Anglican bishops 'were among the vice presidents of the First International Eugenics Congress':[8]

> That same year, the influential Protestant minister, F. B. Meyer ... warned that the high birthrates of Catholics, Jews, and the feebleminded presented a collective menace to society.[9]

I grew up with the assumption that the horrors of Nazi Germany grew from some warped German ideology.[10] In fact, they grew from ideology born, nurtured and flourishing in the English-speaking world which would shortly be at war with Germany.

Germany held a mirror up to the rest of the world and made us see what the outworking of our Great Myth of human progress would look like. For a while we were shocked, and backed away. But we are very like the person whom James describes in his epistle: 'They look at themselves and, on going away, immediately forget what they were like.'[11] We need to face the fact that we have forgotten what happens when we begin to allow in the idea that it would be better for the greater good of society if some should die.

Here we enter deeply difficult territory. Please know that I am not passing judgement on any individual who, within the particular circumstances and pressures and hurts of their lives, support any of the issues I am about to question. In our broken world we are always dealing with both the general and the particular. Something can be in general, *in principle*, deeply wrong and yet in one particular case be the lesser of two (or multiple) wrongs. It is only easy to hold a principle in theory; as soon as we try to apply it in practice we come up against the messiness of reality. Take something as simple as the principles of safe driving. There will be emergencies when ambulances have to ignore red lights or the speed limit. There will be unexpected potholes that force us to cross the middle line. A one-handed person cannot keep both hands on the steering wheel. But while allowing for these situations, we still cannot let the particular exceptions destroy the importance of the principle itself.

We may argue convincingly for the death penalty, for late-term abortion or for euthanasia, and they are all deeply complex issues which in individual instances may be clearly more grace-filled than the alternative. But that does not make them compatible with the incalculable worth of every human life. Nor does that protect us from the real dangers they create.

I have one specific danger in mind. I have experienced being told that my unborn child was almost certainly going to have Down Syndrome. I have experienced facing a specialist who assumed I would terminate the pregnancy; who told my husband and me that having a child with Down Syndrome in the house was like having a dog who would outlive us; whose attempts to manipulate us emotionally culminated in his saying we were being unfair on our other son by bringing a Down Syndrome child into the family. I was a rare, lucky one. I had a completely supportive husband who was aware of the potential difficulties ahead, yet had already made it clear that he would stick by me and bring up this child with me. I do not know if I could have resisted the pressure that society and that doctor put on me otherwise, and I have nothing but compassion for those parents whose situations mean they have to decide differently from us. The vitally important point here is that I was left in no doubt that, to this doctor's mind, *people with Down Syndrome were a drain on society and unquestionably less worthy of life than he and those like him were.*

The eugenics movement started with the 'feebleminded' but moved rapidly to Jews, Catholics and homosexuals. Do you think it is impossible that we today could extend our eugenics practices in a similar fashion to some other group within society? If so – if you believe that we are somehow more virtuous or advanced than people of a century ago – you have just bowed to the Great Myth of human progress.[12]

On what grounds are children with Down Syndrome deemed less worthy of life than children without it? Is it purely the very real difficulties involved in raising a child with Down Syndrome in a society that secretly wishes they weren't there and makes little accommodation for them? Or do we only feel able to countenance the rising levels of such terminations of life because we believe, deep down, that they are not *quite* as worthy of living as 'normal' children? That they do not repay the 'cost' they are to society? That our own lives are more important than theirs?

The reason it is so hard to see the Great Myth of human progress at work is because it is the ocean we are swimming in, the polluted air we have breathed since birth. Its contamination is everywhere.

Here is the nub of it all, and even if you disagree with the past few paragraphs, please read this: if we accept we have the right to decide that some (whether foetus or criminal) will be too much of a burden on society to live, then the corollary is that *our* worth, *our* right to hold a place in this life, depends on us *not* being a burden. This belief has seeped into our consciousness more than we perhaps realize. If my farm has collapsed around me and I cannot support my family, shame and despair join with a sense of no longer *deserving* to live, and suicide is a reasonable choice. If I am disabled from birth or through old age, illness or depression, or am facing long and expensive palliative care, and therefore cannot 'contribute to society' in the ways society deems valuable, then there are unseen, but real, inner and outer pressures to choose euthanasia.

This is where we desperately need to proclaim the good news. The Great Myth of human progress is not the defining myth of human life. The image we are made to be transformed into is not the snake of our own self-interest or the survival of the fittest. It is the image of the Jesus to whom every fringe-dweller or outcast was precious. Our worth does not depend on our 'contribution to society' (as if that were measurable), but on the spark of God within us. Our foundation is not inexorable, blind science, but a God who has made every human being in God's image: each one a unique facet of the Infinite One, each one with the potential to grow that image until it is more and more God-like. The more variety there is within humankind, the richer our vision of God can be. The loss of any one is the loss of someone precious enough to God for him to die for them.

Our goal is not the 'advancement of society' (whatever that might be) but the bringing of each unique person, family or people into the transforming light and love of God, into the pattern of *shalom*, the dance in which all creation moves in harmony. And every piece of that pattern is vital. As C. S. Lewis warns us, every person is a potential god or goddess, to be treated with awe. We should know, from history, what happens when that good news is silenced. What we need to explore with ever-increasing determination is what happens when it is proclaimed.

Notes

1 C. S. Lewis, 'The Weight of Glory' in Walter Hooper (ed.), 2013, *The Weight of Glory. A Collection of Lewis' Most Moving Addresses*, London: William Collins, p. 45. (Sermon first published 1941.)

2 This was what, for many ancient people, the term 'gods' meant: an eternal being.

3 Yet another piece of brilliance on J. K. Rowling's part was to have Voldemort become steadily more snake-like in appearance as he used his power to kill others.

4 C. S. Lewis, 2009, 'The Funeral of a Great Myth' in Lesley Walmsley (ed.), *C. S. Lewis Essay Collection. Faith, Christianity, and the Church*, New York: HarperCollins, pp. 41–57.

5 Lewis, 'The Funeral of a Great Myth'.

6 In this context, it's worth thinking about what beliefs underlie the cry to 'Make America Great Again'.

7 Joseph Loconte, 2015, *A Hobbit, a Wardrobe, and the Great War*, Nashville, TN: HarperCollins, p. 16.

8 Loconte, *A Hobbit*, p. 17.

9 Loconte, *A Hobbit*, p. 17.

10 Notice how my reaction was another variation on the Great Myth. I presumed 'my' sort of people wouldn't ever have supported something as dreadful as eugenics, with the corollary that 'their' sort of people (the Germans) were somehow not as developed as us, and therefore less insightful or innately virtuous. Naturally I would never have consciously thought this, but I didn't need to be conscious of my thought in order to assume it.

11 James 1.23.

12 Those whose hatred of any group in society who thinks differently from them leads them to post death threats and encouragement to suicide on social media are already extending a eugenics mindset to new realms.

24

Good News of *Theosis* (2): Truth and Transformed Vision

I am not sure how this came to my notice, but months ago I found a picture of a man standing next to a cutting in the ground in a prairie in the USA. It was a deep cutting, and from where he stood the top of the soil was higher than the top of his head. The cutting exposed the roots of the prairie grass that still grew on the surface: roots that were as long and deep as this man was tall. The other half of the photo showed the exposed roots of 'cultivated' grass. They ran, at the most, a foot deep. The point of the picture was to show how cultivating prairie land, with its fierce wind and baking sun, could turn it into desert. Only the grass with deep, deep roots could survive.

I have used that picture in numerous talks since then, because for decades now we have been digging up and poisoning off anything that based its truth on deep roots, and replacing it with shallow-rooted, cultivated relativism. Indeed, in the last handful of years, truth has become such an endangered species that we are beginning to raise our young people not even as cultivated grass, but as tumbleweeds that blow with the strongest wind, detached from any root system at all.

We have already spent one 'good news' chapter thinking about truth, but I believe it is such an important issue today that it is worth having a look at it from another angle. In that earlier chapter we thought about the deep importance of there being such a thing as truth at all. Here I want to look at how some of the ideas we have explored in our *theosis* journey might give us an alternative way of *seeing* truth to those we have been offered by either modernism or postmodernism, and that this alternative vision could be a gateway to good news.

The nature of this discussion means that we do have to start by thinking philosophically rather than theologically, but take heart – we will get to the theology (and even poetry if that is your thing) eventually. Alternatively, as I said in the previous truth chapter, there is no harm in skipping this chapter and moving on.

Seeing through the lens of modernism

One of the key characteristics of the period of time we call 'modernism' was that we learned to view the world as an object to be examined, dissected, used and, above all, controlled. We were so successful at this that our collective confidence swelled, and we quickly began to feel we had not only the ability, but also the right, to control everything that affected our lives. When we encountered anything we could not yet control, we either felt affronted by it, comforted ourselves with the assumption that one day science and reason would work it out, or decided it did not exist.

It was only to be expected that Christianity, which is a messy, uncontrollable sort of thing, became a bit of an embarrassment. Therapy, which brings our well-being so conveniently under our own control, was a much more appealing alternative.

Modernism brought us countless blessings for which I am deeply grateful. Scientific and medical discoveries have transformed our lives. I have no desire to return to a premodern world where the smallest infection could kill me. I thoroughly enjoy our modern means of transport and communication, and if I had had to write this book by hand it would never have got this far. But there are two major burdens modernism lays on us.

The first is that anything we control we also have automatic responsibility for. When there was nothing to be done about something, it was no one's fault (except perhaps God's), but if we believe it should always be possible to 'fix' things, then it has to be someone's fault when something goes wrong. Hence a rise in our sense of 'free-floating guilt', a rise in self-righteous indignation and a rise in lawyers' bank balances.

The other burden was expressed succinctly by a French philosopher, Paul Ricoeur, who describes how we have turned 'mysteries we used to ponder' into 'problems to be solved'.[1] Unfortunately, he points out, if there is nothing beyond our reach or understanding – no mystery, no genuine 'depth' to anything – there is, equally, little or no meaning. Think about the sort of art and literature that was lauded in the mid to late twentieth century. Much of it was almost obsessed with the pall of meaninglessness that seemed to have fallen over the Western world. We learned that when you destroy a sense of mystery, you take down meaning with it.

Seeing through the lens of postmodernism

Modernism, then, is solidly connected to the material, observable, measurable, controllable world. The world is the object we dissect to find truth that we can then manipulate to our own ends. In a postmodern world, things are very different. Now the truth is in the *subject*, in the seer rather than in the thing seen.

Think of it this way. In a world of modernism, cameras were invented and images of objects were produced. It was clear that over here was a chair, and over there was a picture of the chair. The chair was the reality, the truth, and the photo attempted to reproduce that reality. That is normal and clear to most of us. However, think about how a postmodernist takes a photo. They can snap it and plug it into a photo-editing app where the rather colourless sky can now be a rich blue (or red or polka-dotted if they like); where a person from a completely different place can be inserted into the scene to sit on the chair, while another person or unwanted object can be removed. Here's the thing: now the image has become the object. The material reality it captured is no longer as important as the way the image depicts it.[2]

For the observer looking at the photo, there is no way of knowing what the original, material reality had been. It does not even matter any more. The focus, and the locus of 'truth' in a postmodern world, is found in our created realities, whether that be a digital photo or the story of our own lives.

Here are two examples of what I mean:

1 A growing section of the population is creating avatars of themselves who will participate in virtual reality experiences. The person themselves is replaced by something created by that person, and that invented being enters into interactions and even relationships with other created avatars. The person themselves effectively sinks into the background.
2 I listened to an interview on Radio National in New Zealand with a man who argued passionately that we should be allowed to choose our official age; that if we felt 20 or 40 or 80 then we should be allowed to *be* that age of choice regardless of the number of years we had been alive. The material reality of our bodies, and even the shared experiential reality of time, are – in his view – unimportant. The truth is to be found in how we, as autonomous individuals, feel.

Although clearly appealing to many, this is a terribly unsettling sort of world to be growing up in. Where do you sink down roots if no ground is stable, if even foundational realities of time and matter become relative? If the only thing to stand on is your own two feet, you are either floating or plummeting down.

An old heresy revisited

Postmodernism, like modernism, has given us many things for which we are (or should be) grateful. One of the necessary correctives postmodernism brought was to shake our complacent certainty that human reason and science could eventually encompass all knowledge. With postmodernism has come a renewed recognition of the place of story in knowledge, for example, and the power of poetry and imagination to perceive and express *experienced* reality. To some extent, mystery has made a comeback. But it has done so while loosening its hold on *material* reality.

I said earlier that there are few, if any, new heresies. Some aspects of postmodernism are encouraging our world to happily embrace one of the oldest and most popular of them: Gnosticism, a religious and philosophical movement that flourished in the first and second centuries AD. It took many forms, but Gnostics shared a suspicion of the material world and advocated a detachment from it. Salvation for most Gnostics involved special knowledge that enabled them to shake off the nasty tendrils of flesh and rise as pure soul. A proper earthly life could either consist of extreme asceticism or, paradoxically, extreme hedonism. The first worked on the principle that we were meant to rid ourselves of earthly desires; the second was based on the principle that material things were worthless and we would be leaving our bodies behind in the end, so why not have fun in the meantime?

Our current Gnosticism is developing a similar disregard for the material world, for 'concrete facts', for allowing physical reality to thwart how we want or perceive things to be. If you want others to believe 'your truth', you no longer need to produce measurable reality or shared human experience to back it up. Instead, you simply repeat it often and loudly and, if needed, aggressively. Hence the prevalence of 'gaslighting'. Hence Vladimir Putin's repeated assertions that Russians do not bomb civilians, which he is able to continue to assert even as photos and testimonies flood in to say the opposite. What are photos? They can be photoshopped. What are testimonies? They are one person's truth, just as Putin's assertions are 'his truth'. And his are louder.

It is all a little depressing, isn't it? Either we go with modernist materialism, which hollows out meaning, or with postmodern Gnosticism which detaches itself from the shared material and experiential world and leaves us afloat.

But ... just maybe there is another way of looking at the world. Just maybe there is something in the story of *theosis* that *is* good news even here.

Seeing a sacramental universe

The following thoughts are a wondering, an exploring, rather than a solution to the situation we find ourselves in. They are based on the idea that perhaps the vision that underlies the story of *theosis* can give us a different way of viewing the world, and therefore truth.

The sacramental vision of *theosis* gives us a material, 'ordinary' world which is fired through with mystery and meaning. If we start, as everything in the *theosis* story does, with Jesus, we find someone who was completely human, solidly material, with normal human flesh that bled and itched and ached like our own. He lived on earth in a particular time and place, was born of Mary, suffered under Pontius Pilate, and so on through all the claims we make in the creeds. But he was God. There was so much more – infinitely more – in him than we could see. 'In him all the fullness of God was pleased to dwell', and yet he was a foetus, a baby, a child, a man.[3] It is one of the deepest wonders of our faith. The beautiful Christmas hymn holds this paradox together in these two couplets:

> Our God, heaven cannot hold Him, nor earth sustain,
> Heaven and earth shall flee away when he comes to reign.

> In the bleak mid-winter a stable-place sufficed
> The Lord God Almighty – Jesus Christ.[4]

It is on the Being of Jesus that we base a sacramental view of the world. The material world is not something ephemeral or valueless, something to be put to one side so that we can build our reality around our inner desires or thoughts. It is the good creation of God. More than that: it is the means through which God was revealed to us and continues to be revealed to us. God took on flesh; Jesus used material things like bread and water, and even saliva, to communicate grace; and our resurrected body will be, if anything, *more* real, more 'solid' than our present body. The material world is an icon of God: a bearer of God's glory hidden just behind the veil. God's energies infuse creation, and even you and I have the spark of God's image in us. We, too, are a mystery.

A sacramental view of the world is based firmly in the reality – the truth, if you like – of the material. To that extent, it is in accord with modernism. But while it has the solid foundation of modernism, it does not have the same limitations. It agrees with postmodernism that logic and science do not tell us the whole truth. The water at the wedding at Cana was genuine H_2O which was turned into genuine wine, and it was precisely in their material reality that the genuine mystery lay.

Think again of an icon, a painting that is made to be looked through, not at, but which provides something *for* us to look through, and which guides that looking. Icons are often described as 'windows'. When we view the world sacramentally, we look into and through the material, not just at it. We know that there is mystery throbbing at the core of the material because God has chosen to create it, to instil it with life or purpose; we know that it is part of the great dance of creation.

This type of vision 'shows us people – and everyday things such as water, bread and wine – as being "more than this" ... [W]e learn to see the mystery.'[5] The roots that give us our foundation of truth reach through, into and beyond this material world to the limitless energies of God. Those are roots worthy of prairie grass.

Good news?

Why might this way of understanding truth be good news? To begin with, it gives us a particular way of understanding ourselves and one another. You and I are who we are, with all our gloriously awkward foibles and physical weaknesses and complexities; we are clothed in the flesh that is a creation and gift of God and to be respected and accepted and cared for as such. But we are also a mystery, a child of God on a journey deeper into God's reality, holding within us more than we or another could ever completely understand.

When a working group from the Archbishop of Canterbury's office were tasked with creating a study series on becoming reconciling communities, one key theme they came up with was 'curiosity'.[6] They suggested that curiosity was underestimated as a tool for peace and love. As long as we are curious about one another, aware of the mysteries we are yet to understand, there is hope that we will approach the other with respect, humility and eagerness.

Second, this vision gives us a foundation to sink roots into. We do not need to leave physical reality behind in order to find the mystery and meaning and *worth* that so many today are trying to create from the thin air of their own expectations and those of others. Such ungrounded creations are so very unstable that maintaining them requires either great stress or great aggression. We have an alternative. There is more than enough mystery and meaning and wonder and worth to be found nestled within each of us as we are if we learn to look at ourselves and others sacramentally.

Third, this vision welcomes science and all the ways it deepens our understanding of this astounding cosmos. Why wouldn't we welcome everything that clarifies our vision of the vessel God has created to receive God's energies? A friend who heads up the New Zealand branch of Christians in Science wondered with me recently whether the centuries-old supposed conflict between Christianity and science was essentially over. Today we are both on the same side of a divide, allies in a cause. We both celebrate the physical world and we both believe there is such a thing as Truth in an increasingly relativistic world.

And, finally, this vision welcomes poets and musicians and artists as those whose eyes have glimpsed something of the mystery behind the mundane, and whose skills have found a way to channel a hint of its fragrance to others. So, for those of you who love poetry and those of you who are happy to try to understand why others do, let's see a little of what one poem can show us.

The poetic vision: a world charged with God's grandeur

Both poetry and religious faith grow from the one vision of the world as a place with more to be glimpsed than is on the surface; more to be divined than the obvious. Both poetry and faith know that imagination can perceive colours where reason sees shades of grey.

One poet who exulted in this connection between poetry and faith with every word he wrote was Gerard Manley Hopkins. Many of his poems deal directly with our *theosis* belief that the sacramental view of the world is a real one; that there is 'something more' to be glimpsed through our material world. His own vision gives us hope that as we journey deeper into *theosis* the way we perceive the world will change: that we may begin to see as God sees.

Here is the opening octet of Hopkins's poem, 'God's Grandeur':[7]

The world is charged with the grandeur of God.
　It will flame out, like shining from shook foil;
　It gathers to a greatness, like the ooze of oil

Crushed. Why do men then now not reck his rod?
Generations have trod, have trod, have trod;
  And all is seared with trade; bleared, smeared with toil;
  And wears man's smudge and shares man's smell: the soil
Is bare now, nor can foot feel, being shod.

Like all Hopkins's poetry, it is dense and complex and, if you are not
already familiar with the poem, it can be frankly bewildering to read.
I hesitate to 'explain' it because poetry is so much more than any prose
explanation, but perhaps you could go back and read it again from the
beginning up to the word 'crushed', letting the words spark images in your
mind of the world filled to overflowing with the energies, the presence,
the grandeur of God which can flash or 'ooze' out before our eyes.

Then there is an abrupt change. 'Why do men then now not reck his
rod?' If this mystery is so embedded in every atom of our world, why do
we not see it, sense it, believe it? Think back to our discussion on being,
and the idea that we had obscured God's image in us by pasting our own
image over the top. Hopkins mourns how we have done the same to the
image of God in our world, smothering and polluting it with our own
obsessions, 'smell' and 'smudge', cutting ourselves off from contact with
that world and all it can tell us of God.

But then comes the last six lines of the poem:

And for all this, nature is never spent;
  There lives the dearest freshness deep down things;
And though the last lights off the black West went
  Oh, morning, at the brown brink eastward, springs –
Because the Holy Ghost over the bent
  World broods with warm breast and with ah! bright wings.

Despite our best efforts to suffocate and obscure it, 'there lives the dearest
freshness deep down things', nurtured, protected and given life by the
mothering Holy Spirit. Unquenchable, ever-new, ever-alive, if we have
eyes and hearts to see it. Good news indeed.

Poets like Hopkins are a gift to us, because through their eyes we too
can see God's grandeur in a flash of light from tinfoil – or in a dragonfly's
flight, or a falcon's swoop, or even a stone tumbling down a well.[8] We
can sense the 'dearest freshness' of life, deep down. Through their eyes
we are given a sense of what it might be to be further along the *theosis*
journey than we are; to be closer to seeing as God sees.[9]

Imagine if we could all see our world and one another embued with the energies of God. Imagine the respect, the wonder, that would call from us. Our modernist selves thought mystery and meaning were dead, but that was because we 'murdered to dissect'.[10] Our postmodernist selves sought mystery and meaning detached from awkward physical reality and found a dark and formless vacuum. Even the sun needs molecules to reflect off if we are to see its light. A sacramental vision honours the molecules that light refracts from, and opens its sleepy eyes to the glory of the multicoloured light itself.

It is not easy to do. We are surrounded by media and well-meaning idealists who are trying to shake our trust in any truth but our own subjectivity. But the *theosis* story offers hope that our vision can be 'transformed' and 'renewed' as we journey towards God-likeness, sinking our roots deep through the material to the energies of God.[11] Then we will begin to see the truth of what things are, in their material and God-filled realities.

Notes

1 Paul Ricoeur, 1978, 'The Language of Faith' in Charles E. Regan and David Stewart (eds), *The Philosophy of Paul Ricoeur*, Boston, MA: Beacon Press, p. 225.

2 I have here enlarged on an idea I found in Anna Marie Aagard, 2010, '"My Eyes Have Seen Your Salvation." On Likeness to God and Deification in Patristic Theology', *Religion and Theology*, 17, pp. 302–28.

3 Colossians 1.19.

4 Christina Rossetti, 'In the Bleak Midwinter', *Poetry Foundation*, https://www.poetryfoundation.org/poems/53216/in-the-bleak-midwinter (accessed 31.10.2022).

5 Aagaard, 'My Eyes Have Seen', p. 306.

6 To find out more about this course, see their website: https://difference.rln.global/ (accessed 31.10.2023).

7 Gerard Manley Hopkins, 1953, 'God's Grandeur' in W. H. Gardner (ed.), *Gerard Manley Hopkins: Poems and Prose*, Harmondsworth: Penguin, p. 27.

8 See his poems 'The Windhover' and 'As Kingfishers Catch Fire'.

9 There is something unusual about what Hopkins is doing here which is worth noting. When poets write about non-human entities (like autumn, or a river) as if they are humans, they don't expect anyone to believe them, to 'take them literally'. But when Hopkins 'catches' the inner reality of something and expresses it in poetry, he does so because he believes the vision is true. He believes there *is* this spiritual centre, something that is both a unique identity and a revelation of God, in each thing, and that sometimes we are able to see, absorb and understand it. He even invented a word for the thing itself ('inscape') and a word for the experience of having it hit you, of grasping or catching the insight ('instress').

10 From the poem by William Wordsworth, 1950, 'The Tables Turned' in Mark van Doren (ed.), *William Wordsworth Selected Poetry*, New York: Random House.

11 Romans 12.2.

25

The Goodness of the Good News

'Aslan,' said Lucy through her tears, 'Could you – will you – do something for these poor Dwarfs?'

'Dearest,' said Aslan, 'I will show you both what I can, and what I cannot do.' He came close to the Dwarfs and gave a low growl ... But the Dwarfs said to one another, 'Hear that? That's the gang at the other end of the Stable. Trying to frighten us ... Don't take any notice. They won't take us in again!'

Aslan raised his head and shook his mane. Instantly a glorious feast appeared on the Dwarfs' knees ... but it wasn't much use ... They thought they were eating and drinking only the sort of things you might find in a Stable ...

'You see,' said Aslan. 'They will not let us help them. They have chosen cunning instead of belief. Their prison is only in their own minds, yet they are in that prison; and so afraid of being taken in that they cannot be taken out.'[1]

This is the final 'good news' chapter in this book, and it is a chance to consider something we need to be aware of: something we will encounter every time we begin to seriously consider good news. It is the insidious power of cynicism.

When I was working for Anglican Schools and doing reviews of their 'Special Character', I would attend a selection of Religious Education (RE) lessons. In one highly elite school, the chaplain was the only trained RE teacher employed, so in order to fill the timetable they asked other teachers to step forward. The teacher we observed had a class of bored 15-year-old boys. She began by showing them the next episode in a television series on Christianity written and narrated by an atheist, which seemed a rather strange choice. She followed this up with a talk on the virgin birth. Now, perhaps she was nervous in front of us, and wanted to show these reviewers that she was not a naïve fundamentalist, but she posed the question to the boys, 'Why do you think Christians believe in the virgin birth?' Not surprisingly, she got no response, so she continued, 'Because it is likely that Mary was raped by a Roman soldier and they didn't want to admit that.'

This was appalling on so many levels. On the straightforward level of education, these were boys who, in all likelihood, neither knew nor cared who Jesus' mother was, so they were hardly going to be interested in (or equipped for) debating one of the more complex theological issues connected to her. On a deeper level, her explanation was not, nor ever was, the 'why' of the doctrine of the virgin birth.[2] Christians who believe this doctrine do so primarily for theological reasons, not historical ones.

The deepest pain I felt, though, was not for either of those reasons, frustrating though they were. It was because both the video and the lecture were encouraging these young people to be cynical long before they had any knowledge of the thing they were being cynical about. Perhaps the teacher did not want to be seen as gullible, or to be 'pushing her faith'. Most likely, she thought that by showing her cynicism she would be 'getting alongside' the boys in her class. Sadly, though, all this approach achieves is to efficiently cauterize any tender shoots of faith in students.

The most effective dampener on good news is not philosophical or scientific objections and arguments, but cynicism. Cynicism is one of the most powerfully destructive tools humanity has come up with. It has all the power of a siren song, luring us in deeper and deeper until it devours all the life in us, yet it is almost irresistible in its appeal. Like its cousin, self-righteous indignation, it gives us the delicious pleasure of feeling superior to other, less insightful, people. Like the Dwarfs in C. S. Lewis's *Last Battle*, we pride ourselves on not being taken in by anyone; on having the insight to see through the wishful thinking or childish faith of our neighbours. And, like the Dwarfs, we run the risk of blinding ourselves to the beauty and riches and wonder we are being offered; of cauterizing our own minds and senses and spirits.

It is not that we necessarily set out to become cynical. Sometimes it grows over us like a protective carapace. We have been disappointed by circumstances and people – and even God – and that hurts. We learn that if we do not build up our hopes, we will not be disappointed too much. If we do not expect too much of life and it turns out better than expected, we may even be forced to be pleasantly surprised. Isn't that a more sensible approach than to risk the vulnerability of allowing ourselves to dream things of beauty and wonder and then be disappointed?

In the face of cynicism, a story like *theosis* is laughable. We fail so spectacularly and regularly – how can we possibly contemplate a life of being transformed into God's image? Where is the evidence that human nature has been even slightly redeemed? Can we seriously believe that our *eternal* being has been saved? Many of us have been so shaped and injured by cynicism that we no longer dare to believe these things. If the hope that they might, after all, be true peeks a tentative head over the edge of our cynicism, we hit it down as rapidly and effectively as if we were playing Whac-A-Mole. It is pie in the sky, and if we find in ourselves a craving for pie, we dare not believe we are being nudged by God in the right direction. Rather, our very desire for it becomes one more sign that it is the creation of wishful thinking. We have to be realistic. We bravely face the mundaneness of what is left of our religion once miracles, the incarnation or bodily resurrection are removed or 'spiritualized', and reassure ourselves that we are intelligent, perceptive, modern human beings. We are not going to be taken in. And we join the Dwarfs in the dark stable.

Can I suggest that if we believe in God at all, it is worth taking the risk of believing the foundational, credal promises of our faith, even if they seem too good to be true? Not just the story of *theosis*, but every story we have considered is bursting with hope and promise and beauty beyond anything our meagre imaginations have been able to conceive. *Our good news is good*. It really is. It is not a watered-down version of our deepest hopes. It is far better, far bigger, far more awe-inspiring than we can imagine or fully understand. We do not have to be apologetic for it. We do not have to dilute it to make it more palatable. Sometimes a sip of something that makes your head spin is exactly what is required.

We need to realize that we can strip away our cynicism without fearing that we will automatically strip away our brains with it. All that will happen is that our spirits and imaginations will find they can breathe again.

If we are going to play Whac-a-mole with anything, here are a few targets that the *theosis* story brought to my mind. You will have your own:

- Let's whack down the desire to restrict God's mercy to something that allows a small number of us a faint taste of God's grace. That is a poor imitation of the grace that God has poured abundantly on the *world* as plentifully as sunlight.
- Let's whack down the odd belief that if something is incomprehensible to us, it cannot exist or cannot have happened. Do we really believe God's mind is no bigger than our own?
- Let's whack down the tendency to spiritualize things that God deliberately made thoroughly material (for example, the resurrection) and remove the spiritual from things that God poured himself into (for example, the incarnation).
- Let's whack down our fear of feeling disappointed by God. We all will, at some stage, and the psalms give us permission to get thoroughly fed up with God when it happens, and to say so. But disappointment will not win. 'Be of good cheer! I have overcome the world.'[3]

- Let's whack down all sense of worthlessness. We need to remember that Aslan, who calls Lucy 'Dearest' and 'Dear-heart' with a tenderness that can still bring tears to my eyes, is only a faint representation of how God feels about each one of us.
- Let's whack down all fear of meaninglessness. Our world, our neighbours, we ourselves, are charged with the fire and life and love and glory of God, and we are set on a path to become nothing less than God-like. Do we dare believe it?

Believing all this is a risk, but the sheer goodness of the good news makes it worth it. Consider the worst-case scenario. Perhaps we will discover after death that we were completely wrong, or perhaps there will be no 'we' to discover anything at that point. Still, I would rather live my life now with that bright vision. I would rather believe I, and those around me, were a part of the purpose of God than an accidental accumulation of atoms. I would rather believe in the worth of every human life than see myself as part of a battle in which only the fittest survive. I want to soak in the beauty and amazement of creation knowing that it is a gift and a promise of even more glory to come. I would rather gamble on all the unprovable things I am convinced of being true, whether they be my belief in my family's love or my belief in Christ's resurrection, than live a life outside the stories of our faith.

Maybe this all proves that Christianity is the product of wish-fulfilment. Or maybe it suggests that this story that so perfectly matches, meets and fulfils our deepest longings does so precisely because it is true.[4]

Notes

1 C. S. Lewis, 1998, *The Last Battle*, Chronicles of Narnia, London: Harper-Collins, pp. 155–7. Original edition 1956.

2 It is a theory that has appeared occasionally but rarely been taken seriously.

3 John 16.33.

4 George MacDonald, as always, puts it so much better, this time in the mouth of a young curate: 'Even if there be no hereafter, I would live my time believing in a grand thing that ought to be true if it is not. And if these be not truths, then is the loftiest part of our nature a waste. Let me hold by the better than the actual, and fall into nothingness off the same precipice with Jesus and Paul and a thousand more, who were lovely in their lives, and with their death make even the nothingness into which they have passed like the garden of the Lord. I will go further, and say I would rather die forevermore believing as Jesus believed, than live forevermore believing as those that deny Him' (George MacDonald, 1876, *Thomas Wingfold, Curate* in Michael Phillips (ed.), 2018, *The Cullen Collection*, New York: Rosetta, chapter LXXV.

PART 6

Final Thoughts

26

Faith, Story and Identity

The foundational story

In this book we have pulled out four dusty lumps from under the carpet of 2,000 years: four ancient ways of telling the foundational story of Christ's atonement, chosen from a gloriously varied selection of possibilities. You may wonder why I have focused on these four, and the answer is simple: because I was writing the book I could choose the ones I found most interesting. That is one decided advantage the author has over the reader. Clearly, though, this is only a taster of the stories the New Testament writers knew and used in their attempts to communicate the mystery and meaning and power of Christ's work.[1]

What I hope has come through all our varied explorations and ponderings is that the foundation of our hope is *what Jesus has done*, not the particular way in which we *understand* what Jesus has done. Jesus' incarnation, life, death, resurrection and ascension is the foundational story. That this story happened 'for us and for our salvation' is our foundational creed. The smaller stories given to us by the biblical writers to try to understand the 'how' and 'why' of this salvation are misty windows allowing us one glimpse after another of an eternal wonder. They are poems whose words open our hearts to something we had never experienced before; they are pieces of music that awaken a longing for something we can never find on earth; they are portraits drawing out a side of someone we had not seen before; they are, above all, icons guiding our sight as we look through and beyond them to the mystery. They are to be valued and studied and honoured, but they are not the thing itself and our salvation does not depend on them. It depends on Jesus.

This should be deeply comforting, primarily because of the reassurance it gives us that our own confused attempts to understand God's work cannot shake what Jesus has done. But there are other benefits in recognizing the difference between God's action (the foundational story) and our means of talking about it (such as the stories we have explored). The fact that I have grown up believing one atonement story and my neighbour another does not mean I have to convince her that I am right. I do not need to feel threatened, because the reality of Jesus' atoning work does not rely on us agreeing. Her love for one story does not mean mine is 'wrong' any more than her appreciation of the way Shakespeare writes of love in Sonnet 18 means that my appreciation of Donne's poem 'A Valediction Forbidding Mourning' is devalued or wrong. Maybe if we stopped being defensive, both of us could be enriched by learning from the other. Both poems give glimpses into the mystery of love. Each atonement story gives glimpses into the mystery of what Jesus has done.

Remember, though, that this is not the same thing as relativism. There are limits to this openness to other stories. If someone were to promote stories that claimed there was no such thing as love, or that Jesus did not come 'for us and our salvation', they would not be looking through alternative windows on the same truth. They would be claiming that there is no such truth there to see. The truth of God's atoning work stays stable, however we understand it, but to say it is not there at all is to attempt to destroy it, not illuminate it.

Put simply, we are to have faith in Jesus, not faith in our own faith. As Christian people we have not always remembered that. When we ground ourselves on the uncertain and unstable foundation of 'faith in our own faith', we soon find it necessary to guard our beliefs carefully against the threat of different understandings; we may feel driven to split away from those who espoused an alternative understanding; we may even feel justified in using violence to defend our own understanding of what we should believe, because the outcomes are eternal. If our own carefully constructed faith is the foundation of salvation, we would do anything to preserve it. In the history of the Church, we *have* done anything and everything at our disposal to preserve it.

But in reality, our faith is in Jesus and what Jesus has done. That is the foundation, that is the cause and means of our salvation. That is the good news, and no amount of debate or confusion or contrasting atonement theories can ever shift it. Thank God.

The misty windows

With that foundational story in place, we are then free to enjoy the myriad sub-stories that give us glimpses into the mystery and truth of it: the 'misty windows' we peer through. As we have seen, some of these stories have been more helpful than others at different times in the Church's history, since each is responding with good news to some form of bad news. If the particular piece of 'bad news' the story addresses is no longer high up in people's consciousness, the message it gives us will not be seen as 'good news' in that time and culture, no matter how beloved the story may be to some within the Church.

We have a couple of possible ways of approaching that problem. We can choose, as I have in this book, to dig a little deeper into some traditional atonement stories to find where the good news still is for our contemporary bad news. We can also delve into the unfathomable riches of our scriptures to see what other treasures God has in store for us there: other stories that give us insights into the key foundational story, and provide solid good news for our day.

I think both these options are important for us to consider carefully. Note that I am still focusing on 'stories' rather than 'theories' or 'arguments'. As Christians, that is where we start. The Bible is a library containing numerous literary genres, but at the heart of it are stories. These stories have then been drawn on and elucidated and argued over by ancient historians, evangelists, priests, prophets and philosophers, which is how we end up with the Bible as we know it, but it is the stories themselves that hold the good news.

One of the loveliest descriptions of this truth I have found was, appropriately, in the opening chapter of a children's Bible:

> Now, some people think the Bible is a book of rules, telling you what you should and shouldn't do. The Bible certainly does have some rules in it. They show you how life works best. But the Bible isn't mainly about you and what you should be doing. It's about God and what he has done.
>
> Other people think the Bible is a book of heroes, showing you people you should copy. The Bible does have some heroes in it, but (as you'll soon find out) most of the people in the Bible aren't heroes at all. They make some big mistakes (sometimes on purpose), they get afraid and run away. At times, they're downright mean.
>
> No, the Bible isn't a book of rules, or a book of heroes. The Bible is most of all a story. It's an adventure story about a young Hero who comes from a far country to win back his lost treasure. It's a love story about a brave Prince who leaves his palace, his throne – everything – to rescue the ones he loves. It's like the most wonderful of fairy tales that has come true in real life!
>
> It takes the whole Bible to tell this story. And at the center of the story, there is a baby. Every story in the Bible whispers his name. He is like the missing piece in the puzzle – the piece that makes all the other pieces fit together, and suddenly you can see a beautiful picture.[2]

Think about the two wonderfully evocative stories that Sally Lloyd-Jones has suggested here. Would the Church look different today if the prime understanding of what God had done for us in Jesus was couched not in terms of payments or punishments, but within the story of a bride being rescued by the prince who loves her? Or if the parable of the treasure in the field was not interpreted as us discovering the kingdom, but the King discovering us where we had long been lost and buried?

This choosing and shaping of stories is not simply a light-hearted, imaginative game. It is a serious task, for stories shape who we become: they form our identity.

Stories and identity

While I have not directly addressed 'loss of identity' as one of the 'bad news' stories of today, it has been a factor behind much of what we have explored. Identity is one of today's most pressing needs, most pressing hungers. Something that previous generations barely worried about, since it was a natural part of life, has recently become the elusive White Hart we spend our lives searching the forest for. In Arthurian legends, this Hart was ever just ahead, ever eluding capture, but ever drawing the knights on.

Our basic sense of identity has been destabilized in many ways: by relativism, by individualism, by easy long-distance travel, by the endless scope of the internet, and by modernism's suspicion of 'metanarratives' (or, in normal language, big stories). We once belonged to a family (which is an increasingly fluid concept), and a particular place in the world (whereas I, for example, have lived in 27 houses in 8 countries); we once belonged to a religious tradition. Family, place and religion all gave people deep roots and big stories that surrounded them, cradled them, shaped them. Some people may have felt restricted by these 'belongings', but they prevented the situation many find themselves in now, where they have no place within or without to call home.

Current Western culture encourages us to seek this White Hart of identity through an ever-increasing obsession with our individual self, as if we could recapture an escaped guinea pig by obsessively examining its hutch. Other cultures know better. Residents of Aotearoa New Zealand learn that when you meet a group of people for the first time, or are about to give a speech, the polite way to begin according to Māori protocol, '*kaupapa* Māori', is with a *pepeha*, a greeting that establishes the speaker's identity through their *whakapapa*: their genealogy and connections with the world. In delivering this *pepeha* we are taught that our identity starts with the mountain we belong to, the river we belong to, and the *waka* that brought us to this land. Then we ground ourselves in our *iwi* or tribe, our *hapu* or sub-tribe, our grandparents, our parents, and only then – only after all this has been established – do we say our name. Without all that comes before, without those connections to place and family and culture, our name has no substance. Once all that is established, our name has identity.

That outline is the simplest possible *pepeha* that I, like other *Pakeha*, learned to stumble my way through. In contrast, when I invited the Māori Archbishop of Aotearoa to speak at an Anglican Schools' Conference, the Archbishop started his *whakapapa* before the Maui of legend, and traced it all the way through hundreds of years of generations to himself. Nor was his tale a string of names and places. The overarching story was filled with smaller stories along the way to bring these *tīpuna*, ancestors, to life for us; stories that gave the big story richness and colour and depth, and brought those same qualities to the identity of the man before us.

Our identity is formed by our connections, and those connections are communicated best through story – as another ancient people knew so well. Here is Rabbi Jonathan Sacks:

> Identity needs memory, and memory is encoded in the stories we tell. Without narrative, there is no memory, and without memory, we have no identity ... *We are the story we tell ourselves about ourselves.*[3]

That fascinating last sentence became a key motivation for this book: 'We are the story we tell ourselves about ourselves.' What stories are we telling ourselves about ourselves as Christians? Particularly, given the centrality of the concept of atonement to our faith, what stories of Christ's atoning work are we telling ourselves? It is vital that we take this question seriously, because the stories we choose to tell will shape who we are. Our stories are powerful and, as we discovered when thinking about blood, something with power for good can, if used wrongly, become an equal power for evil.

The Jewish people were and are deeply conscious of the seriousness of story. Rabbi Sacks reminds us that when Moses is giving instructions to his people in Egypt before they head for the desert, there is a sense of urgency, a need for haste. That is why there is not even time for bread to rise. Yet in the middle of all the hasty instructions, on three occasions Moses slows right down in order to instruct them to tell this story to their children and grandchildren and *their* children all through the generations.

Three laborious reminders in the midst of haste – because this will be the story that shapes their identity. From that time onwards, the identity of the people of Israel is that of a people whom God has set free, has rescued when things were as bad as they could be. From that time, the people of Israel were to be a people who experience the worst horrors of the world, and yet have hope:

> With the hindsight of thirty-three centuries we can see how right Moses was. A story told across the generations is the gift of an identity, and when you know who you are and why, you can navigate the wilderness of time with courage and confidence. That is a life-changing idea.[4]

The survival of the Jewish people through one unimaginable horror after another, century after century, is a witness to the strength of their sense of identity, grounded in story.

Do we, as Christians today, feel anything approaching that strength of belonging to our stories? Do we recognize them as *ours*? For here is a key thing: it is not enough to relate tales of history. They have to be *our* history, to belong to us. 'History tells us what happened. Memory tells us who we are.'[5] Are our Christian stories something we observe and re-tell from outside, or something we want to belong to?

For our Christian genealogy is not reliant on biology. We too are children of Abraham, grafted by grace on to that ancient, glorious and flawed tree of the people of Israel. Our thread of belonging is woven through to prehistory. But we too have our own distinct story: the story of Christ and (for better or worse) of the Church. Our Christian stories are our family stories. They are not primarily something to analyse, but something to connect us, something to shape us, something to form our identity. That means that each of the stories we have explored in this book are *our* stories: not to be observed and considered from outside, but to belong to.

Who do our stories of atonement say we are?

I come back, then, to the question: what stories have we as Christians chosen to belong to, and what are the driving stories behind who we are today? What is our identity as followers of Christ? What are the stories we are telling ourselves and living by, and therefore telling the world? And, as a result of all this, what identity are we offering people who are hungering for a story?

The reality, as we all know, is that much of the secular world sees our identity as being one that has nurtured power-driven abuse: sexual abuse on the parts of the Anglican and Catholic churches, financial and spiritual abuse on the part of TV evangelists, domestic abuse among too many evangelical churches. I know we are wearied with the pain of all this, but we also all know there are questions that we have not finished addressing.

Here is a central one: *What stories did we tell ourselves about ourselves that made it possible for abuse of the vulnerable by the powerful to happen?* For we are not allowed to blame it on a few bad people who sneaked in. We have to ask ourselves where and when the stories of our structures of power, and the honour and set-apartness of our clergy, became a stronger part of our identity than the story of our loving, foot-washing, self-sacrificing God?

And how do our stories of atonement inadvertently support this?

Perhaps it is time that stories which involve satisfying the honour of a divine hierarchy, or propitiating an angry God with death and suffering, or divine victory being achieved through violence, are gently put to one side as tales that once had their time and place but which, today, are not helpful. As we have seen, we can do so without downplaying the severity of our sin nor our need for grace nor the power of God. We do need to reclaim our ancient atonement stories, but where the power within them has darkened we need to reclaim the light. And we need to explore other stories, nestled within the unending richness of our scriptures: stories that will strengthen in us the difficult, glorious identity of a people who live love in the face of hate, faith in the face of cynicism, peace in the face of uncertainty and division, self-giving in a culture of self-idolatry, and hope when all are despairing.

There are many more such stories to be found in our scriptures: stories known to us all which may not yet have come to the fore as the good news stories of atonement for our time. Before we close, then, here are two connected suggestions for consideration.

Homecoming

Think for a moment of those three wonderful kingdom parables: the lost coin, the lost sheep and the lost son. We do not normally call the third parable by that name, admittedly, but it emphasizes what they all have in common. Something is lost, and then is found. When that language is so familiar to us, I wonder why we do not have an atonement story based around it. We sin and are cleansed: sacrificial atonement. We deserve punishment but another takes it for us: substitutionary atonement. We are captive and released: victorious atonement. We are sick and healed, estranged and reconciled. But what if we are lost, as so many are? Lost in a bewildering world of change, uncertainty and fear; lost sometimes even in our own identities? Surely 'being found' is as much a part of atonement as being healed, or being paid for, or being cleansed by Jesus' blood? And our story is one of the King of kings giving up everything in his quest to go to a far country, find us in the wilderness to which we had wandered, and bring us home.

Or what about another ancient story, closely connected to this, that runs through the whole Old Testament and finds wonderful fulfilment in the New Testament: the story of exile and return? Here people are not so much lost, as somehow not where and who they want to be, not where they belong. How many people feel like exiles in their own countries, cultures, homes, families, or even their own bodies? In our Western world now, populated by the loneliest generations in history, by individuals confusedly fighting for their individual rights while longing for community, by people searching wildly through social media for the meaning and purpose they can no longer find, by young people whose heartbreaking level of suicide is the ultimate self-exile – is there anything more important we can offer them than belonging?

Through Christ, we who were far off have been brought near. What was once a chosen people marked by race is now the family of God, open to all. We are no longer in exile here on earth, lost with no identity, but instead are God's people. And, through Christ, we have the promise of a return not only to a community of love here on earth, but to a place in the house of many rooms that the Father has prepared for us. Our identity is of a people who have been searched for by God, and found; a people who have been welcomed, who belong, who have been sought in the wilderness and brought home.

If we recaptured the biblical atonement stories as we have in this book, or if these two final stories became our central stories in the next century, how would the Church change? Who would we become? 'We are the stories we tell ourselves about ourselves.' Perhaps we need to take this more seriously than we often have, so who we are and what we proclaim can truly be good news for our world.

Notes

1 I suspect it would be impossible to write a book on atonement that was anything other than a taster.

2 Sally Lloyd-Jones, 2007, *Jesus Storybook Bible*, Grand Rapids, MI: Zondervan.

3 Jonathan Sacks, 'Writing my Own Chapter', *Covenant & Conversation*, https://www.rabbisacks.org/covenant-conversation/bo/writing-my-own-chapter/ (accessed 20.05.2022).

4 Jonathan Sacks, 'Once Upon a Time, a Long Time Ago', *Covenant & Conversation*, https://www.rabbisacks.org/archive/once-upon-a-time-long-ago-there-was-a-nation-in-slavery/ (accessed 20.05.2022).

5 Jonathan Sacks, 'Memory Is My Story', *Covenant & Conversation*, https://www.rabbisacks.org/quotes/memory-is-my-story/ (accessed 23.05.2022).

Epilogue

We began this journey by wondering how we can use words to express the mysteries of God, particularly the central mystery of atonement. God's mysteries are big enough to have space for words of every form: for reason, for discussion, for debate, as well as for imagery and story, and I have used them all in these pages. But story, of course, has been central. The world of the Bible, both Old Testament and New, is not our own, and entering into the experience of the stories they tell and use is not straightforward. Yet neither is it completely beyond us, because our imaginations are made for taking us into worlds that are not our own, for letting us sense and live through experiences that have never happened to us. Imagination is to understanding what reason is to knowledge, and together they are our best hope of being able to speak of divine mysteries.

I have drawn on many more recent stories to help our imaginations along on this journey, and want to close by turning once more to C. S. Lewis, whose books have given life and depth and warmth to the faith of countless people in the past 70 years.

In *The Voyage of the Dawn Treader*, Lucy encounters a book of spells, one of which is not so much a spell as a story. It is titled 'For the refreshment of the spirit'. She reads it through, quickly becoming so immersed in it that she forgets she is reading it, not living it. On finishing she wants to re-read it immediately, but finds that the pages cannot be turned back. Even worse, she realizes that she is beginning to forget it. 'It was about a cup and a sword and a tree and a green hill, I know that much. But I can't remember, and what *shall* I do?'

Shortly afterwards, Aslan appears, and Lucy asks:

'But please –'
'Speak on, dear heart.'
'Shall I ever be able to read that story again; the one I couldn't remember? Will you tell it to me, Aslan? Oh do, do, do.'
'Indeed, yes, I will tell it to you for years and years.'[1]

This story of the cup and sword and tree and green hill is the story we are invited to enter, to be part of, to belong to. It is a story God is telling us all the time, no matter how quickly we forget it. It is a story that we catch glimpses of in rare moments of beauty or poignancy or nobility or grace that can bring tears to our eyes, although they are not sad. 'They are not the thing itself; they are only the scent of a flower we have not found, the echo of a tune we have not heard, news from a country we have never yet visited.'[2] It is the story that all our smaller stories can only hint at, and it calls on all that we are – our being, our reason, our imagination, our emotions, our spirit – in the joyful quest to hear it in its fullness.

Notes

1 C. S. Lewis, 1980, *The Voyage of the Dawn Treader*, Chronicles of Narnia, London: HarperCollins, p. 147. Original edition 1952.

2 C. S. Lewis, 'The Weight of Glory' in Walter Hooper (ed.), 2013, *The Weight of Glory: A Collection of Lewis' Most Moving Addresses*, London: William Collins, p. 31. (Sermon first published 1941.)

Bibliography

Aagard, Anna Marie, 2010, '"My Eyes Have Seen Your Salvation." On Likeness to God and Deification in Patristic Theology', *Religion and Theology* 17, pp. 302–28.

Abelard, Peter, 2011, *Commentary on the Epistle to the Romans*, Steve R. Cartwright (trans.), Washington DC: Catholic University of America Press.

Alter, Robert, 1981, *The Art of Biblical Narrative*, New York: HarperCollins.

——— (trans.), 2019, *The Hebrew Bible*, vol. 1, New York: Norton.

Anglican Church in Aotearoa New Zealand and Polynesia, 1989, *A New Zealand Prayer Book – He Karakia Mihinare o Aotearoa*, Christchurch, NZ: Genesis.

Anselm, 1969, *Why God Became Man*, translated and edited by Joseph M. Colleran, Albany, NY: Magi Books.

Athanasius, 1944, *St. Athanasius on the Incarnation*, translated and edited by a religious of CSMV, London: Mowbray.

Augustine, 1961, *Confessions*, R. S. Pine-Coffin (trans.), London: Penguin.

Aulen, Gustaf, 1970, *Christus Victor*, London: SPCK.

Baker, Mark D. (ed.), 2006, *Proclaiming the Scandal of the Cross*, Grand Rapids, MI: Baker Academic.

Barker, Margaret, 2009, 'Temple and Liturgy', a paper presented at Lambeth Palace, London, June.

Barna Group, 2019, *The Connected Generation*, Ventura, CA: Barna.

Boersma, Hans, 2004, *Violence, Hospitality and the Cross*, Grand Rapids, MI: Baker Academic.

Bolz-Weber, Nadia, 2020, 'Be Not Afraid', *The Corners* by Nadia Bolz-Weber, https://nadiabolzweber.substack.com/p/be-not-afraid-um-yeahok?r=3dw94& utm_campaign=post&utm_medium=web&utm_source=copy&fbclid=IwAR-02biCFWZ8KlCdlWItkd_ehToqeY4ejbf4pDX9NPE-_pvrIkZ65SIsdWg4 (accessed 18.09.2022).

Bouteneff, Peter, 2008, *The Orthodox Christian Church: History, Beliefs and Practices*, lectures narrated by Peter Bouteneff, Learn25Audio.

Boyd, Gregory A., 2001, *Satan and the Problem of Evil: Constructing a Trinitarian Warfare Theodicy*, Westmont, IL: InterVarsity Press.

Charlesworth, James H. (ed.), 1983, *The Old Testament Pseudepigrapha*, vol. 1, New York: Doubleday.

Chesterton, G. K., 2011, 'The Red Angel' in *Tremendous Trifles*, Overland Park: Digireads. Original edition 1909.

Clare, Cassandra, 2008, *City of Ashes*, Mortal Instruments trilogy, London: Walker Books.

———, 2007, *City of Bones*, Mortal Instruments trilogy, London: Walker Books.

Creasy Dean, Kenda, 2010, *Almost Christian: What the Faith of Our Teenagers Is Telling the Church*, Oxford: Oxford University Press.

Darwin, Charles, *The Descent of Man*, accessed through *Classics in the History of Psychology*, https://psychclassics.yorku.ca/Darwin/Descent/descent5.htm (accessed 18.09.2022).

Donne, John, 1957, 'Batter my heart three person'd God' in Helen Gardner (ed.), *The Metaphysical Poets*, London: Penguin, p. 85.

———, 'Death be not proud', *Poetry Foundation*, https://www.poetryfoundation. org/poems/44107/holy-sonnets-death-be-not-proud (accessed 21.10.2022).

———, 1997, 'Meditation XVII' in *No Man is an Island: A Selection from the Prose of John Donne*, London: Folio Society.

Fiddes, Paul S., 1989, *Past Event and Present Salvation: The Christian Idea of Atonement*, London: Darton, Longman and Todd.

Finlan, Stephen, 2007, *Options on Atonement in Christian Thought*, Collegeville, MN: Liturgical Press.

———, 2005, *Problems with Atonement*, Collegeville, MN: Liturgical Press.

Goldingay, John, 1995, 'Your Iniquities Have Made a Separation between You and Your God' in John Goldingay (ed.), *Atonement Today*, London: SPCK, pp. 39–53.

Guite, Malcolm, 2012, *Sounding the Seasons: 70 Sonnets for the Christian Year*, Norwich: Canterbury Press, Scribd ebook, p. 34, available from https://www. scribd.com/book/367616576.

Gunton, Colin, 1988, *The Actuality of Atonement*, Edinburgh: T&T Clark.

Hengel, Martin, 1981, *The Atonement: The Origins of the Doctrine in the New Testament*, London: SCM Press.

Hopkins, Gerard Manley, 1953, 'God's Grandeur' in W. H. Gardner (ed.), *Gerard Manley Hopkins: Poems and Prose*, Harmondsworth: Penguin.

Irenaeus, 'Adversus Haereses', http://www.earlychurchtexts.com/public/irenaeus_ on_recapitulation_in_christ.htm.

Johnson, Luke Timothy, 2006, *Hebrews: A Commentary*, Louisville, KY: Westminster John Knox Press.

Kelly, J. N. D., 1960, *Early Christian Doctrines*, San Francisco, CA: Harper and Row.

Lewis, C. S., 'The Weight of Glory' in Walter Hooper (ed.), 2013, *The Weight of Glory: A Collection of Lewis' Most Moving Addresses*, London: William Collins, pp. 25–46. (Sermon first published 1941.)

———, 'A Slip of the Tongue' in Walter Hooper (ed.), 2013, *The Weight of Glory: A Collection of Lewis' Most Moving Addresses*, London: William Collins, p. 189. (Original publication date 1949.)

———, 2002, 'The Funeral of a Great Myth' in Lesley Walmsley (ed.), *C. S. Lewis Essay Collection: Faith, Christianity, and the Church*, New York: HarperCollins.

———, 1998, *The Last Battle*, Chronicles of Narnia, London: HarperCollins. Original edition 1956.

———, 1982, 'Sometimes Fairy Stories May Say Best What's to Be Said' in Walter Hooper (ed.), *On Stories*, Orlando, FL: Harcourt, Inc., pp. 45–8.

———, 1980, *The Silver Chair*, Chronicles of Narnia, London: HarperCollins. Original edition 1953.

———, 1980, *The Voyage of the Dawn Treader*. Chronicles of Narnia, London: HarperCollins. Original edition 1952.

———, 1959, 'Against Too Many Writers of Science Fiction', *My Poetic Side*, https://mypoeticside.com/show-classic-poem-16799 (accessed 8.08.2022).

————, 1952, *Mere Christianity*, Glasgow: Collins.

————, 1950, *The Lion, the Witch and the Wardrobe*, Chronicles of Narnia, Harmondsworth: Penguin.

Lloyd Jones, Sally, 2007, *The Jesus Storybook Bible*, Grand Rapids, MI: Zonderkids.

Loconte, Joseph, 2015, *A Hobbit, a Wardrobe, and the Great War*, Nashville, TN: HarperCollins.

Lunn, Nicholas P., 2009, 'Jesus, the Ark and the Day of Atonement: Intertextual Echoes in John 19:38-20:18', *JETS (Journal of the Evangelical Theological Society)*, 52.4, pp. 731–46.

Macdonald, George, 2018, *Thomas Wingfold, Curate* in Michael Phillips (ed.), *The Cullen Collection*, New York: Rosetta.

————, 2012, *Unspoken Sermons*, Summit, NJ: Start, Kindle ebook.

Macquarrie, John, 1997, *A Guide to the Sacraments*, London: SCM Press.

Martinez, Florentino Garcia, 1996, *The Dead Sea Scrolls Translated*, Wilfred G. E. Watson (trans.), English edition Leiden: E.J. Brill.

Marx, Karl, 1844, 'A Contribution to the Critique of Hegel's Philosophy of Right', *Deutsch-Französische Jahrbücher*, 7 and 10 February, https://www.marxists.org/archive/marx/works/1843/critique-hpr/intro.htm (accessed 22.09.2022).

Matthews-Green, Frederica, 2015, 'Theosis Part 1: Glowing with the Light of Christ', YouTube video 2:59, posted by Theoria, https://www.youtube.com/watch?v=Zr2avLzFSV4.

Merton, Thomas, 1967, 'Blessed are the Meek: The Roots of Christian Nonviolence', *Catholic Peace Fellowship*, http://www.catholicpeacefellowship.org/wp/wordpress/1960s-cpf-pamphlet-blessed-are-the-meek-the-roots-of-christian-nonviolence-by-thomas-merton/ (accessed 01.11.2023).

Milgrom, Jacob, 2004, *Leviticus: A Book of Ritual and Ethics*, Continental Commentary, Minneapolis, MN: Fortress Press.

Nix, Garth, 2003, *Abhorsen*, Old Kingdom Trilogy, Crows Nest, Sydney: Allen & Unwin.

————, 1995, *Lirael*, Old Kingdom Trilogy, Crows Nest, Sydney: HarperCollins.

————, 1995, *Sabriel*, Old Kingdom Trilogy, London: HarperCollins Children's Books.

Och, Bernard, 1995, 'Creation and Redemption: Towards a Theology of Creation', *Judaism* 44.2, pp. 226–43.

Parsons, Martin, 2007, 'Binding the Strong Man: The Flaw of the Excluded Middle' in Peter G. Riddell and Beverley Smith Riddell (eds), *Angels and Demons*, Nottingham: Apollos.

Phillips, Macon, 2011, 'Osama Bin Laden Dead', *White House*, 2 May, https://obamawhitehouse.archives.gov/blog/2011/05/02/osama-bin-laden-dead (accessed 01.11.2023).

Reardon, Patrick Henry, 2015, *Reclaiming the Atonement: An Orthodox Theology of Redemption: Volume 1: The Incarnate Word*, Ancient Faith Publishing, Kindle edition.

Ricoeur, Paul, 1978, 'The Language of Faith' in Charles E. Regan and David Stewart (eds), *The Philosophy of Paul Ricoeur*, Boston, MA: Beacon Press, pp. 223–38.

Riordan, Rick, 2010–2012, *The Kane Chronicles*, New York: Hyperion Books.

————, 2009, *Percy Jackson and the Last Olympian*, London: Penguin.

————, 2005–2009, *Percy Jackson and the Olympians*, London: Penguin.

Rowling, J. K., 2007, *Harry Potter and the Deathly Hallows*, London: Bloomsbury.

———, 2005, *Harry Potter and the Half-Blood Prince*, London: Bloomsbury.

———, 2003, *Harry Potter and the Order of the Phoenix*, London: Bloomsbury.

———, 2000, *Harry Potter and the Goblet of Fire*, London: Bloomsbury.

———, 1997, *Harry Potter and the Philosopher's Stone*, London: Bloomsbury.

Russell, Jeffrey Burton, 1977, *The Devil: Perceptions of Evil from Antiquity to Primitive Christianity*, Ithaca and London: Cornell University Press.

Sacks, Jonathan, 2017, *Numbers: The Wilderness Years, Covenant & Conversation Book 4*, Jerusalem: Maggid.

———, 'The Core Idea', *Covenant & Conversation*, https://rabbisacks.org/wp-content/uploads/2020/05/CandC-Family-Behar-Bechukotai-5780.pdf (accessed 03.10.2022).

———, 'Writing My Own Chapter', *Covenant & Conversation*, https://www.rabbisacks.org/covenant-conversation/bo/writing-my-own-chapter/ (accessed 20.05.2022).

———, 'Once Upon a Time, a Long Time Ago', *Covenant & Conversation*, https://www.rabbisacks.org/archive/once-upon-a-time-long-ago-there-was-a-nation-in-slavery/ (accessed 20.05.2022).

———, 'Memory Is My Story', *Covenant & Conversation*, https://www.rabbisacks.org/quotes/memory-is-my-story/ (accessed 23.05.2022).

———, 'Succot for our time', *Jonathan Sacks: The Rabbi Sacks Legacy*, https://www.rabbisacks.org/ceremony-celebration-family-edition/succot-family-edition/ (accessed 04.07.2021).

Sage, Angie, 2005, *Magyk*, London: Bloomsbury.

St Teresa, https://www.worldprayers.org/archive/prayers/invocations/dear_jesus_help_us_to.html.

Studdart Kennedy, G. A., 1927, *The Unutterable Beauty*, London: Hodder and Stoughton.

Tolkien, J. R. R., 1964, 'Tree and Leaf' in *Tree and Leaf, Including the Poem Mythopoeia*, London: HarperCollins.

Turia, Tariana, 2011, 'Parihaka – A Legacy of Non-Violence', *Catholic Worker*, http://catholicworker.org.nz/the-common-good/parihaka-a-legacy-of-non-violence/ (accessed 03.10.2022).

Tutu, Desmond, 1995, *An African Prayer Book*, New York: Doubleday.

Vennard, Martin, 2018, 'Death of Hitler: How the world found out from the BBC', *BBC News*, https://www.bbc.com/news/world-europe-44131106 (accessed 23.04.2021).

Wikipedia, 'Stalin Monument', Wikipedia, https://en.wikipedia.org/wiki/Stalin_Monument_(Budapest) (accessed 23.04.2021).

Williams, Margery, 2015, *The Velveteen Rabbit*, Toronto: HarperCollins, Kindle edition.

Williams, Rowan, 2005, *Pause for Thought*, Terry Wogan Radio 2, 18 October, https://soulspark.online/sunbathing-with-god/ (accessed 14.03.2022).

Wooding, Dan, 2013, 'The Day Mother Teresa Told Me, "Your Poverty Is Greater than Ours"', *Patch*, 6 April, https://patch.com/california/lakeforest-ca/bp--the-day-mother-teresa-told-me-your-poverty-is-gree85a671097 (accessed 18.09.2022).

Wordsworth, William, 1950, 'The Tables Turned' in Mark van Doren (ed.), *William Wordsworth Selected Poetry*, New York: Random House.

Wright, N. T., 1993, *The Climax of the Covenant*, Minneapolis, MN: Fortress Press.

www.ingramcontent.com/pod-product-compliance
Lightning Source LLC
LaVergne TN
LVHW041123310325
807191LV00004B/18